W9-BMS-172

Savor
the
Spices
of
Life

Chef Shaw Hanna Rabadi

Restaurateur

A Mediterranean story-cookbook
of one man's journey to a better life
and the recipes that took him there

FOOD
FOR
THOUGHT

NOTICE TO THE READER

The Publisher makes no representation or warranties of any kind, including but not limited to, the warranties of fitness for particular purpose or merchantability, nor are any such representations implied with respect to the material set forth herein, and the publisher takes no responsibility with respect to such material. The publisher shall not be liable for any special, consequential, or exemplary damages resulting, in whole or part, from the readers' use of, or reliance upon, this material.

The information contained in this book is to be used for educational and informational purposes only, and is not intended to diagnose, treat, cure, or prevent any health problems or disease. The information contained in this book is not a substitute for professional medical advice or medical examination. Consult your physician with any questions or concerns you may have regarding your condition. The author is not responsible or liable for any claim, loss, or damage arising from the use of the information obtained herein.

COPYRIGHT © 2011
Shaw Rabadi
1736 Western Avenue
Guilderland, NY 12203

All rights reserved. ©2011 Shaw Rabadi. This publication, or any part thereof, may not be reproduced or transmitted in any form or by any means, electronic or mechanical, including photocopying, recording, storage in an information retrieval system, or otherwise, without prior permission of the publisher.

Published by Food for Thought Press
11 Peel Street
Selkirk, NY 12058

DEDICATION

With love, great respect and admiration, I dedicate this book to my mom, dad and grand-parents, especially to all of the women in my family who have influenced and guided me in learning and perfecting the artistry of cooking food.

This book is also dedicated to all those who offered tips and guidance, from the simple Mezza to the elaborate dinner parties that are fit for kings, queens, and all my friends.

To my family:
my wife Victoria,
my sons Brendan and Philip,
and my daughter Lexi,

I love you very much.

To: John Ingemire
Here is to your
Health. Enjoy all the spices
in your life.
my Best
Shawn

Many waters cannot quench love.

CONTENTS

ACKNOWLEDGMENTS

Writing about food and working on this cookbook has been one of the most fascinating, challenging, and, perhaps, enjoyable experiences of my life. This, of course, would not have been possible without the help, dedication, and generosity of my family members, brothers, sisters, friends, and colleagues.

First, I would express my love and utmost gratitude to my mom Hilaleh and my father Hanna, or John and Helen, their adopted American names. Their love and sacrifice for their children, country, culture, and traditions has motivated me my entire life. Despite all their hardships, their love of family and food have inspired my desire to carry on the tradition of cooking and eating like a Mediterranean for a lifetime. This book is my chance to share the joy and love of food with you in the same way I experienced it growing up.

This book is designed and written with two ideas in mind: first, a personal story that took me on a journey at age 16 from Jordan through Lebanon and the Middle East, and finally to the USA, or "Amreekah," as we called it. Second is to explore and present you with key elements of Mediterranean food the way I lived it, both past and present, including the health benefits that are derived from such a "diet," or, as it is known to me, a lifestyle.

Certainly, the book benefited greatly from the inspiration and ideas of those with whom I worked in professional kitchens and in my own restaurant for more than four decades. For more than twenty years, I have been professionally involved and interested in the restaurant and catering business. Many of those recipes are included in this book.

My special thanks to my friend and editor Carolyn Johansen. She poured her heart and soul into the editing process and examined the true meaning of each word and recipe, even testing many of them in her own kitchen. Carolyn's dedication and genius gave cohesion and a sense of organization that touched the heart and soul of the book. My thanks also to Mr. Johansen for his constant support, appetite, and the many chats we had over dinner and a glass of wine or two, as we discussed everything from food to family, politics, and especially our kids.

A big thank you goes to so many dedicated souls who helped me in assembling this book. Their hard work and diligent review of everything, from my bad handwriting to understanding and even interpreting my vision of the whole project, made this all come to fruition. Amanda Pierce, whose amazing typing skills exceeded my expectations and forced me to keep on writing and rewriting to stay on pace with her. Many others who contributed to the book include: Sarah Bradbury, Lesia Gribbin, Ronen Barokas, and many others. I thank them for their patience and understanding in testing, making, and even eating many of these recipes.

My big thanks to Judy Pfeiffenberger, who has been nothing short of a lifesaver. She is my all-in-one instant Web researcher, baker and cake decorator, party set-up artist, fact finder, and reliable friend.

Special thanks to Laura Laz for her support, encouragement, and assistance in the overall idea for the book. In addition, a great debt of gratitude goes to Ms. Stephanie Petrik for her professional insight and attention to every detail and the many aspects of the recipes, especially and including the nutritional analysis, meaning, and interpretation.

My thanks and admiration go out to my son Brendan Rabadi, who kept busy ensuring that all documents were saved and secured in many formats and locations to avoid loss of information, to print and reprint the many hard-copy drafts for editing and review. Also, I am grateful for his endless hours of reading and researching the subjects of publishing, photography, design, and web technology.

Big hugs and kisses to Ms. April Rabadi, nutritionist and niece extraordinaire, who used her knowledge, skill, and advice to craft and provide the initial database for the nutritional analyses for all the recipes in this book.

I am also grateful to Dr. Paul Lamanski, Director of the Center for Preventive Medicine and Cardiovascular Health of Prime Care Physicians, PLLC, who encouraged me to team up with the Center to develop a wide range of menu choices to promote the highest dietary standard of a heart-healthy diet. His encouragement led to the establishment of our cooking classes, which, in turn, led to the beginning process of documenting, analyzing, and sharing of our recipes in this book. Visit www.centerforpreventivemedicine.com for more information on the Center's commitment to working with individual patients for better health and better life.

In addition, my special thanks to Dr. Mark Nelson for his passion and tireless professional pursuit to influence the various government agencies, school officials, and leaders in the food industry to realize the need to change our school lunch programs to include healthy alternatives for our children. Joining Dr. Nelson on many of his presentations to school teachers, officials, and students to share samples of healthy food was an inspiration to me and contributed to my starting my cooking classes and launching this book.

There are so many who have given time along the way to make this happen. My friend, Dr. Dan Tobin, who offered his great insight, boundless enthusiasm, and bundles of energy, plus "The Seven Challenging Questions," which you can only imagine made me pause, then kept me moving on the right track.

Of course, my graphic designer, Cathleen Berry—I call her "my Fav." Cathleen is a genius. She, without hesitation, agreed to help with the book by saying, "I'd love to; this is exciting!" She took every word I said at our initial project meeting and turned them into art. She captured and created the mosaic of the two worlds I lived in. She patiently and professionally listened to my goals, managed to do the impossible, and designed this book to what it is. She made the combination of text, pictures, and recipes inviting and easy to read.

Our talented photographer, Lucy Fremont, worked hard with me to capture the essence of the dishes and visually translated them into outstanding pieces of art. In addition, I would like to thank my brother and photographer, Talaat, who contributed the intriguing cover photo, which I feel truly captures the essence of the book and starts readers on their journey through the Mediterranean.

To Sara Catterall, who, under the guidance of my publisher, understood the overall goals and unique content of this book and did an outstanding job with the indexing.

To Harriet Hart and her efficient line-by-line proofreading and fine tuning of the words that brought us to a confident place.

Finally, my publisher Vince Potenza (SoundLightMind.com, Food for Thought Press), who promised me, "We will get this book done for you, and we will do what it takes to get done on time." He made it happen. Vince is my hero and my friend. Thank you for your vision and support of everyone's effort. He orchestrated and organized a plan to propel and guide the production of the book forward with a firm hand and a gentle soul.

Thank you to you all.

A book is like a garden carried in the pocket.

ENDORSEMENTS

Jeffrey Perkins, D.O.

COMPREHENSIVE INTERNAL AND PREVENTIVE MEDICINE

April 29, 2011

There are cookbooks and then there are other cookbooks. Shaw Rabadi's new book, "Savor the Spices of Life" is not just a book of wonderful healthy family Mediterranean food recipes but is also a primer on nutrition, specifically Mediterranean food nutrition and a healthful lifestyle.

I have been practicing preventative and general internal medicine for over 35 years. I have been a long-term proponent of the Mediterranean-Middle Eastern diet. From personal experience, I benefit from the wonderful cooking of my beautiful wife Jeanette as she is an experienced Middle Eastern cook. The foods are not only delicious but extremely healthy for you.

The Mediterranean diet has always involved a way of eating that favors high-fiber, healthy fats primarily from olive oil, nuts and avocado, limited amounts of meat foods and an emphasis on fish and poultry. Legumes, all sorts of greens, colorful fruits and whole grains are an intrinsic part of this way of eating.

Why is this important? Our food affects the molecular configuration of all of our cells and the health of those cells. The typical American diet, derived from the British puritanical diet promotes an environment of inflammatory chemicals which increases our risk for the all too common degenerative diseases of aging. The foods, herbs and spices that are a natural part of the Mediterranean way of eating have the opposite effect. This is translated in lower incidences of vascular disease including heart disease and stroke, hypertension, cancers and even Alzheimer's disease and those people who follow this way of eating.

The Mediterranean diet improves lipid profiles. I have seen my patients lower their cholesterol, improve their HDL levels. I have seen diabetics have better blood sugar control and require less medication by following the Mediterranean way of eating

I heartily endorse this book. Remember it is not just a cookbook or a collection of recipes, it is a large part of the path one must take to live a longer, healthier and more satisfying life.

Jeffrey Perkins D. O.
Chief, Division of Internal Medicine, St. Peter's Hospital
Albany New York

1873 Western Avenue, Suite 101, Albany, New York 12203

Phone: 518 690-0171
Fax: 518 690-0174
Email: preventdoc@medscape.com

Over the last several thousand years, a grand experiment has been conducted by providence on the people who live in the basin of the Mediterranean Sea. It is an experiment which has been determined by a unique climate and geography, which, in turn, have defined a unique flora and fauna, which, finally, have led to a cuisine and a way of living which we call Mediterranean. Yet, it is only in the last few years that the results of this experiment have been determined and fully understood by medical science. And the results indicate that a Mediterranean diet and lifestyle can powerfully help to reduce disease and sustain robust health.

The challenge for medical science is how to bring the benefits of a Mediterranean diet and lifestyle to people who were not raised in this part of the world and for whom such an approach is not instinctive. The challenge is perhaps best met by individuals in the culinary community who have an understanding of the science behind the cuisine and who also have a talent to distill and define that which is most appealing to an American palate. Shaw Rabadi is such an individual.

Shaw's upbringing is Mediterranean, but his outlook and perspective are decidedly American. He bridges both world views and in the process can help those who have not been raised in a Mediterranean country get a flavor not just for the cuisine, but for the lifestyle, as well. *Savor the Spices of Life* is a book that is grounded in the human values exemplified by the Mediterranean family, and it presents this cuisine as a brilliantly creative response to making the best of what was and is available. The dishes presented preserve the best of the traditions of Mediterranean cuisine, but emphasize the ease of preparation and flexibility so necessary in our contemporary American culture.

I hope that this good and wise book helps you to implement in your daily life more of the Mediterranean diet and lifestyle which have been shown by medical science to be so beneficial to health.

Paul E. Lemanski, MD, MS, FACP
Director, Center for Preventive Medicine and Cardiovascular Health, Prime Care Physicians, PLLC
Assistant Clinical Professor of Medicine, Albany Medical College

■ ■ ■

Healthy food is good for you physically and good for your soul. It is a sad fact that many of us "Amreekans," for ease and for convenience, have forgotten that fact. We have paid for it dearly and are now in the midst of an epidemic of obesity, diabetes, heart disease, and depression. We are less healthy today than we were a generation ago and becoming unhealthier. We look for quick answers to everything. It surprises me how many of my patients would rather be prescribed a pill for their ailments than take on the responsibility of eating a heathy diet. But when the message does get across, it delights me when health is re-achieved. Shaw's cookbook is nothing short of masterful. It is his journey in life. It is personal, insightful, and full of information, both anecdotal and scientific. The recipes are easy to follow and give the reader the sense that Mediterranean cooking and a healthier lifestyle is achievable by us all. Let it become our journey.

Elizabeth C. Gath, MD
Internal Medicine, Primary Care
Owner, Primarily for Women, Albany, NY

■ ■ ■

BFS Restaurant is on the top of the list of our family's favorite restaurants, because everything on the menu is delicious and visually appealing, but most important of all, heart healthy! And we now know that what is good for the heart is also good for the whole body.

Enjoying eating and, indeed, eating healthy can be as easy as coming to BFS Restaurant, sampling their delicious menu items, then learning how to make them at home with the easy recipes in this cookbook or taking one or more of BFS's cooking classes. When I heard about this cookbook, I knew it would be the one I would use the most to bring BFS owner and chef Shaw Rabadi's culinary recipes for delicious taste and wellness right into my own home! This beautiful cookbook, with its simple directions and helpful photographs, provides the guide for heart-healthy eating in the style of haute cuisine.

As a physician of 46 years and a specialist in physical medicine and rehabilitation for 34 of those years (now retired), I have seen the devastating results in those who neglected to take care good care of their health. Besides exercising, drinking plenty of pure and hydrating water every day, getting proper sleep, and managing stress, we also need to pay close attention to what we eat as a key ingredient to our healthy lifestyle recipe. What we put into our bodies has a lasting and powerful impact on our health . . . indeed, we are what we eat!

The Mediterranean diet is now the diet recommended by the American Heart Association for heart health—as the heart is, so is the body. Similarly, all major health organizations around the world recommend the abundant intake of fruits and vegetables, nuts and grains, the use of olive oil as the principal source of fat, low-to-moderate consumption of fish and poultry, low consumption of eggs, sugar, and especially meats, and moderate consumption of wine, normally with meals.

The recipe for better health can be as easy as eating a Mediterranean diet. Rich in plant food, nuts, legumes, and grains, this diet is the best source of dense nutrition and disease-fighting vitamins and antioxidants. These foods offer an unparalleled array of nutrients—thousands of them in each one that simply cannot be found in a vitamin pill—working in synergy and providing disease prevention at the cellular level, as Mother Nature intended.

Using the principles of the Mediterranean diet in creative and appealing ways is the hallmark of Shaw Rabadi's recipes. So do yourself, your family, and your friends a favor by sharing this amazing cookbook with them, and in so doing, making Shaw your "partner in disease prevention," as you enjoy his delicious recipes! Together, let us share the gift of health and enjoy a culinary journey to a long and healthy life!

Emma U. Aliwalas, MD
Designs in Wellness

■ ■ ■

For years I came to depend on Chef Shaw Rabadi's BFS Restaurant when I felt nostalgic for the family food that I grew up on in Jordan. Mediterranean cuisine is not only heart healthy, but flavorful, while not spicy hot. Now, his authentic recipes are combined in this beautifully designed cookbook with photographs of prepared meals, fresh herbs, and spices. Shaw's family journey tales bring a Mediterranean atmosphere to the American cook.

Hani Marar, MD
Capital Radiology Associates

■ ■ ■

I have known Shaw for years, and in this wonderful book he shares what what is important to him in life: his heritage, his family, and the convictions about health and eating that have shaped his life and his business. This book is a much more than a collection of recipes . . . it is a roadmap to a healthier life, and a delicious path, at that. Buy it for the recipes; read it for the story.

Richard A. Rubin, MD, FACP
Internal Medicine Physician, Slingerlands, NY

■ ■ ■

Shaw Rabadi's *Savor the Spices of Life* is an important book, guiding the reader to a healthy way of preparing food in modern, hectic times. Shaw is a wonderful man, father, storyteller, chef, and friend. Here's to healthy life, family, friends, and love.

Dan Tobin, MD

■ ■ ■

This is no ordinary cookbook. The author brings to life authentic Mediterranean cooking through reliving his life experiences of food and family. It is clear from the start that the author's family played a major role in his passion for food and cooking. He has a wonderful ability of bringing personal life stories and seamlessly integrating them into the book and recipes. The book has almost a motivational tone to it. The author enthusiastically encourages living a healthier life by incorporating a healthy active lifestyle, by refining the way you eat, and emphasizing the importance of family.

It is well established that the Mediterranean diet is a heart healthy diet. Studies have shown that those who follow a Mediterranean diet and active lifestyle have reduced rates of heart disease and cardiovascular mortality. There is also evidence that following a Mediterranean diet can reduce the risk of some cancers, Parkinson's disease and Alzheimer's disease. Not surprisingly, the author's restaurant has been recognized and promoted as a heart healthy restaurant. The Mediterranean diet and the recipes within this book contain many key components to a heart healthy diet. There is an emphasis on consuming fresh, preferably home grown and organic, fruits and vegetables, and the use of whole grains, nuts and legumes. Many of the recipes within this book replace butter with healthier and more favorable olive oil. The use of olive oil in cooking not only brings out the natural flavors of foods but also has clear beneficial affects on lipid profiles. The use of herbs and spices in place of salt also has clear cardiovascular benefits.

The layout of the book is visually pleasing and efficiently organized. There are many wonderful pictures throughout the book that bring to life the ingredients and recipes. I really enjoyed the Discussion section of this book. The information contained in this section is a valuable reference for anyone interested in food and cooking.

A true review of a cookbook should include testing some of the recipes. Unfortunately, I was unable to do this. I have, however, worked with enough chefs and have used many cookbooks to know that the format of this cookbook is very user friendly and complete. I especially enjoyed the "notes" at the end of each recipe. These notes add a nice personal touch to the book. This book would be enjoyed by the novice as well as the seasoned cook.

A good cookbook not only gives you the recipes, but also should give you the motivation, excitement and power to learn about the food itself. This book accomplishes this with ease. The author's sincere excitement about food, family, and life are apparent from cover to cover.

Anthony J. Navone, MD, FACC

■ ■ ■

At last, a cookbook for the busy lives we lead that keeps it healthy and exciting. As a nurse practitioner specializing in heart diseases, I am happy to finally have a cookbook to whole-heartedly recommend to my patients. Shaw's recipes serve up healthy ingredients without stereotypical, blah health foods. He makes it effortless to cook with healthy foods and methods while keeping it tasty. Page after page you will find ingredients, recipes, and menu suggestions that will have you serving food you feel good about, and eating food that will help you feel good.

Coleen Balch, MSN, RN-BC, ANP, AACC

■ ■ ■

Shaw Rabadi takes us on a memorable cultural journey of the Mediterranean lifestyle. He leaves no stone unturned to reveal all the health benefits his culture provides, from the heart healthy use of olive oil to the abundance of fresh fruits and vegetables to the modest consumption of meats, all of which he wraps in layers upon layers of spices and herbs to satisfy our palette. Enjoy your journey to a healthier lifestyle.

Linda Donnelly, RD, CDN

■ ■ ■

With the millions of supposed "quick-fix diets" scattered across the media over the years, to this day, three keys to a healthy diet have not changed: moderation, variety, and balance. After having the great honor of working with Shaw Rabadi during the creation of this beautiful cookbook, I have seen, first-hand, the application of these three key characteristics of a healthier diet. As just one step closer to a healthier you, I ask you to cook your way through Shaw's cookbook and absorb its wealth and variety of fruits and vegetables, fresh herbs and spices, nuts and grains, and heart healthy fats. Even more, I dare you to slow down and savor each and every bite for not only the delicious flavors but also the abundance of disease-fighting agents.

Stephanie Petrik, MS, RD

■ ■ ■

This book has delicious healthy recipes, wonderful nutrition tips and a beautiful story of family history and love. I highly recommend this resource for everyone seeking optimal health.

Marianne Romano, RD, CDN
Registered Dietitian & Certified Nutritionist, Private Practice, Albany, NY

■ ■ ■

This is a beautiful and passionate cookbook experience. It expresses a vision for excellence and shares that vision with the reader who also takes on some of that passion through the recipes and the story of one man's journey. The relationship with food is seen through new ways and many tips for making it creative and fun and above all healthy.

Carol Beller
Nutritionist/Coach, Albany, New York

■ ■ ■

Shaw Rabadi has written a cookbook which brings a personal glimpse and an approachable new clear vision as to the positive effects of the Mediterranean diet on our bodies. Mr. Rabadi's recipes are simple yet inspiring, urging us toward the brightest, freshest and smartest (BFS) ways to use an extraordinary array of delicious ingredients. With the nation intensely focused on health and nutrition, his timing could not be more perfect. Fascinating stories, brilliant photography and mouthwatering recipes make this cookbook a must for your kitchen repertoire and a wonderful new healthy lifestyle. In essence, *Savor the Spices of Life* will nourish mind, body, and soul! I know that it will nourish mine!"

Dale L. Miller
US Certified Master Chef, (WACS) Global Master Chef

■ ■ ■

Research has shown that a traditional, natural, "Mediterranean" diet improves health and reduces the risk of several chronic diseases. With his emphasis on whole, fresh ingredients; a variety of fruits, vegetables, nuts, and healthy fats; as well as a simple appreciation of food, Mr. Rabadi has captured the essence of balanced, mindful eating. His methods prove that, with the right perspective, healthy eating can be effortless and need not require deprivation.

Sonya Irish Hauser, PhD
Assistant Professor of Nutrition, MS Program Director

A Note from the Author

The problem I had with writing this book was knowing what recipes to include and when to stop. With all the recipes and variations from around the Mediterranean to choose from, I could have literally written volumes. Add to that all the other culinary ventures and explorations I could have taken you on, and this would have become an encyclopedia! So to keep the book portable, I offer you my interpretation of a sampling of mostly eastern Mediterranean dishes, without sacrificing the ultimate nature, simplicity, and taste of the original dish. Wishing you good health!

—Shaw

In Middle Eastern customs, as a guest after eating,
when you leave the table you should say, "Safra daeyma,"
which translates to "May your table always be full."

Do You Have Ta3m?

How does a great cook reach a level of balance using fresh ingredients that will evoke great flavor, color, and texture without any single seasoning dominating the dish? The ultimate pleasure in food is the enjoyment of all flavors in harmony. In the Arabic language, even in Jewish kitchens, cooking and reaching that special taste is called *ta3m*. That's what separates good cooks from great ones.

All recipes have a list of ingredients and a method of preparation. Two cooks will most likely prepare the same dish achieving slightly different results, based on their interpretation of the procedure and the use of key ingredients. However, both cooks will strive to achieve *ta3m*. The cook must use, whenever possible, a special ingredient that kicks the flavor to a new level or depth. I don't mean the use of more salt, sugar, or fat! I am referring to fresh and pungent flavors. For example, grilling an eggplant instead of roasting it will yield that deep, smokey, rich taste when making babaghanooj.

A little imagination goes a long way in achieving *ta3m*. You'll find throughout this book that fresh herbs, spices, olive oil, tomatoes, garlic, legumes, grains, dried fruit, nuts, low-fat dairy, honey, and brown sugar, aside fresh fruit and vegetables of all shapes, colors, and sizes are the ingredients that play the prominent roles in Mediterranean cuisine. At the same time, these items will lend a helping hand to achieving *ta3m* that makes cooking, sharing, and enjoying vibrant and tasteful dishes with your family and friends something to remember. Cook with *ta3m*, and you'll never have a boring meal again!

PROLOGUE

I have many memories of the first seventeen years of my life, when I was growing up in Jordan. Most of these are about food and the way that our life revolved around it, from planting it, growing it, harvesting it, storing or selling it, to cooking, serving, and sharing it. I also remember the many people who influenced every aspect of my life, teaching minor and major lessons, and even affecting the decisions I made throughout my life.

Now, forty years later, I want to share with you my personal story as well as my experiences in the restaurant/catering business. I will do my best to be short, to the point, and not B.S. a lot. (Later, I will explain what B.S. is and how to B.S. a lot regarding cooking, trust me!) Intermingled within these pages are the lessons I learned and the values I have absorbed about family, food, and cooking, set in a favorite format of mine . . . a story cookbook.

I will definitely feel successful in this endeavor if my story entices you to journey to the kitchen and explore your love of food. Perhaps you will share your own story with friends and family, and encourage them to do the same, while savoring something you have just prepared (preferably one of my recipes!) and enjoying a glass of wine. This is what I call a "sit and enjoy your life" moment.

I also want to pierce through the fabric of my life's journey to give you a glimpse of a fantastically complex family full of love and compassion toward each other, as well as everyone they came to know. My mom and dad lived with honor and dignity. Dad was firm and confident, expressing his feelings boldly and pointedly; Mom lived simply and quietly, with a strong connection to and reliance on family, friends, God, and good food. Dad was king and Mom was queen, and a great cook at that. I miss them both.

■ ■ ■

In memory forever! Mom and Dad. Good people! Proud parents. Celebrating Mom's birthday April 13, 1986.

Vivid blue skies, olive trees, pines, and lots of sunshine bathing the white buildings. All is in God's 'hood. Summer 2008.

The vivid blue skies over the mountains in the distance, the rolling hills, lush valleys, and prairies of Jordan are just a faint memory now. But I can still see in my mind's eye the bright orange reflection of the sun bathing the sides of the small clay homes, the rugged yet elegant one- and two-story stone homes, and the more contemporary multi-story, hand-crafted limestone homes. Their walls bear cracks because of the intense heat of the sun, but these cracks are superficial; the walls thick and strong. Love, passion, and honor fill these walls and seep out into the air that is breathed by all. That is what makes a community despite the hardships of work, endless rain, unbearable sun, and unpredictable winds. The Mediterranean people have dealt with hardship, poverty, and whatever life sent their way with grace, hope, and preparedness, but never with despair.

In the village, my aunts, grandmother, and all the women in the family cared for my family members and even the flocks of sheep and goats, both at home and along ancient trails. Proud men and women, young and old, walked intently like soldiers with a mission to do the day's work away from home, out in the fields and harvest God's gifts they were blessed with for generations before them.

I remember the silence of the fields, and can smell again the rich fragrance of lemons and mint growing in gardens that overflowed onto the fences around each house. I can still hear

During a recent visit to the Souk (market) in Jordan. Take a deep breath! One brother posing. Summer 2008.

Nothing like a fresh pita or flat bread in the Souk. Summer 2009.

the animated conversations and the laughter that came from small cafés, taverns, and "soukes" (sidewalk cafés), where people drank Arak and smoked water pipes. Merchants and buyers swelled the streets, and the fragrance of fresh herbs and spices, bread baking, and coffee brewing filled the morning air.

The townspeople all knew one another. Some were relatives, friends, or even in-laws. They marked another day of commerce and trade, visiting for a brief time and catching up on the day's news.

I tell you, I miss those days. Today, modern equipment, technology, transportation, and a generation uninterested in the past have taken a toll on those fundamental traditions and delightful morning strolls in the village center market. People now buy ready-to-eat, prepackaged meals and frozen dinners from super food centers, instead of wholesome food from village markets. When I was growing up, our plant-based diet was simple, tasty, and healthy, and everyone ate together at mealtime. Today's animal-based diet and on-the-run eating habits are the total opposite.

■ ■ ■

My grandparents. The ultimate love story. The most perfect, kindest, and hardest-working people I have ever known. And yes, I love you and miss you. My grandmother was a true poet, and my grandfather was a romantic soul. Summer 1963.

Serving good and healthy food has always been the hallmark of my approach to cooking. This philosophy was a way of life at my grandparents' home in the northern mountains of Jordan and in my mom's kitchen, and it continues in my home and at BFS. Whether I am cooking a meal to impress two people or two hundred, happy occasions are a good reason to celebrate the gift of good food. In the Middle East, these occasions are always accompanied by great music (Om-Kalthoom), Rababbeh (an instrument made of sticks and goatskin in the shape of a violin) and Oud (a handcrafted guitar), as well as great food and good company at a humble outdoor setting. Now that's good enough to celebrate and enjoy the spices of life any day.

Traditional customs of eating Mensuf. Yum! A gesture to welcome you and enjoy in good health. Fall 2006.

At holiday gatherings, three-day wedding extravaganzas, engagement festivities, birthday parties, or other occasions, the same people were usually there, no matter who was hosting the event. The menu (mensef, mujedarah, upside down chicken and rice) was pretty much the same each time, but when mom cooked the meal, it was something special. My mom was a master at all of these dishes.

Hand-rolled pita bread or flat bread, coming from your front door step, with Mom's love, IS PRICELESS. Summer 1999.

My mother would labor all day to make a banquet out of every meal, whether it was a simple lunch or an important dinner. I was compelled to dive in, not knowing what I was doing, to lend a helping hand. After all, she was feeding at least a dozen people at a minimum every day for every meal. Of course, Dad's point of view was that the door was always open for more guests to just drop in, and that they did. My dad and mom (after her arrival to "Amreekah") continued to bless and enrich their siblings with the same traditions, good and plentiful food, great memories, and a wide-open heart and home to all.

We sat to eat a meal on the floor, on a handmade quilt, with our legs folded underneath. Pillows surrounded us, and the food was set on a large tray (Tabaqu) in the middle. The drinks, mostly milk, water, coffee, and sweet tea, were conveniently located nearby. Whenever we sat to eat, the eldest present would pronounce the presence of God (Allah) and give thanks to God Almighty and the Creator of things, before we all started to eat. Then, depending on the occasion, we would toast the event, the person, or even the long day of hard work. Breaking bread with family and with friends or others who dropped by was as important as the food itself.

We respected food in general, and specifically bread, as the gift of nature and the gods. My mom and my grandmother before her would pick up a fallen piece of bread off the floor, kiss it, and place it on her forehead. She would then ask God for forgiveness and thanked Him for the eternal gift He gave us. Such respect for the gift of food, and the importance of sharing it, has been slowly slipping away. My parents and grandparents would roll in their respective graves if they knew what happened to the time when a family sat to enjoy a meal all together.

Long after the evening meal was served, friends and families stayed late to sip on coffee and a number of healthful and zesty snacks. The topics of discussion changed from politics to harvest to the weather and then back to politics. This is what is referred to as "Sahra" or "Chat 'n' Chew," a little bit of many things such as Mezza-like appetizers and a wide selection of assorted spirits and drinks. The Mezza is a very simple treat of warm bread, cheese, nuts, sliced cucumbers, ripe tomatoes, Laban, and variety of olives and pickled vegetables (peppers, baby eggplant, turnips), along with fruit, hummus, and Zaatar.

Traditional Mezza dishes.

My family loved company, loved to share with everyone, especially new visitors or friends, and my dad used to go out of his way to ensure that they were welcomed and comfortable. He constantly urged the guests to test this or try that, insisting that they would be inspired to eat even if they weren't hungry.

During a warm spring day, and a visit from Grandfather in front of the two-room house. The oldest two, enjoying similar weather in Europe for college studies. Spring 1967.

In my mother's kitchen, and my grandmother's before her, the most amazing and simple collection of a few brass pots, some cast-iron sauté pans, multiple clay jugs, and some odds and ends of utensils produced an undeniably grand array of foods from tasty treats to appetizers to an entire collection of various plates forming a delicate and natural balance of colorful food and great flavors. Most importantly, it was all healthy; from national dishes (mensaf) to baked fish in tahini to roasted lamb and plenty of salads.

Even today, we siblings, as grownups with children of our own, still wonder—how did my mother do it? How did she keep the household in good order, or even remember

At the conclusion of a holiday celebration, I joined the family and my sisters for pictures. I am taking advantage of the camera being around. I was never shy in public! Spring 1965.

the kids' names, let alone keep track of us and everything else in the house—food, clothing, sports, travel, etc. In addition, by the time my oldest brothers were about to graduate from college, my mom was about to give birth to our youngest brother.

Her secret was organization skill and time management. And she had a little help! She recognized my knack for working with food, which I now understand perfectly and appreciate more and more. As a true and brilliant "manager" with soft authority and efficient delegation, she would assign to me mundane cooking tasks such as peeling potatoes, rolling stuffed grape leaves, or stuffing squash, rolling couscous, and making butter and Leban, and even rolling yogurt cheese balls. Mom loved fish but she frowned at the prospect of cleaning fish, because it reminded her of the skin of a snake. Therefore, it became my job to scale and clean the "fish du jour."

My mom was the source of love, the voice of humility and kindness. Brought up in a small village on a family farm, she learned to be self-sufficient. She never had a "job," never attended school and did not know how to read or write. I don't remember her dressed in anything but the black robe-like clothing as seen lately on the TV evening news as images of faraway Mid-Eastern places flash across the screen. She never donned the black veil to cover her face, though—she just wore a cotton or silk head scarf. Her clothing and shoes were simple and inexpensive. She wore no make-up and used no hairspray on her naturally curly hair. It wasn't until the late 70s or early 80s that, here in America, she started to wear lipstick and other makeup.

■ ■ ■

My dad tried very hard to succeed and prosper in Jordan, which is a very poor country. Finally, he decided that he should follow in his friends' footsteps and venture to the "promised land," America (which many pronounced "Amreekah"). His decision was not a selfish one, but rather a way to rescue his wife and children (nine boys and two girls).

From time to time my dad would invite his friends, relatives, and our beloved Italian-Arab priest over for dinner or dessert. "Father Mario," God bless him, I know he is in a better place, used to love to visit my family. Coffee was brewing, sweet minted tea was being poured, and fruit and nuts were being served in abundance. In the meantime, we kids were milling around, teasing stray cats, wanting to be a part of the evening. As we heard the laughter, the chatter, and the munching, we always wanted to crash the party, but mom kept us on a tight leash in the next and only room left in the house. As we squirmed around and had grand pillow fights on the homemade mattresses which had been stuffed with our own old ground up clothes as the filling, we would suddenly hear the conversation: "So, did you hear anything yet, Hanna?" "No, but Insha Allah. Soon, very soon." We all wondered what it meant.

After a dozen or more years of waiting and obtaining an American sponsorship, he managed to get a work visa to come to America. As some of you know, moving from one house to another is trauma enough. However, leaving not only one's country, but also a continent, to go to another is epic in comparison. Hardest of all is leaving one's parents and other relatives, the "hood," personal property, and inheritance from prior generations. Amazingly, it seems little planning went into this monumental decision.

My dad was a proud man, very smart, considerate, and compassionate. He was very knowledgeable and assertive, yet thoughtful, and in command of any situation he encountered. He was a good listener and teacher. He was book smart, and he loved poetry and learning. For someone like my dad to leave the homeland for another country took courage, character, and determination to do the right thing, overcome every obstacle, and sacrifice all for a cause bigger than himself.

■ ■ ■

I was sixteen when my dad found his path to dreamland and immigrated to this country. My two oldest brothers were studying in Venice, Italy, courtesy of Father Mario as thanks for my dad's generosity and my mom's good cooking. My brother directly older than myself (that puts me at number four from the top) was studying to be a priest in a Catholic school in Jerusalem prior to the famous Six Day War in the Mideast. That left me, a sixteen-year-old student, a Christian minority, with very few friends, in charge of the family while my dad was in America. I had seven siblings and a mom to care for, worry about, and help with various chores, including food production and cooking. Don't get me wrong, my mom was a great cook and capable of producing great amounts of food in no time, but frankly, knowing what I know now, I don't know how she did it with limited resources and very limited kitchen facilities. Remember, everything was harvested, prepared, cooked, and stored

Two rooms, a lemon tree, two girls, nine boys, and one flat roof, perfect for sun-dried fruits, vegetables, nuts, wheat, and anything else. Summer 1999.

by hand. I guess this is where I get my minimalist approach to cooking while managing to create great dishes (so I am told). After school, the normal chores, cleaning, feeding the younger ones, and studies, I had to help unfold the huge mountains of mattresses, creating a sea of beds wall to wall for everyone to sleep on. These mattresses were handmade of course, light yet comfortable, and were topped with heavy, stuffed quilts, giving us firm beds to sleep on and comfortable covers to sleep under. As you know, the desert gets cold at night even though it is hot during the day.

With no TV to watch, no games to play, and no easy access to markets, malls, theaters, or neighborhood clubs, we were pretty much homebound. We spent a lot of time at church, not only for religious purposes, including helping the priests and nuns at the altar, but also playing ping pong, volleyball, or soccer with the neighbor's kids. Radio was a prominent fixture in my life for music and news, and for listening to dramatic plays, poetry reading, and popular radio puzzles, especially during the Muslim holy month of Ramadan, the Islamic celebration of fasting from sunrise to sunset. Ramadan was a challenging time for those who did not practice this religion or observe the tradition, because it was impolite to eat in front of those who were fasting. But of course, when the time came to break the day's fasting, it was an all-out feast. The market buzzed with buyers, and the air was filled with delicious smells of falafel, shawarama, baked bread, and fried sweets. Every night was a festival to enjoy and remember.

■ ■ ■

Open market, water pipes, Arabic coffee, the smell of delicious food, and the sound of life and music. Summer 2008.

With the pen I am using, the wine I am drinking, and the music (Arabic) I am listening to, I honestly can't control the flow of words and emotions. So I am going to keep on going until it is all out of me or the ink runs out. Don't worry! I bought at least a dozen pens. Excuse me, I need to put my pen down and go get a napkin to wipe my tears off my face. They are making a mess of my ink on this page, making my paper wet, and the pen isn't writing on wet paper. Sorry, I am back now.

■ ■ ■

It was at a school play, the hall is filling up with parents, crazed kids, teachers, vendors, etc. The 7:00 P.M. show time is approaching, and my wife (Irish, German, American heritage—go figure), married five years prior to me, this tall, dark-skinned Middle Eastern man, is standing next to me holding on to the hand of my first son tightly and nervously. He is about to go on stage in a few minutes. I am, to tell you the truth, a nervous wreck, but I do not show it. My hands are sweaty and feel clammy and cold. My face, however, shows that look of pride, but my heart is racing underneath my freshly pressed shirt, maybe a tie, I don't remember, and like usual, there are no pictures—my wife never believed in the picture documentary. She enjoyed the police shows, drama stories, and the soaps. OK, there were no pictures to show what we were wearing. Still, I wanted my son to be the best on stage. I wanted him not to be afraid; I wanted him to be cheered and applauded the most. OK, that sounds really selfish, self-serving, and stupid. After all, he is a kid, maybe 4 years old, but to

Never too late? Or Is it never too early? The hat is $1, the dialogue and surprised look is priceless, and learning the etiquette of how to hold a glass of red wine is timeless! June 1986.

me it's his debut. As parents mingle and have those famous small chats, "small talk," here I am coaching/drilling my son to stand straight, fix his shirt, look straight ahead, and smile. Suddenly, the lights flicker. The announcer asks for all the kids to go up front with their teacher so they can be arranged seated or standing, at which point I am going nuts, hoping that my son would be standing in front, preferably in the middle of the set. You see to me he is special, like all other kids to their parents. But my take on it was much deeper than that. Let me elaborate. He was handsome, tall, top of his class, had a new cute outfit, new shirt, tie, jacket, slacks, as well as shoes and socks. You see, this is what I knew at the time and what I know now. I had the best-looking, best-dressed kid on stage. "He has to come through for daddy," I asserted to myself under my breath. As the kids quiet down, the audience is being seated, anticipating the performance of their kids' lives on a stage. This collection of fidgety, semi-crazed, grinning kids, and wow, in front my son is one of them. The piano teacher keys a couple of notes to quiet everyone and then . . . that is when my son, standing up straight, looking straight ahead tries to search into the audience for dada and then he utters with a clear, magnified, soft voice, "DADDY!? I LOVE YOU!!" Not only that was an unexpected debut, but it was an impromptu solo performance—wow—and the timing was absolutely perfect!

That is when I discovered the meaning of a father-son relationship and the assertion publicly that I was Dad and he was my son, unlike the experience, exploration, and excitement of the birth of one. Of course, the audience cheered, laughed, surprisingly with approval, clapped, and my son intermittently turned around to see his teary-eyed parents, nodding thank you with great pride and gratitude. What the audience did not know is I am thinking "mission accomplished. The show is over early. How can I reset, sit quietly, and listen? How can anything top this?" Of course, two humble, teary-eyed, young parents obliged and stayed throughout the whole remaining amateur performance. Later, of course, we were rushed, perhaps overwhelmed, with well-wishing and congratulations, smiles, high fives, etc. I am not trying to upstage or take away from the other parents. I know they all felt the same way about their own kids.

This episode in my life, and what it meant to me then and still does, I am sure, is a direct reflection and exact duplicate of my own performance, coaching, and attempt as a result or conclusion similar to that of my own. Growing up in a close family, whenever it was my time for that life lesson, I was taught by my dad all these things. But somehow, I realized this same lesson of how proud a parent could be as was directly taught to me by my own son in one single line, a simple place, and an unpredictable night.

Those are perhaps the same words of wisdom and nurturing nudges I got from my own father long ago, sometimes entirely unassuming and nonchalant, but often deliberate, mostly direct, and to the point.

■ ■ ■

Back in the U.S., my father's Promised Land jobs were more or less an extension of his jobs in the old country. The "Promised Land" never promised him anything and was short on hope. One of his first jobs was an all around "most willing to do anything" job at a VW car dealership which was owned by a second- or third-generation Lebanese family.

Dad lived alone in a one-bedroom apartment with a tiny kitchen and shared a community bath/shower room. After having been in America for two months, he went into a small Greek diner to have something to eat. After a few visits, "Jimmy," the gregarious Greek-American owner, convinced my dad to take a job part time. He would be a dishwasher of course, since I have never seen my dad cook anything, he being the only son of a family with three sisters and a farming mom and dad. I am sure he was spoiled and never even had to fry an egg for himself. Through this job, my dad was able to socialize with new friends with similar cultural backgrounds, religious followings, and values (not the language, however; loneliness is a terrible thing). He would eat Greek food and some Lebanese salads and pilafs, watch the news on a second-hand black-and-white television, and speak Arabic to Andy, one of the longtime cooks, an overweight, fast-talking Lebanese man. Andy spoke broken Arabic, but well enough to delight my dad, and it definitely eased his loneliness. Andy also lent Dad his support on the job, which made it a little easier. My dad was also able to earn a little extra money, which he saved and sent back to the oldest kids in Europe and the rest of the family and kids in Jordan. This continued for some five years until the next chapter unfolded, resulting in the mass immigration of the entire clan in 1973.

I know that his full-time jobs and part-time jobs earned him enough money to support himself in his new land and his family and siblings back in the old country. But it did not stop there. He wanted to learn the language, support his large family, get his kids a quality education, and prove to himself and the rest of the relatives, clans, and parents that he could take a risk, accomplish his goals, send money home, and look like a rich person. You see, all of this is a status symbol, a great front that many who came to America adopted. You couldn't be poor in a rich country like America. It was the goal to somehow fuel the egos and convince others, perhaps, to follow the same road to "Amreekah."

My dad learned the language, not from studies, but from absorbing the spoken language at work, the diner, and with Andy, who spoke Arabic as poorly as my dad spoke English (that's one reason they related to one another and learned from each other). Another thing that also helped was his interaction with the neighbors he encountered in the common area at his resident apartment. Dad adopted the name "John," which is the same as Hanna in Arabic. Surprisingly, all his new friends in America had very short names too, like Joe, Cy, Nick, Gus, Bob, Ann, Ed, Barb—they were easy for him to remember and to practice and use later. My dad's friends adored him and loved his generosity, great self-awareness, the way he was comfortable in his own skin, and his confidence. To some, he was their hero, because he did something they had never done, and they were amazed at the selfless life he led. Dad had no relatives nearby in his newly adopted hometown, so he spent a lot of time with these people. There were a few he would have been better off without (we've all experienced that), but some became longtime friends.

My father was a generous, loving man, yet he was lonesome at times. If time permitted, he would travel by train to nearby Yonkers to visit relatives and friends from the same village back in Jordan, spend the weekend, and satisfy his need to hear fresh news from home brought back by recent visitors to the homeland. These visits enabled him to reconnect with some childhood buddies and compare "war stories." Each went to great lengths to claim that his journey had been longer, more difficult, and more tedious than anyone else's. All would sit around and discuss their accomplishments, their jobs, how many two family homes they purchased, who made the best deal lately, or who had more money. Each would tell a story bigger than the previous one, just to upstage the other guy.

■ ■ ■

This risky journey to start a new life in another country on another continent was the start of the domino effect of the many things life brought bearing down on our family. Once we moved to the U.S., life was never the same again. Don't get me wrong, on balance it was a good, even great move. It was worthwhile and made us who we are, a close and strong family that knows how to deal with adversity. It is not about how much was lost, or why the decision was not discussed with us. Our family was not a democracy, but a monarchy; Dad was the king and rightfully so. After all, we had a great model in "King Hussein" and his ancestors before him. Rather, it is about how much we learned, changed, and gained.

This new culture did not change the values and the moral fabric of this great large family, however. We all held onto and are still holding onto the dream and the struggle to survive. We are driven to achieve and ultimately succeed. Looking back, I am still trying to figure out what that "thing" called success is!

We struggled to be an immigrant family in a distant land attempting to fit in during a strange time in America (1967–1974), while trying to figure out what it was like to be an American, "Amerkani," and possibly even a successful engineer, doctor, or lawyer. My dad instilled in all of us the desire and determination to excel, and he always pointed this out as the reason why we came to "Amreekah."

■ ■ ■

As I was growing up, my grandparents, farmers to their core, taught us the meaning of the harvest, the respect it deserved, and how blessed we were to have this great land and the fruit it provided us. Sometimes, my grandfather would sit on the dark red soil, mostly rich clay, and rub his hands together with the soil between his palms, explaining that it makes us who we are. We are people of the land, and that is good and honorable.

Our permanent home was in the village, but during the summer season we moved to make-shift houses where the crops grew. For example, vineyards were located in one part of the village, the wheat fields were in a different part, and the olive groves were scattered in several distant locations. So when summer grew closer upon us, we would build makeshift tree houses, fully equipped with the necessities to live for two or three months. Supplies for daily use were transported by horses or mules every couple of days or as needed. Most times, the trips from the farm camp "tree house" to the village was a two- to three-hour walk each way on foot. For us kids, this was an exciting adventure, dis-covering something new to bring back to the village to play with and to share the story with others over supper. The family laughed with the kids, captured by their imagi-nation, interest, and innocent cu-riosity about the different places we went to. Often, the conversation would lead to who was more scared or who found the smoothest, shini-est, or more perfectly shaped piece of limestone. Often, we sang folk or popular songs, only to be rescued by others because we did not pro-nounce words correctly, forgot the

The only way I knew how to harvest the olives! In great anticipation of tasting the harvest. Fall 2008.

Peace on earth, Heaven on earth, God bless this gift of beautiful land and its people. Summer 2008.

lyrics, or messed up the rhythm. We would all laugh and enjoy the company until bed time. We all rose hours before the sunrise. My grandfather and grandmother were the first ones up to make sure everything for that day's trip was packed, especially food for the hardworking teenage laborers of the day. Plenty of water, flatbread, cheese, olives, and vegetables made it into our supplies trunk to be enjoyed in the shade after a long day of work.

Forgive me if I sound like a proud member of a farming family when I talk about our "farm," even though I am, and that's how I feel. The truth of the matter is, I have always loved the life of a farmer, and even today, I still love the farm-fresh markets and all that they offer. Farmers' markets, either in my neighborhood or discovered on the side of a highway during my travels, are the best places to find the finest, freshest fruits and vegetables. As a foodie, I am always intrigued by the variety and choice you can find there, and I am inspired to create great-tasting dishes.

Just the thought of handpicked vegetables and fruits combined with grain, legumes, and nuts inspires people to eat well and healthy naturally. All through my life, there has always been a bowl of fruit on our table, prompting us to eat fresh fruit daily without even trying. You see, when you can pick your fruit and make it your center of attention, you will eat it, enjoy it, and savor the great taste of the moment . . . all the time.

Early on, as I was watching my grandmother and my mother prepare a meal, the thing that struck me most was the use of fresh herbs and spices in the daily food they prepared. As great cooks, they knew the right spices, mostly freshly ground, and used them skillfully and with artistic flair, without using measuring cups or measuring spoons. You see, they were using these herbs and spices in place of salt to bring out the *ta3m*—the rich taste or flavors— in food. Not only did they know salt was not good for you, but they also knew that these herbs enrich food and stimulate your appetite in a very healthy way. I have lots of happy memories of my grandmother's and my mom's simple methods, techniques, and approaches to cooking. Today, cooking professionally and teaching, I reflect passionately on those days; those memories inspire me to use only fresh and good ingredients in my cooking.

Every medical organization, health publication, and other associates all speak and promote the benefits a Mediterranean diet (lifestyle) has on our health. So one can say that what began for me fifty years ago is once again rising to the forefront of healthy cuisines. There is major emphasis on fresh fruits, vegetables, legumes, whole grain, olive oil, fish, and herbs. So as we move forward as cooks and professionals of all types, we certainly can learn from history when it comes to food and from the people who preserved and honored those traditions. We can then continue to honor them into the future.

My attempt here is to seduce you into your kitchen to start your own "renaissance," so that you will create simple and delicious food without fear or hesitation. My intent is to provide enough guidance to allow you to achieve successful results and great tasting dishes, yet these recipes are also designed to be flexible, easy to prepare, and fun to execute. They were developed, adapted, perfected, and tested at many of my cooking classes held at my restaurant, BFS Restaurant. Generally, many of these recipes, from the Middle East and from around

the Mediterranean, are considered heart healthy, but I have made some modifications to keep true to the heart-healthy approach as much as possible.

I hope that this book captures the flavor of the many favorite recipes of my family, my best recollections of the simple delights of my early childhood years, all the time spent in the kitchen throughout my adulthood, and twenty years of developing great-tasting food in my restaurant. The ever-changing and ultra-modern kitchens, high-tech equipment, availability of specialty foods, imported spices and seasonings, and the abundance of fresh fruit, vegetables, and herbs year round make cooking and eating like a Mediterranean that much easier and fun. So what are you waiting for? Start a whole new way of cooking and enjoy life!

LEFT: Was not fashionable then, and not yet in fashion now. I was making a statement for the high school yearbook. Wow! That was a long time ago, yet it seems so near. One never should lose the culture or values. Be rooted and connected, even in the smallest things. You will always reflect fondly on the meaning and the goodness of it all. Fall 1970.

RIGHT: All are Invited! Eat! Summer 1999.

BELOW: God has a great view of this blessed land! The land of the prophets. Late summer 2008.

ABOVE: For years this was known to all as the Rabadi Castle. Now it is known as the Ajlune Castle. This will never change in my mind. But it is a great view of three surrounding states. Go visit this historic place. Summer 2009.

ABOVE: Arabic coffee at its best—especially at the foot of the Rabadi Castle in Ajlune, Jordan! Capitalism flourishes even in the least suspected places. I love it. Summer 2009.

LEFT: My overgrown village, Ajlune, after years of poor development and expansions. I used to live in it but do not recognize it now. Its called progress! I call it poor planning! Leave it alone. Summer 2009.

ABOVE: A souk, or open street market. Sweets, nuts, and halava candy. Oh my! Summer 2004.

RIGHT: A traveling beverage salesman. Gourmet coffee and tea on the go! With all the bells and whistles, ready to serve. Summer 2009

A person is what he eats.

ABOVE: Legumes, grains and couscous, too! Summer 2006.

LEFT: Mezza at one of the food tables at a recent gathering.

BELOW: Earthly Heaven! Rolling hills, distant fields, red soil, and the vivid blue skies. Fall 2007.

LEFT: A pose in front of the Christmas tree, on a short visit during holiday break from college. Proud parents. Christmas 1974.

BELOW: Flowered shirt, glass of wine, checkmate, and a loving kiss from Dad. Fall 1973.

ABOVE: A comforting mom. A moment after the "rising son." A large dose of Arabic coffee is much needed. Get a haircut! Fall 1975.

RIGHT: A photo and patterns in plaids! A moment with my grandmother on her short visit to the USA. Conversation and remembrance. She loved it! Winter 1975.

The Journey Begins

Ajlune, Jordan

I joined my dad in the U.S. when I was 17. Nine years later, my dad encouraged me to go back to Jordan for a visit. Initially, I wasn't interested—I was too busy getting my PhD in management/corporate dynamics; I wanted to understand how corporations work, and why some succeed and some fail.

After a while, however, I began to question whether I was on the right path. My college buddies began visiting with their new jobs, nice sports cars, and girlfriends. Here I was, in debt from college loans and working, in addition to pursuing my degree. My social life was, at best, minimal, because much of my time was consumed by graduate schoolwork. I did lots of research, which required focus and quiet time, and I was in a relationship on a path to failure.

During this time, I befriended a great fellow student who also was from Jordan. His family, whose name I won't mention, was of the Jordanian elite, rich and politically connected. In the interest of protecting his identity, I will call him HM. For two years, as he was completing his PhD, we became very good friends. In fact, I introduced him to his girlfriend, and ultimately he married her.

Upon his graduation, his family came to America to attend his graduation. Dr. HM and his family invited everyone, including my family, to a celebratory luncheon. It was a splendid time. During this festive gathering, I was invited to visit my friend

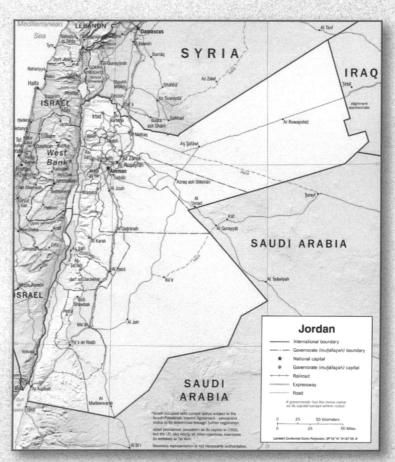

Obligatory passport picture—borrowed jacket, tie and vest. No fashion statement here. Didn't know any better. The look of "back to the future!" Summer 1968.

and his family in Jordan. While I thanked them for the invitation, I didn't seriously consider accepting, but said that I would let them know when the time was right.

However, I still didn't entirely understand why I wanted to get my PhD and I began to think, "What on Earth am I going to do with a PhD? Two more years of schooling left, and what about Jordan!?"

Prior to all of this, my desire to visit my homeland had waned over time. My dad and other family members traveled back and forth almost every year. The talk in our house back then, of course over a massive table filled with food that kept reminding us of where we came from, was about who was there now, who was going back soon and who had just arrived with the latest news. It seemed like we had weekly and even daily updates about the land we had left behind. With this recent invitation, my sense of longing for and connection to Jordan began to grow.

After deciding to end my PhD studies in the fall of 1977, I received my second Master's degree, and in December of the same year I accepted a position as a junior consultant in a statewide organization that provided management consulting services to members of a health care institution. I would start the new job in mid-January and anticipated a busy travel schedule.

Dad could not have been more proud. Even though I did not have a PhD, my willingness to go to Jordan to achieve another goal or close another chapter, and at the same time visit my family and newfound friend in "high places" in the Kingdom of Jordan, made him very happy.

Was this first trip to Jordan a business trip?

En route to Jordan, we had to vacate the plane during the lengthy layover in Amsterdam, so I toured the various shops and eateries just to kill time. I was also eager to take in the sight of travelers from all over the world. The crowded airport stretched for as far as the eye could see in all directions. Endless lines of passengers from many ethnic backgrounds uttered their excitement and anxieties in many languages.

It would have been great to converse in Arabic with another traveling passenger, but that didn't happen, so I kept busy reading two day old Arabic newspapers to brush up a little on the written version of the language. I also practiced speaking, in my head, with ordinary people, those in "higher places," and business travelers I might have a chance to meet. I listened to Arabic music, and although I didn't recognize the new artists and their songs, the basic sound of the music was close to the music I grew up with. Not much had changed, I thought.

As the airplane began its final leg of the journey, I started feeling anxious. Perhaps it was fear of the unknown, or that my childhood might not be as I had remembered it. More likely, it was because this was my first return to a country that I left under false pretenses with fake documents to avoid being drafted into the army. What if I were discovered, captured, imprisoned and punished? As I was trying to get some shuteye, the roar of the engines, the background chatter and the voices of the stewardess speaking to the passengers competed with my swirling thoughts about how to deal with these possibilities. In my jacket pocket, I had two passports. With great relief, I realized that as an immigrant with dual citizenship, I needed only to present my American passport, my possible ticket to freedom again, to the authorities.

Heavenly landscape! On Earth as it is in Heaven! Fall 2008

Olive grove! This is what it is all about and where it all started. Caring for the land, the source of love and food, and yes, values, culture, and way of life. Fall 2008.

The giant 747 finally arrived in Amman, Jordan. As I descended the stairs, I was greeted by the brilliant sun, the hot, dry, dusty Jordanian air and the uniquely blue Jordanian sky. Suddenly I realized I was "home," and slowly every part of me began to relax a little, but the feeling was short-lived. All around us and everywhere you could see were fully armed soldiers with automatic machine guns; land rovers and army jeeps topped with turret guns, gunmen at full attention, roamed around the tarmac. This was the scene much of the time in the late sixties and early- to mid- seventies, but I certainly didn't expect this level of security on that early January day! Perhaps this was the normal state of affairs for a country seemingly always in a state of war. My anxiety and fear returned. My heart beat faster, but one thing I learned over the years is that no matter what, "Don't let them see you sweat." I figured, what are the odds of their discovering my status as a past citizen of Jordan a decade prior? How would they know that I bribed a Bedouin to escape and evade the draft for a war I did not believe in? Let me take you back a bit . . .

■ ■ ■

A few weeks before I left Jordan, I was waiting to get my visa and proper official papers in order to leave the country. At that time the country was in a state of alert—a state of war—

and for a seventeen year old adult, leaving Jordan turned out to be next to impossible due to the draft policy in effect. Born to a large family of nine boys and two girls, my position as the fourth child from the top made me a perfect candidate to be drafted into the Jordanian army. It was time to leave.

With my Dad already in the U.S., I began to worry about Mom since she would be left all alone to manage the household, care for six children, and make sure that they stayed out of trouble during a time of war, in a country in which they were a Christian minority.

My mother and I were put in touch with a deep-voiced man with an aura of authority who had connections and a reputation for having certain "ways" to get things done. He was tall, dark, very husky, and draped in Bedouin-like attire: headdress wrapped over his mouth and nose and all around his big head, black and gray striped jacket, and an oversized, gold-trimmed shawl wrapped around and over the rest of his clothing. In exchange for a large sum of money (a bribe) he would use his connections to get me the needed approval for a visitor's visa and passport so that I could leave Jordan "legally" by car through Syria to Lebanon for a period of ten days. All of this was under the guise of visiting my mother's relatives in Beirut, Lebanon. And so began an unforgettable journey.

■ ■ ■

My neighbor was an English teacher at the local school, and his aunt and other relatives were tenants in one of our apartments adjacent to our house. As the time grew closer to my semi-secret departure on this "short trip" to visit my mother's ancestors, he was kind enough to offer to join me, this 17-year-old virgin traveler, on the taxi ride to Amman.

As we traveled, he recited English words and small phrases that might be useful during my travels. He also advised and warned me about what I could and could not say, and cautioned me not to speak to strangers. That's funny, I thought. Leaving home as a teenager, going through three countries to get to my ultimate destination on another continent, everything is strange and everyone is a stranger. "How can you tell?" I naively asked. He said, "If they don't know you, your father, your family's name or where and what village you are from, then they are strangers. The only ones you should talk to are the security people and those who ask questions about official business. Don't go anywhere or do anything you are not supposed to." He gave me a piece of paper on which he had written the phone number of the church across the street from my home. "Keep this in a safe place and don't lose it," he said. He gave me some money to use if I needed to eat something.

Amman's bus and taxi terminals were noisy, filled with the smell of burning diesel, and teeming with departing passengers. Passengers traveling from Amman to Damascus were to line up in a designated spot on the street curb, completely ready with our luggage, belongings and a paid ticket to board the next taxi in line. After 15 or 20 minutes, there was still only me and one other passenger. We deposited most of our belongings in the trunk of the taxi, with some luggage tied securely with ropes on the roof of the car, the double ropes wrapped around into the inside of the car through the windows so we could hold onto them as well. As we waited for more passengers, we heard loud haggling and arguing between our driver and the driver of the taxi behind us. Our driver leaned into the car window and shouted at the two of us to remove our belongings and place them in the taxi behind us. Reluctantly, the other passenger and I vacated our taxi to make way for a group of five passengers traveling together. After going through the same maneuvers of securing the luggage with rope, etc. we got in the second taxi and waited. Another 20–30 minutes went by until two more passengers arrived, and the driver impatiently decided to take off rather than wait for a full load of five, as it was getting late.

Traveling north from Amman, Jordan to the Syrian border, there was little to see and not much to talk about, especially to "strangers." The taxi was hot, smoky and noisy, the air thick and dusty. I sat back and tried to rehearse the English words and phrases my neighbor had taught me. As the taxi pressed on through the empty landscape, I could hear the gurgling sound of music coming from the radio in the front of the car, interrupted from time to time by announcers, religious readings and news. My heart trembled, my eyes teared, and my mind was unsettled; I was conflicted between the home I just left behind and the unknown world I was about to enter. I could still feel Mom's kisses on my cheek and taste the last meal she prepared for me before my departure.

Can't resist the yearning for and the belonging to this land. I miss being there. Fall 2008

The vast emptiness of this bleak land suddenly came to life. Traffic backed up on the one-lane highway connecting the two friendly countries. Sheep and shepherds, flocks of goats, donkeys and an occasional cow or two shared the road with vehicles. I lowered my window and was overwhelmed by the dry, hot air, and the smells and sounds around us. Bells around goats' necks tinkled rhythmically; sandy dust kicked up by the moving herds of animals coated the car window, making it harder to see. I could barely distinguish people from animals in the distance. At the driver's demand, I closed the window. The noise grew fainter for a moment. Suddenly, police cars raced by, sirens screaming; the crowd grew larger, and sheep and goats, with disgruntled blats and cries, wandered unattended. Cars stood still, motors running, with all doors open; passengers stood and stared at billowing smoke in the distance, covering their eyes, noses and faces to avoid the burning smell. The sound of "call to prayer" began to ring across the landscape under blue skies. The black smoke towered over the horizon as the traffic inched forward, then stopped again. That's when we got word from passersby and horrified onlookers that an out-of-control car had crossed oncoming traffic going south, barreled over the make-shift barrier, plummeted into a deep gully and burst into flames. I was shocked to discover that it was the taxi we had initially boarded and been forced to vacate. Everyone in our taxi prayed and thanked God for our safety. After riding together as strangers all this time, we now felt connected by our survival and incredible luck. After a short while, several of the passengers recited the Koran, prayed and bid those mortals a peaceful journey to their God and creator, asking God to forgive them and bless their families and loved ones.

I was consumed with thoughts of what could have been. Call it fate or call it luck, I guess you could say that my life's journey was not yet complete.

It was late afternoon when our taxi reached the Syrian-Jordanian border checkpoint. Only two hours earlier, I had escaped death by crashing and burning in an exploding taxi. Now a second roadblock to my journey occurred when my passport/visa was confiscated by the border police on orders of the same man, the Bedouin, who had been paid handsomely to ensure my safe and secure exit out of Jordan. Of course the reason was greed and the abuse of power. For the second time in less than eight hours, I was ordered to vacate the taxi, and was taken into custody by the border police.

It was nearly a day before I was allowed to contact my mother. I was desperate and I begged and eventually was permitted to make a phone call so I could leave a message for my mother with the nuns at the church across from our home. Of course, just the mention of nuns, priests and church drew ridicule, laughter and teasing remarks.

The nuns ran across the street to get my mother to the phone. Out of breath, crying, fearful, her voice trembling, she asked anxiously what went wrong. I began to explain the tale of the journey so far, where I was and what I needed her to do. I had been instructed to tell my mother that my papers were not complete and that she needed to get in touch with the Bedouin to clear things up. In reality, this vicious thief held me as a hostage on the border to extort more money from my lonely mother knowing that she would, of course, pay up. As my mother heard this, she began to sob, and then her fear turned to anger. She was determined to get me out of this dilemma, and vowed that this man would be responsible for instructing the border guard to release me immediately.

I spent a sleepless night in a stable filled with goats, chickens, a couple of mules and a whole lot of hay that was soaked with animal urine and smelled of manure. I rested on a bed of dry hay, only to be disrupted and kept awake by passing sirens, the resident rooster, and other animal companions milling around.

By midmorning, one of the border guards let me know that all of my papers were now in order and that I was free to go and take the next taxi. I quickly gathered my belongings and stood by the checkpoint on the side of the highway, hoping for a ride to Beirut through Syria. After waiting for a couple of hours, I was able to board a taxi that had room for one more passenger. I sat squeezed into the front middle semi-seat, and was barely able to move. After one of the passengers departed somewhere in the Baaka Valley, west of Damascus, the ride became a little more comfortable and I began to enjoy the sight of beautiful green pastures and valleys as we traveled westward to the eastern shore of the Mediterranean.

It was late afternoon on a gorgeous mid-June day, the breeze fragrant with water and mint, when we arrived in the Paris of the Middle East—Beirut. The taxi dropped me off in the hotel's circular driveway. I managed to secure my belongings in the hotel storage room, since it would be seven or eight hours before the airport limousine would pick me up and take me to the KLM gates, where I would begin the final leg of my journey. By then my dad had been informed of my unexpected delay at the border and was given the new arrival times and plane information so he could pick me up from the airport.

As I passed through the hotel lobby, I was fascinated by the sight of so many people from faraway places. Music played softly in the background, and I could smell coffee, minted tea, falafal, and something with lamb. I was tired, thirsty, and very hungry, so I set out to find something to eat in the nearby neighborhood. I was craving something simple and familiar, like a shawarma sandwich or falafel and hummus, and perhaps a side of tabboule with sweet minted tea. I had only enough money to purchase a small meal at a sidewalk café, but the experience was a feast for the senses. The street was brightly lit, cars whizzed by, and loud music came from every corner. Tantalizing aromas filled the air as waiters served food amid the laughter and conversation of the customers, a mix of natives and visitors. I'd never experienced anything like this in Jordan, where things were more subdued, and untouched by the French influence.

As I strolled back to the hotel, the sounds of the festivities faded in the background. I found myself at the back door of the hotel kitchen. Through the wide-open door I heard music

Pita bread baking in a brick oven.

and voices that sounded familiar, and I suddenly realized that the two people in the kitchen were not "strangers." They spoke the Arabic language and the dialect like I did without the modern twang of the French-influenced Lebanese speech.

I stopped briefly, and as I greeted them by saying "Assalam-Alykoum," they immediately recognized that I was from the same northern part of Jordan as they were. They greeted me with a warm handshake and the traditional Arabic greeting with three kisses, and welcomed me as if I had been lost and then found.

After sharing with them my 48-hour ordeal, they quickly asked if I was hungry, which I was since I only ate what I could afford an hour ago. With true Jordanian hospitality, they insisted that I should eat well because I had a long flight and their food was much better than the airline's. They invited me to sit in the outdoor area, a patio on a nearby landing only a few yards from the sandy beach. The patio was furnished with white cast iron tables and chairs, and was surrounded by short stone pillars topped with a ledge of stone, on which vases of flowers were spaced evenly, looking like extensions of the columns below. The setting sun bathed the Mediterranean in an orange glow as dazzling rays bounced off the sea. I wish I could paint this magnificent scene.

I felt happy and relaxed, forgetting the ordeals of the last two days. What a send-off gift! Here I was, in an elegant setting, viewing my last Middle Eastern sunset, enjoying the limitless hospitality of two new friends and eating some of the best food I'd ever had. I feasted on hummus, warm pita, rice pilaf with braised lamb brain and sweet onion, and baby carrots in clear broth with spinach. A uniformed waiter brought me sweet minted tea in a copper pot, an ornamental tea glass, and sugar cubes in a hand painted ceramic pot, all on a silver platter. It was enough to make me feel like one of the carefree tourists I had seen in the hotel lobby. What an unexpected, delightful dining-out experience! Yum! Zakie.

■ ■ ■

On June 15, 1969, at approximately 6:00 P.M., I arrived in "Amreekah." The pilot of the jumbo jet came on the jet's intercom and began to speak in English, which I didn't fully understand, then in Arabic, welcoming us all and confirming that we had just landed in the international airport called JFK, named after President John F. Kennedy, in New York of the United States of America (U.S. of A.) . . . Amreekah . . . nothing can describe the feeling that came over me at that moment. I'll never forget it.

As we taxied toward the gate, the passengers burst into a joyous exchange of well wishes in many languages and with enthusiastic gestures (high fives, thumbs up and fist punches in the air) celebrating their newfound freedom.

The lines were long for "checking-in" (or should I say "checking out," because of the life I was leaving behind?), as I awaited the start of this new path for freedom, hope, and prosperity in my newly adopted home.

Finally, ah! Approved, passport freshly stamped to confirm my acceptance and entry to this land of freedom. All my trials, tribulations and bad experiences faded into the background as soon as I stepped into the concourse to see my father and two brothers for the first time in months. I will never forget the huge hugs and kisses, lots of pats on the back, and the relief on everyone's faces, especially mine!

Forty years later, as I am writing on this anniversary, I still recall that it was a rainy, cold, and windy night. I will always remember walking through the brightly lit, air conditioned concourse and then stepping outside onto the busy sidewalk to take in the first breath of my new home and new life. We stepped into a yellow taxi, secured my belongings, and drove away from the airport. The darkness slowly took over and the rain pounded the windows of the taxi cab. As I peeked outside through the raindrops that coated the windows, I started to feel safe. No soldiers or guns were in sight.

We arrived at my aunt's house in Yonkers, New York, intending to stay just briefly, but at my aunt's insistence, we stayed overnight to visit with my relatives. We enjoyed a vast array of foods—Mezza—and drinks of all kinds amid their welcoming hugs and kisses.

The next morning we drove to my Dad's place in Poughkeepsie, New York. This was one of many houses in a row, a multi-apartment house of three levels. My dad's apartment was made up of one large bedroom on the basement floor with a closet, a storage space, and a kitchenette just large enough for an oven, small sink and space for one person to stand in. The refrigerator was pushed into the storage space under the staircase. In the bedroom there was one large bed and two other folding mattresses and quilt-like covers that reminded me of the same stuff back home in Jordan.

The bathroom/shower was located on the first floor, and was shared with the first floor tenants. I don't recall those tenants ever emerging from their respective rooms and we never associated with or befriended them. I thought, "There go those afternoon gatherings with Mezza, laughter and the company of your neighbors, appreciating life while listening to music and telling stories."

I immediately ventured outdoors to find the olive groves and grape vines, the scent of basil and mint, and the thick greenery climbing the fences. To my total disappointment, this yard did not have anything that resembled green except a few trees and a bunch of neglected thorny shrubs. A couple of abandoned tires and an old grill added to the bleak appearance of the place.

Suddenly I had lost the connection to my childhood memories of gardens, grapes, olives and lemon trees, the chickens, goats and sheep milling around . . . these images were slowly slipping away from me as I experienced such a thing called "Amreekah" and my first inter-action with real Americans, "Amreekanis" in this city.

I have to admit, at first this is not what I have expected to see or experience. I was somewhat disillusioned, and yet part of me thought this is going to be "OK." The belief that this was and "IS" a better place, gave me the confidence, despite the shock of separation from every-thing I knew and grew up with, that things will turn out to be good not only for one "me," but for the whole "my family" in the long run.

The Writing Begins

It's June 7, 2009, the 63rd Tony Awards are on television. It seems everything is upside down or backwards, yet totally new and hopeful again. As I listened to the remake of the music and the movies of the early seventies, the eighties and even the sixties, Sir Elton John's opening song (Electricity) from the 1970s era was playing. It only took a moment, or perhaps even after the first lyric, to bring me back to that place and point in time where I first heard this song upon arriving in Amreekah.

As I paused, listened, and reflected a little, I realized that, somehow I would have to come to terms with my distant and past life and thought of the things I learned and still needed to take with me into the future. You see, suddenly all I heard was the revival of the old songs and they were being made new. Although I heard these songs decades ago, I felt nostalgic about those days, even though I did not understand the lyrics, back then. I was happy and surprised to hear these songs three decades later and appreciating them more now. Yet, I was moved by the words and encouraged as I reflected on the writing of this chapter. You see, in my mind, as is the case in many of us, these songs and words also revived the meaning of "back to basics" or back to the future, as if it were, motto again.

I was reminded of those old days and that point during the French Open Tennis Tournament with Raphael Nadal playing Roger Federer, when I noticed in the background the presence of one of the greatest players who made the game what it is today, Bjorn Borg, with his elegant, stylish and imposing figure, as he cast his shadow over those two young players.

As a reader you may know, the late sixties and early seventies were also a time of uncertainty in the world, as we witnessed and experience a new era born as depicted in the making of the real Woodstock of 1969. The feeling of freedom, love, peace and equality for everyone flourished then, now and forever, still overshadowed the troubles of the time. My intention here is not to endorse, condone or condemn that era, but rather to reflect on how it conjures up the feeling that even then, food was basic, wholesome, important, and natural.

Hence, here is my attempt at getting back to my childhood and the basics of enjoying good food, family and friends, serving natural food for better health and the well-being of us humans and the earth we inhabit. Thank you for letting me share this with you and for joining me on this journey.

Shaw Rabadi

Every age has its book.

LEFT: The first Christmas visit for my youngest at the time. At Grandad's. Say cheese! Christmas 1986.

BELOW: As best man, at the wedding of one of my brothers. With my wife Victoria, sons Brendan and Phillip, and daughter Lexi. April 1995.

BELOW: Jane Fonda (!!) and one of the extras during the filming of *Rollover!* Appeared as a westernized business executive extra in a movie that did roll over then. But look around today at the U.S. financial problems and the foreign investments in our economy. Maybe they should bring back (or roll back) this movie. It was fun to do! Summer 1980.

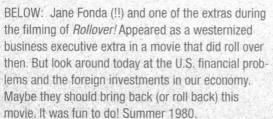

BFS Restaurant . . .

Good health is a
crown on the head
of the healthy, that
only the unhealthy
can see.

. . . and Catering

food fills
the heart
with love.

Grapes are
eaten one
by one.

WHY THE MEDITERRANEAN DIET?

The "Mediterranean diet" by nature is a very loose term and applied by many with a wide array of interpretations. Whether it's the country's location or geography, however, the Mediterranean region shares many common attributes regarding people, history, culture, climate, religion, and most definitely food.

Regardless of how you define the Mediterranean diet, it is still well known that Mediterranean food is the best food to eat for better health and lots of fun to prepare. Mediterranean lifestyle and cuisine are the very things that have primarily shaped the people, their devotion to and love of the land that has built an undeniable passion for their way of life, and cooking. The result is a world-wide appreciation for Mediterranean cuisine as the ultimate for its tasty and healthy options.

A common misconception I have come across is that many people believe that the Mediterranean diet consists of a relatively small number of staple dishes. In fact, the beauty of the cuisine is that there are distinct differences in flavors, spices and other specialty ingredients as you go country to country . . . and yet, there remains a common string of characteristics throughout the region and individual countries. These are the essential elements of the Mediterranean diet, including food lower in saturated fats, high fiber content, a great emphasis on fresh fruits, local vegetables, legumes, grains, fresh herbs, lots of olive oil, and an abundance of spices.

Ahh! Olive harvest time. I can just smell and feel the air. I adore the experience although, from a distance. Fall 2008.

Make no mistake about it, one of the most crucial aspects of this diet is the active lifestyle as its cornerstone. The use of locally grown foods and fresh ingredients, the scarcity of red meat, and the geography all influence Mediterranean cuisine. Red meat is an occasional treat, especially around the holidays and special events. On the other hand, fish, poultry, eggs, and cheese play a prominent role in the cuisine. Yet, this will vary in degree from the eastern to the western parts of the Mediterranean region. You will also see the differences in the consumption of wine, especially as dictated by societal and religious acceptance, tolerance, and influence.

Regardless of geography or climate, there is an abundance of olive oil (the main fat), thus making it the main ingredient, influencing cooking style, life style, and providing an important link in the diversity and healthy aspect of Mediterranean cuisine. During my childhood in Jordan and still to this day, olive oil is the most important ingredient in all of Mediterranean cooking, as opposed to butter. Olive oil and canola oil are the healthiest fats for cooking.

Many studies have been documented in support of the Mediterranean diet and the lifestyle and culture of the people that live in the region. Even with all the studies attributing good health to this diet, lifestyle also plays a large part in this determination. Let's not forget that physical activity and daily walking or exercise does go a long way in contributing to and reaping the benefits of such a diet.

So what exactly is the Mediterranean diet? This is the description that was delivered at a 1993 conference held at the Harvard School of Public Health: plenty of fruit, vegetables, legumes, grains, with olive oil as the principle fat; lean red meat consumed only a few times per month and in small portions; moderate consumption of dairy products such as cheese, yogurt, fish, and poultry, and moderate consumption of wine at meal time.

To make the change in your diet to that of the Mediterranean style is really simple. This is because the food types, cooking methods, and even tastes are very much familiar to most, if not all of us. The changes needed should be small, gradual yet deliberate and must be sustainable to ensure comfortable success for the long term.

Having grown up in the Mediterranean region and having lived and experienced the culture, it was the way of life and way of thinking, and the respect for the land that enabled us to produce and grow the food we ate. Paying attention and being aware of what food is and where it comes from was considered sacred, a gift of the Gods, and it was treated that way . . . we were not "above" food. It is with this attitude that food was treated whether it was raised or grown on the land we knew, owned and loved. It is with this sentiment, attitude, the love of food, and the enjoyment of sharing, that I now write these pages for you.

The Staples of the Mediterranean Diet Include:

- Diligence regarding eating times and serving portions
- Use of olive oil in all cooking and dressings
- Use of whole grain, legumes and beans
- Eating vegetables and fruit daily
- Reducing the amount of saturated fats, especially the amount of red meat consumed
- Eating fish and nuts rich in omega-3 fatty acids
- Serving red wine with meals rather than other alcoholic drinks
- Reducing the amount of salt and sugar in cooking, limiting processed foods
- Visiting your local farmers market more frequently
- Choosing an exercise regimen consistent with your doctor's guidance
- Eating Better, Fresher, Smarter overall, and you will be happy you did!

About Your Health and Wellness

Taking control and making changes to your heart health, as well as general health, is not an easy endeavor. Deliberate, small changes, made gradually with minor sacrifices and sustainable means are the keys to success. Here are some general tips that are fundamentally good for your heart health and apply to most everyone.

- Cut back on eating processed foods, or what I call the four S's: Salt, Sugar, Saturated fats, and Snacks!

- Get to know YOU, and your health numbers (e.g., cholesterol, etc.). Learn your risk factors associated with heart disease, hypertension, and diabetes.

- Get the facts. Ask your doctor how to control those risk factors and how to reverse them. If you are a smoker, try to quit! If you have high cholesterol or high blood pressure, check it regularly. If you are inactive, like some of us, get some level of exercise. Ask yourself, "Am I overweight?" Be honest. Your doctor can help you control your weight by exercise and medical treatments.

As you adhere to what your doctor says, you should begin to take the right steps to learn more about yourself. Change your eating habits, and some aspects of your lifestyle, so you can be on the road to a heart-healthy life. Only YOU can ultimately take the responsibility for better health.

As of this writing, BFS Restaurant, celebrating 20 years in business, was recognized by Dr. Paul E. Lamanski, M.D., Director of the Center of Medicine and Cardiovascular Health, as a heart-healthy restaurant. Our customers do not have to worry about how much saturated fat, sodium, or cholesterol is in our food, and trust me, they don't miss any of it.

Now, let's have a chat about good fat. Omega-3 fatty acids have been a topic of interest everywhere in health news. In order to reap the benefits of this nutrient, it is important to know which foods contain Omega-3 and how these fats are beneficial to our health.

Okay! So what are the facts? What do we need? From birth and throughout the rest of our lives, studies have told us that we need these essential fats in our diet for their benefits to our general health and more importantly our heart health. So where does this stuff come from and how can we get it in our diet?

- Supplements, such as fish oil (e.g., salmon)
- Foods that have been fortified with Omega-3 (e.g., eggs, yogurt)
- Natural foods (e.g., fresh salmon, tuna, flax seeds, and nuts, to name a few)

While you need to consult with your doctor regarding your personal health needs, one thing for certain is that it is necessary to start eating healthier by incorporating foods containing Omega-3 fatty acids into your diet. Omega-3 fatty acids have been proven to be very good for you. One easy way to consume Omega-3 fatty acids in your diet is to eat heart-healthy foods such as fish and nuts and to cook with good olive oil, 3–4 times per week.

Appropriate portions to get the optimal effect of the consumption of these fatty acids should be recommended by a nutritionist or a physician as you incorporate them into your diet. So, got Omega-3?! If not, you should! Eat and drink like a Mediterranean!

Let's Resolve and Reset

As always, the coming of a new year also brings the need to "reset" our goals, hopes, dreams, and promises. All the resolutions we make for personal changes possess some level of challenge for all aspects of our lives, family, health, wealth and much more.

We must have the will to follow healthier habits, and a plan for how we will do this, in order to achieve a healthy weight. However, everyone and everything around us influences our will, our daily habits, and eventually, the outcome. As individuals, we cannot just "will" the outcome of a healthier weight without modifying our eating habits, lifestyle, and behavior to make real and lasting change.

We need to promise to learn our life lessons—especially new lessons. You may achieve the end result by engaging in what it means to eat healthy. Start by making small, gradual, deliberate, and realistic changes in order to succeed. For example, learn to know the foods that are good for you and the food you should avoid as much as possible. As I said before, avoid the four S's: Salt, Sugar, Saturated fats and Snacks. In addition, learn how to cook and eat healthy at home and while eating out.

I promise you: nothing changes unless you successfully demand it from yourself and others around you. There is no single or simple answer to changing your eating habits and there is no "bailout" for our personal lifestyle. No "fat tax" or incentive can offer you an out from the choices you (we) make.

Eat and drink like a Mediterranean!

So let's reset! Be your own advocate and chief agent of change for better health and a healthy lifestyle. My advice is to cook and eat healthy like a Mediterranean! Eat Better, Fresher, Smarter. You will find within these pages tips and hints for the enjoyment of shopping for fresh local ingredients, cooking delicious food and eating healthy. I wish you many years of happy and healthy cooking!

Patience is a virtue.

ABOVE: BFS Restaurant and Catering.

LEFT & BELOW: I'm ready for the guests!

It's About Our Kids

I don't need to warn you or raise your anxiety level any higher. As parents, we share in the concern about obesity in kids today. Three out of ten children across all socioeconomic groups are considered overweight. Obesity should be declared a national health emergency of catastrophic proportion and should be dealt with urgently without delay. We know the real impact and risk associated with obesity: heart disease, diabetes, etc.

Parents, teachers, doctors, and politicians have long recognized this concern and the need to help our kids. The road to fixing the problem, however, is riddled with financial and political obstacles and conflicting priorities. These difficulties are found in the schools, at home, the funding issues, and frankly, the politics of it all.

As parents we should take control and begin to help drive major changes at the home front, in the schools' food programs and even the choices we make while eating out. It sounds like a tall order, but hey, look at what is at risk here. It's our kids' health and their future.

Ok! Then what can we all do to introduce such changes? We should teach our children healthy eating habits starting now. The following are the top ten ideas we should adopt which will go a long way to helping our kids to eat and live healthier lives.

We (You) Need to:

- Be a role model; set a good example as a parent and get to know the food facts!
- Be a proactive parent; turn off the TV and video games and get some exercise.
- Be a motivator; help encourage your children in making the right food choices.
- Be empowering; instill in them the value, knowledge, and importance of healthy eating.
- Be a savvy shopper; know your good food and shop for the right stuff (avoid the middle aisles—that's where the processed food is).
- Be a trader; trade the bad for something good or better, and have a treat but don't cheat!
- Be a better cooking team; share with them the fun aspect of cooking in the kitchen—get cooking!
- Be a decider; you should decide where to go out and eat, not just anywhere the kids want to go (the right vs. easy choice).
- Be colorful; fill your days with colorful meals and add the colors of fruits and vegetables to make eating fun.
- Be goal oriented; set small goals for small manageable changes that you can achieve, not major leaps or sacrifices.

My daughter Lexi, my son Philip, my wife Victoria, me, and my son Brendan at a nephew's beautiful wedding. Good times. Lots of dancing, and yes, the food and wine! May 2010.

Be your kids' best advocate; don't limit their interests or deny them what they like without first seeking your doctor's advice. Certainly family history, eating habits, and lifestyles of family and friends will all impact our ability to influence our kids to make changes. There has been no more urgent time to act than now.

Eating healthy will go a long way to help our children deal with the challenges they will face as adults by keeping them as happy and healthy as possible. Let's all act now before it's too late.

After the first, there is a second. If there is no first, there will never be a second behind it.

Discussions

DISCUSSION ON CALCIUM

Bone health is paramount. Our bones consist of two primary materials: proteins (mesh-like structure) and calcium phosphate (hard, strong filler). Because our bone tissue is constantly being built and rebuilt throughout our adulthood, we require constant replenishing of these two essential elements to ensure healthy bones and joints. Sufficient dietary calcium, regular exercise to stimulate the bone building process, and a balanced diet rich in vitamins and minerals from plant-based foods help reduce the risk of osteoporosis (weak bones).

We can get calcium from many foods, such as milk, fish, beans, nuts, corn and dark, leafy greens. Vitamin D has been shown to help in the efficient absorption of calcium and phosphorous from the foods we eat. Known as the "sunshine vitamin," vitamin D is produced by our bodies when we are exposed to the sun's ultraviolet rays. It is also added to milk and may be found in eggs and fish.

Research has shown that diets high in salt and in saturated fats from red meat (and other sources) lead to a loss of calcium from our bodies. Therefore, salt and saturated fats should be kept to a minimum to maintain optimal levels of calcium. High salt consumption also causes our bodies to shed other essential minerals like potassium and magnesium.

Remember, proper and balanced levels of essential minerals will work in harmony for bone health, heart health, and overall general health. So, eat less salt, less red meat, and other foods high in saturated fats, and more of the calcium-rich foods that our bodies need.

Habit is the sixth sense that dominates the other five.

DISCUSSION ON DESSERTS, PASTRIES AND SWEETS

Desserts containing butter and sugar are high in calories. Where possible in this cookbook, the amount of sugar and butter was reduced or natural substitutions were made without compromising taste or method. For most of the Eastern Mediterranean countries, e.g., Lebanon, Greece, Turkey and Israel, the use of semolina, shredded wheat, and filo dough (paper-thin pastry sheets) are widely used in many dessert preparations. In addition, custards, puddings, pies, fritters, and butter cookies are traditional type desserts.

Nuts of all kinds are widely used in desserts like baklava, pie crusts, pie fillings, fritters and cookies as well as Halva (sesame-based candy). Since traditional Mediterranean foods are rich in fruit and nuts which are readily available year round, these are served before or after each main event. Generally, dessert is served later in the evening with Arabic coffee. As a hostess, my mom would always serve the dessert, coffee and any fruit at a different setting or another area such as the dinner table or in the living room. The event, occasion, the type of holiday (e.g., Christmas, Easter or Ramadan), as well as traditions and customs dictate the right dessert for the gathering. However, the setting, the comfort and the perceived hospitality provided to ensure the pleasure of the guest was the ultimate goal for the host.

So for those of us who are interested in some of those secrets or tips, here are a few.
- Use drawn butter or a mixture of butter and (no trans fats) vegetable oil based butter.
- Cinnamon, saffron, anise, orange water, allspice, cloves, rose water, caraway seeds, honey, food coloring, and vanilla are used.
- Honey syrups, molasses, fruit syrups, coffee, and yogurt are used in great amounts.
- Knafi [katifi] dough, filo dough, puff pastries, farina, semolina, flour, couscous, bulgur wheat, rice, cheese, rice flour, whole wheat grains, dates, nuts, oranges, apples, lemon, eggs, raisins, dry fruit, chocolate and many other variations and combinations are used for filling, mixing or interchanged with other ingredients for other variations and combinations as used by the dessert makers.
- Spices or flavoring such as mahlab, mistik, orange peel, ginger, and caramel clearly set things apart from other cuisines.

DISCUSSION ON DRESSINGS

When it comes to salad dressings, the first thing that comes to mind is convenience versus quality. What I mean by convenience is ready-made, off the shelf from the refrigerated section or on the shelf of the dried goods section from your local supermarket. Certainly we are inundated with the variety of dressings available to us. On the other hand, when it comes to quality, I refer to the quality of the ingredients as well as the number of ingredients themselves that make up the dressing. As you can probably tell by now, I believe the best dressing is the one you make yourself. This means it's simple to make, has fewer ingredients, and excludes certain unnecessary ingredients that neither you nor I can afford to have or pronounce (e.g., hydrogenated oils or fats, msg, sugar, coloring compounds, and salts). As part of my philosophy and desire to promote quality food, to me it's all about the simplicity and freshness of the ingredients you use to produce the best dressing.

Growing up we have always used the simplest and most available ingredients in making a dressing which include but are not limited to: extra virgin olive oil, wine vinegar, fresh lemon juice, garlic, mint, basil, or even pomegranate juice. Any combination of these ingredients would yield a terrific, fresh tasting dressing. While many dressings that are available in your supermarket have great taste, they have too many ingredients that are not conducive to healthy eating. Let me give you an example: 2 tablespoons of your favorite brand of ranch dressing may contain 16 grams of fat, and 90% of the calories come from fat; plus, it comes with a high amount of sodium. We all look for flavor or rich taste (*ta3m*—Arabic for rich flavor) in the food we eat. However, I am here to tell you that great taste and richness of food doesn't necessarily come from sugar or salt laced food, or foods with an abundance of saturated fats (oils). I have come to know from experience that we seek multiple flavors of layered components that give us great taste while giving us a satisfying finish. It is no different than having a great glass of wine.

One other contention of mine is how much dressing we use on our salads, regardless of its origin (store bought or homemade). I suggest that dressings should be drizzled on, not spooned over or poured on. Have your favorite dressing served on the side and use sparingly.

Creativity in Sassy Salads

Salads are served as an appetizer or after the main course, depending upon what region in the Mediterranean you are visiting. The climate, freshness, ingredients, and simplicity offer so many inspirations and possibilities for spontaneous salads. The abundance of fresh ingredients and variety of leaves provide a multitude of taste, texture and color. Try different vinaigrettes besides the standard olive oil and lemon juice. Many independent gourmet markets as well as your local grocers carry fine ingredients for lots of variety. So eat healthy, compose your own salad as a first course or substantial enough as a meal. The following are general tips for that ultimate salad.

- Seek multiple flavors from fresh and different ingredients
- Layer tastes for contrasting flavors
- Create complex finishes that linger
- Be able to taste all ingredients without overwhelming each other
- Use fresh herbs/spices where possible, especially in season
- Use variety of greens (e.g. spinach, arugula, chicory, radicchio, spring mix, etc.)
- Go sassy! Add dried nuts, dried or fresh fruit, olives
- Make your own unconventional dressing (try extra virgin olive oil, Dijon mustard, rice vinaigrette, sherry vinaigrette, red vinegar, balsamic vinegar, garlic)
- Make it a meal
  - Add marinated, grilled or roasted vegetables
  - Add feta or low fat cheese
  - Add nuts (pine nuts, walnuts, almonds) and seeds
  - Add unusual spices like five-spice mixes, Chinese, Ras-el-hanout, Moroccan, etc.

What else do you like? Be adventurous and enjoy.

In summary, when it comes to salads I always look for contrast in flavors, creative additions to the salad itself, and I consider it to be my first elegant course of a meal. So toss away that boring head of iceberg lettuce and introduce the vibrant colors of spinach, spring mixes, chicory and arugula. In addition, always make your salad a "sassy," singing salad full of vibrant colors and interesting ingredients (e.g. artichoke hearts, olives, radishes, diced lemons), as well as dried fruits and plenty of nuts. Do not forget such additions as chickpeas, pomegranate seeds, salmon, tuna, or grilled meats for great flavor.

He who wants to eat honey should endure the stings.

DISCUSSION ON FIBER

Fiber is a key part of foods obtained from plant sources rich in whole grain, fruits, vegetables, legumes, nuts, and seeds. For the most part, fiber is an indigestible food material (undigested starch), yet it is associated with reducing the risk of cancer, heart disease, diabetes and obesity. The following is a brief presentation on Dietary Fiber. There are two types of fiber.

Soluble Fiber: This type of fiber is found in oats, barley, dried beans and many familiar fruits such as apples, pears and plums and is also found in many vegetables like artichokes, carrots, peas and Brussels sprouts. Soluble fiber helps lower blood cholesterol and sugar levels in our blood.

Insoluble Fiber: This type of fiber is the component of plant foods that cannot be digested by our body. They are considered roughage, yet they help in moving waste material through our digestive tract. Also, these foods may help in weight control and reduce the risk of colon cancer. Some good sources of insoluble fiber are whole grains, multigrain breads and cereals, brown rice, some fruit and eggplant.

Many research studies have shown that a diet rich in fiber from plant based foods promotes good digestive health and lowers cholesterol levels. Insoluble fiber passes through our stomach and intestines. It absorbs water and bulks up our body waste and helps in moving it through our digestive tract. On the other hand, soluble fiber slows down the passage of food through the digestive tract and turns into a gel. It prevents cholesterol, fat and excess sugar from being absorbed by the body, slowing down the absorption of sugars. This results in reducing glucose (sugar) in the bloodstream and, therefore, it prevents spikes in blood sugar levels.

The main goal here is to encourage you to work fiber into your diet. This requires very little effort and little creativity. The FDA recommends an intake of 11.5 grams of fiber per 1000 calories, or 25–30 grams per day for a 2500 calorie diet.

You should review additional information provided by the American Journal of Clinical Nutrition, Journal of the American College of Cardiology Foundation, and The FDA and the American Dietetic Association.

DISCUSSION ON GRAIN

As ancient as time itself, the wheat grain crop is still one of the primary sources of food and nutrients in the world today. Wheat was always viewed and treated as the Staff of Life, portrayed as sacred, and played an important religious role in many cultures throughout the world and certainly in my culture in Jordan. I dream of the wheat fields we planted, watched over, and harvested. Next to olive oil, cheese, eggs and yogurt, wheat is a dietary staple of most Mediterranean cultures and it is available in many forms—wheat flour, berries and bulgur. It is considered among the richest source of nutrients and vitamins needed for good health. Wheat is found in breads, pastas, crackers, cakes, and breakfast items, which is just a short list of many foods. Unrefined and unprocessed wheat, which is in its natural state, offers the most important natural ingredients, such as complex carbohydrates, protein and minerals.

Whole wheat is one of the staples of the Mediterranean diet which provides substantial health benefits including reducing insulin resistance and lowering your risk of cardiovascular disease, obesity and Type II diabetes. Rich in antioxidants, fiber and vitamins, wheat is a great way to consume your dietary requirements from one single source. It is most valuable when unprocessed and in whole grain form.

Dietary fiber (insoluble) such as whole wheat contributes a great deal to lowering blood fats (triglyceride) and acts as a laxative.

Growing up in Jordan with a farming family, we harvested wheat the old fashioned way. We plowed the earth with two mules, planted the seeds by hand, sawed the wheat with a hand held tool, dried and crushed the straw, and separated the wheat from the hay.

Wheat was then manufactured into many forms, like flour and bulgur wheat in three different sizes. Wheat was used for everyday consumption as in bread, or was boiled, sun dried, and crushed to be used during the off season in salads, pilafs, soups and kibbee. Wheat was also used and mixed with yogurt to then be dried and preserved.

Many of the following recipes will explore the use of bulgur wheat using many different techniques. Some of the other most popular grains include rice, oats, barley and corn. For the practical cook, these grains are readily available, inexpensive and play an important role in our diet, regardless of cuisine or culture. You will find whole grain in breads, pastas, desserts, salads and breakfast cereals as well as popular healthy snacks.

The proteins in the wheat form a substance known as gluten, to which some people are intolerant. Where possible, other substitutions will be identified in place of wheat or other ingredients high in gluten.

Wheat has many forms and functions depending upon the way it is processed, including:

Wheat berries (the whole wheat grain) May be used in breads, soups, stews, or mixed with rice or other grains for pilafs. For best results, the berries should be soaked overnight, then boiled in plenty of water until tender.

Cracked wheat Made from crushing the wheat berries and maintains all the whole wheat nutrients. May be used in pilafs and cereals.

Bulgur Wheat Made from the wheat berries, but unlike cracked wheat, the berries are first cooked, then sun dried and crushed to different sizes ranging from fine to coarse. Used in salads (e.g., tabbouleh) or combined with lentils for great, wholesome pilafs.

Couscous Made from steaming, drying then crushing durum wheat. Traditionally steamed in meat broth or vegetable stock. After steaming, fluff the couscous with a fork. Most popular use or preparation as a salad, pilaf or dessert. It has a wonderful, grainy texture, and the ability to absorb the flavors of the accompanying meat, chicken or fish dish.

Semolina Made from the wheat kernel once the bran and wheat germ is removed during the milling process. Similar to couscous, it is made from durum wheat. May be available fine or coarse. Used in cereals, cakes, making pasta and cookies.

My advice is to buy from stores that have high volumes of sales and good turnover of inventory, regardless of what wheat form you purchase. Always buy in small quantities, store in a cool, dry space and rotate your purchases by dating them. Most whole wheat products should be good for up to three months. Whole grain products should be good for up to six months. The most important thing is to keep dry in airtight containers to avoid the products turning rancid.

DISCUSSION ON MEDITERRANEAN HERBS AND SPICES

When I think of herbs and spices, some of the first things that come to mind are great aromas, flavors, colors and *ta3m*, or taste. This chapter will simply explore the uses of herbs and spices in Mediterranean cooking. At the same time, I want to reinforce the idea and the healthful concept of trading herbs and spices in place of salt and saturated fat to enhance the flavor and taste, *ta3m*, of all the food you are about to explore in this book. The other intent here is to bring you closer to those wonderful herbs and spices and to encourage you to take this journey with me for a pleasurable and useful experience.

Mediterranean cooking is like being in the middle of an orchestra where every major piece or section plays a very sensual melody to complete the full flavor and irresistible aroma. From garlic to grappa or from capers to cumin, and let's not overlook oregano, basil, mint and thyme, all are used extensively in the medley of flavors. Like an orchestra, you will be delighted with the essence or perfumes of rose petals (rose water), the spice mixture of harissa (paste of chilies) and the aromas of cumin, cinnamon and mint. Like music and musical instruments, each has its own note and role to play. A single flavor or seasoning never dominates a dish, masks or overtakes the performance or flavor *ta3m* of the other ingredients. Instead, they are all used in such a way to preserve and enhance the natural flavor in a harmonious and tantalizing way.

As you begin to cook healthy Mediterranean food, you will discover the use of herbs and spices is a very important component to creating that great flavor or that *ta3m* you desire. Since I discourage or minimize the use of saturated fats throughout these chapters, you are, however, encouraged to adopt a spice(s) or love an herb(s) of your choice and add to your creation, as the kicker ingredient for that *ta3m*, rich taste, you seek. Now you have arrived at the gates of healthy-eating heaven. You will see how herbs and spices enhance and, perhaps, with little finesse and balance, create the true *ta3m* and great flavors in a very wholesome and natural way. Of course this is a good way to avoid the dependence on saturated fats or salt, to achieve the desired taste, and the detrimental nature they have to your health.

So using herbs and spices is like tuning a musical instrument; you must play it time after time, play it by heart, by ear and by mouth (taste buds) and replay it again (to enjoy the perfect balance)!

With all of this, I want you not to forget the daily use of nuts commonly used in many dishes in several Mediterranean countries. For example, almonds, pistachios, pine nuts and walnuts are the most popular and regularly used.

The following is a partial list of the most popular spices and herbs used in Mediterranean cooking. For a much more expanded list, culinary and perhaps medicinal uses, and origins, one can refer to many available resources and reference books dedicated solely to this vast subject. My intent is not to duplicate the voluminous amount of information available in book form or on the internet. Rather, my intent is to help with a quick reference and to identify the spices and merely reinforce the ideas and importance of spices in cooking not only for the great flavors, but also the benefits they provide when used as a substitute for salt, fatty oils, butter and animal fat. Used artfully, you can spice up your dishes for a lifetime.

Remember, generally spices are the flowers of plants and herbs are the fruit, buds, bark, roots, leaves or seeds of certain plants. Herbs and spices are often grouped into varying categories from sweet and savory to aromatics and stimulants of your taste buds. So go ahead, get a little spiced up, explore the boundaries of their pleasurable gifts and venture into your culinary world. Yet remember, like many before you and me, the many roads traveled, seas charted, countries conquered, or continents discovered, kingdoms perished, kings and queens overthrown, and pharaohs were embalmed and preserved until the present day all because of the spell of herbs and spices. As you may know, spices and herbs were and are used in worship and war, trade and treason. These are a few important things these treasures have done and they are definitely enough to whet your appetite.

The pleasures of using the right herbs and spices in today's food and cooking, specifically Mediterranean cooking, is what turns an average cook into a masterful chef.

Selected Herbs and Spices

Allspice The dried, unripe berries or fruit of a small, tropical, evergreen tree also known as pimento. It is used in dishes such as soups, sauces, pickles and sausage. It can also be a healing remedy for colds and upset stomachs.

Anise A plant as well as a Mediterranean herb. It is used for flavoring cakes, curries, pastries and candy. It has a licorice flavor. Anise seeds are used for tea and can help improve memory.

Basil An herb belonging to the mint family. It is used for healthy eating and cooking in most cuisines. Sweet and pungent. Think pesto.

Bay leaves Dried aromatic leaf. Widely used throughout the world. Used for savory food that has been simmering for a long period of time like soups, stews, and vegetables. Buy fresh or dried.

Bouquet garni Bundle of herbs tied together with string. Used for soups and stew. Very fragrant and must be used fresh for best results.

Capers Unripe flower buds of *Capparis spinosa*, a prickly perennial plant. It is found in the Mediterranean area and some parts of Asia. Capers are a distinctive ingredient in Italian cuisine, especially in Sicilian cooking and other cuisines in the region. Use for salads, fish, and tomato sauce.

Caraway seeds It's a biennial plant found in Europe and western Asia used as a spice, especially in rye bread. It is also used in liquors, casseroles, and other foods.

Cardamom The aromatic seed or pod of a tropical Asian plant *Elettaria cardamom* of the ginger family. Cardamom is used as flavoring for soups, stews, and drinks (e.g., coffee).

Celery It is grown for its petioles or leaf stalks which are most commonly eaten as a salad but occasionally cooked as a vegetable. It is an ingredient in almost every soup.

Chervil California, Florida, and Michigan are important producing states. Chervil is an annual Eurasia herb in the parsley family. The leaves of this plant are used for seasoning or garnish. It has a distinctive sweet and anisy flavor.

 **Chilis** It is the fruit of the plant from genus *Capsicum*. Depending on the flavor and freshness, their culinary use varies from a vegetable to a spice. Chilis are used in the cuisines of Mexico, South American countries, Morocco, Spain, and Turkey.

 **Chives** This is the smallest spice of the onion family. They grow in clumps rather than as individual plants. Culinary uses for chives involve chopping its leaves for use as a condiment for fish, potatoes and soups.

 **Chocolate** Fermented, roasted, shelled, and ground cocoa seeds often combined with a sweetener. Cocoa trees originated in South American river valleys. Chocolate anyone?

 **Cinnamon** The dried aromatic inner bark of certain tropical Asian trees in the genus *Cinnamomum*. It's used to flavor both sweet and savory dishes, coffee, tea, and gum, in addition to scenting incense and perfumes.

 **Cloves** They are rich, brown, dried, unopened flower buds. Cloves come from Madagascar, Brazil, Penang, and Ceylon. Cloves are used in spice cookies and cakes.

 **Coffee** Brewed beverage prepared from roasted seeds, coffee beans of the coffee plant were discovered in the highlands of Ethiopia. Got coffee?!

 **Coriander leaves** Also known as cilantro, coriander is a soft, hairless plant similar to parsley with a unique, pungent taste. It is native to southwestern Asia and northern Africa.

 **Coriander seeds** The most common use of coriander seeds is in curry powder. The seeds can be likewise used in stews and soups. It is used in many tasty Indian recipes and is native to the Middle East and Southern Europe. Coriander powder is used often for quick preparations.

 **Cumin** It is the pale green seed of *Cuminum cyminum*, an herb in the parsley family. Cumin offers a nutty, peppery, earthy taste. An ancient spice, cumin is native to the shores of the Mediterranean Sea and Egypt.

Dibs (dates) These are the fruits of a dozen or so feather-palms which grow in sub-tropical and desert areas throughout North African, the Arab States, California, and Australia. Dates are often combined with meat in cooking. The fruit was used as a sweetener. Often eaten as fresh dates.

Dill An aromatic herb native to Eurasia. The leaves or seeds of this plant are used as a seasoning. Most of the production of dill seed oil is used in the pickle industry for flavoring dill pickles. Dill seed is used as a spice. India is the primary producer of dill seed for culinary use.

Dried mushrooms The word mushroom refers only to edible fungi (e.g., porcini mushrooms) belonging to a diverse group. It's neither plant nor animal. Offers great earthy, robust taste.

Fennel It is known for its fine, wispy leaves which are used as a herb, and its seeds as a popular spice. It is native to the Mediterranean. Fennel has a sweet, anise-like flavor great with fish, dressing, sauces, and soups.

Fenugreek The whole plant gives a curry powder aroma and a tangy taste. It is used in homemade curry powder. It is also used in many Indian dishes and some Mediterranean dishes. On the whole, the plant leaves are full of protein, vitamins and minerals.

Garlic Ah, garlic. Anywhere in the world, few cooks would be found without this amazing ingredient. Generally the smaller the garlic bulb, the stronger the flavor. Garlic grown in hotter climates also yields a pungent taste. Garlic is also known for its many health benefits including prevention of heart disease, lowering cholesterol, and aiding the absorption of vitamins. Garlic may be used chopped, sliced or whole in all aspects of Mediterranean cooking like soups, marinades, stews, roasts and dressings. Also, great and exciting garlic flavor may be enhanced by roasting or smoking whole heads of garlic.

Ginger Considered one of the most popular spices across most cuisines. Ginger has a refreshing and lemony aroma with varying degrees of sharpness. Ginger is found as fresh roots, dried, ground, pickled, and preserved in syrup, even candied and crystallized. It is extremely popular in chutneys, marinades, and braised and stir-fried dishes.

Grappa A strong, almost like brandy, drink made from grape skins, stems and seeds. It has an Italian origin. It is used for an after dinner drink.

Harissa A North African hot red sauce or paste made from chili peppers and garlic. Harissa is used both as a condiment and as an ingredient in recipes, like couscous and other northern African dishes.

Honey A sweet aliment produced by honey bees and derived from the nectar of flowers.

Lemon (citric) A common name for citrus lemon. It comes from a small tree or spreading bush of the rue family. The fruit is used primarily for its juice, though the pulp and rind (zest) are used for dressings, sauces, soups, and fish. The juice of the lemon is a characteristic ingredient in many pastries and desserts.

Mace An evergreen tree indigenous to the Banda Islands in the Moluccas of Indonesia or Spice Islands. Mace is the dried, lacy, reddish covering or arillus of the seed. Mace is often preferred in light dishes for the bright orange color.

Mahlab An aromatic spice that comes from a wild cherry seed. Find it in Asian or specialty stores.

Marjoram Similar to oregano yet has a sweeter taste and perfuming aroma. It is a great addition to stews, casseroles, tomato sauces, and braised lamb dishes. This is well regarded as a delicious, sweet, minty aroma in many Mediterranean style dishes.

Marsala A dessert wine that goes into puddings and pastry making. Also used to make delicate vegetable dishes and sauces.

Mastic The resin which exudes from the mastic tree. Little white beads used in milk pudding, stews, and baking.

Mint This herb has many different types, each with subtle differences in flavor and aroma; spearmint is the most used. It is grown and used around the Mediterranean and is used extensively in most cuisines. It is used as a flavoring agent in a wide range of dishes from salads, stuffing, yogurt, soups and even hot or cold drinks as well as desserts.

Mustard Comes from seeds of an annual plant. Mustard originally came from Europe, Southeast Asia, and the Mediterranean area. Great as a condiment and in vinaigrette.

Nutmeg A fruit of an evergreen tree has a sweet taste and glorious aroma. It may be found whole or ground. Freshly grated or ground nutmeg gives the best flavor. It is used and added to pasta, spinach, rice, sauces, baked goods (cookies) and creamy toppings for sweet and savory dishes.

Onion Throughout the world, onions are the number-one most-consumed vegetable. There are several different varieties of onions. Most onions are fried until soft or golden brown. This gives them great depth and flavor.

Orange peel The peel, or zest, of an orange. A common ingredient in fish dishes and soups.

Orange water The distilled essence of orange, used mainly in baking and flavoring desserts and beverages, giving orange fragrance and flavor.

Oregano Considered of the same family as marjoram but has a more robust flavor. It is used greatly in most cuisines, especially Greek cuisine and specifically in tomato sauces and vegetable dishes. It may be found either dry or fresh. It is also used to flavor oils and vinegars.

Paprika It is made from mild flavored peppers and can be sweet or hot (Hungarian). You can also find the smoked variety (Spanish). Paprika is known to be rich in vitamin C. It is often used to flavor stews, soups and sauce. Frequently, one will find paprika as one ingredient in meat rubs as well as cheeses and sausages. Keep it in a cool, dry and airtight place.

Parsley It is widely used in Mediterranean dishes. It makes a nice, colorful garnish on dishes like tomatoes and rice. Also used to make tabouleh salad and in many recipes in this book.

Preserved lemons Lemons or limes preserved in salt develop a mellow flavor much used in Mediterranean dishes. The seeds are edible.

 **Pomegranates** Have been a symbol of fertility since ancient times. Venus the goddess of love was said to have given pomegranates as a gift to her favorites.

 **Ras-el-hanout** Typically a blend of a variety of different spices used in North African or Moroccan cuisine. The components are different amounts of several spices (cumin, coriander, cinnamon, etc.) based on taste and preference of the vendor.

 **Rosemary** It is the leaf of a woody evergreen and is legendary for its unique fragrance, aroma and use by many as flavoring for hearty bean dishes, vegetables, and grilling meats and fish. It may also be used while grilling and smoking by laying the sprigs over the coals while the meat is grilling.

 **Rose water** This distilled essence of rose petals is used mainly in Eastern Mediterranean desserts, giving it a mild rose fragrance and flavor.

 **Saffron** The dried stigma of a plant of the crocus family with an orange-yellow filament picked by hand. It is considered the world's most expensive spice. It has a very distinctive and great aroma and striking coloring features. Its exotic, rich color is widely used in many rice dishes including paella, risotto and fish stews. It is also used in fancy rolls, biscuits and custard-like desserts. For best results, crush the saffron strands and soak in warm water before using.

Sage It has a potent aroma and musky flavor (and should be used sparingly). It is commonly used for flavoring meat stuffing, sausage and veal. You can combine it (making a bouquet garni) with other herbs like parsley and basil to flavor stocks, rice and bean dishes and for infusing olive oil.

 **Sahlab** The dried, ground bulb of a variety of orchid that has a delicate flower. It is a thickening agent used to make ice cream and milk drinks. It is hard to find and very expensive.

 **Sesame seeds** It is the flat, oval seed of an herb used widely in North and South America in baked goods and many pastry foods. Sesame is grown in Asia, India, Turkey, Syria and Pacific areas. Sesame was first found in Harafa, India.

Spring onions (scallions) Are simply an early maturing variety of onion that have sweet, mild flavor with a fresh, crisp taste. Best used in salads.

Sumac This spice is the red berries of the sumac bush that grows wild and is cultivated throughout the Eastern Mediterranean region. It is heavily used in Lebanese, Syrian and Turkish foods. With a unique pleasing sour-lemony flavor, this spice is often used as a substitute for lemon. It may be rubbed on chicken or fish. It is also used as a marinade and salad dressing. Sumac is used to make Zaatar, the famous blend of thyme, sumac, roasted sesame and olive oil.

Thyme An herb of the mint family, thyme grows wild in the hillsides. It is indigenous to Greece. It is best with roasted, grilled fish and meats. It offers a strong, savory, and slightly bitter flavor.

Tarragon It is one of the most popular herbs. It is most widely used in French cooking. It is used mostly in eggs and chicken dishes. It makes a delicious béarnaise sauce and is also used for flavoring vinegar.

Turmeric It is a root of the ginger family with a bright yellow color and appetizing aroma. It is often used as a coloring agent in place of saffron. Turmeric is native to India and the Indonesian islands. It is best used as an ingredient in curries and curry powders. It is used in chutneys and pickles.

Vanilla It is a seed pod of a tropical climbing orchid. Vanilla is mostly used in sweet cooking, added to cakes, biscuits and other desserts as well as preserves.

Zaatar This is a blend of freshly harvested herbs like thyme, sumac, and sometimes marjoram. All stone ground and rubbed with olive oil, seasoned with sea salt and then mixed with toasted sesame seeds. This herb is used to flavor pita breads before baking and to encrust chicken and fish. It is also used as a flavoring spice mix in stews and other meat dishes.

Savor the Spices of Life!

DISCUSSION ON OLIVE OIL

Olive oil, the main fat used in Mediterranean cooking, is more than just food for all those who grew up with it. I have many childhood memories of the olive tree from planting it to harvesting it. It was treated as a gift from the Gods and was like liquid gold. Olives and olive oil are used in varying ways such as food, medicine, gifts to the worshipped, and a great symbol of peace, love and glory. They are celebrated in war and in peace, in religion and politics.

Olives, which are as ancient as history itself, were first cultivated in the eastern countries of the Mediterranean, spreading westward to the rest of the Mediterranean countries like Italy, Greece, North Africa, Spain, and southern France. Perhaps, even today, one can argue that olives, and therefore olive oil, are one of the most sought after commodities in the region and the rest of the world.

Olive orchards are widespread, so much so that they are all the eye can see from the top of the mountains, to the depths of the valleys, and to the countryside. During the warm summer days, my grandfather would start his day with us by his side, caring for and pruning the trees and plucking weeds to ensure the health of each tree. He treated them as family members, almost calling them by name, how good they were, when they were planted. He would gently tap the stem or the branches of each tree as we moved around with graceful respect on this rich clay-like soil, which was colored red, white, and sometimes brown. We could hear the Earth whispering, the trees whistle, and the birds sing in harmony and anticipation of the soon-to-come harvest season. We could feel, smell, and see the connection between man and Earth. In fact, we could feel it in my grandfather's rough but gentle hands, see it underneath his fingernails, and most importantly, just below his white headpiece, you could see it reflected in his hazel eyes. That, to me, spells pride and joy of a long, hard day and job well done. As the trees grew taller, most of the time in silence, and in pride and strength, it was as if they were reaching out to the Gods in thanks and glory.

Grandmother used olive oil as an ointment or cure, and made hand soap, believing in the benefits it offered in healing and beautifying the skin. I recall grandmother would offer each one of us a small shot of extra virgin olive oil in a demitasse cup, insisting that we should drink it in one gulp so that our knees would not squeak as we grew older. Somehow, I believed her then and I now understand and believe her more. Olive oil is also used as a preservative for the food, but more importantly as a balm for the soul.

For the first sixteen years of my life, growing up in the region, I knew and loved my grandparents' land, felt the ancient soil and breathed the air that was filled with the majestic smell of the olive tree. As far as I could see, trees shimmered under the glorious Mediterranean sun. Those are the olive trees I knew and remember. The trees awaited the arrival of a treasured season that produced a valued and most golden gift: extra virgin olive oil. My grandfather attributed this gift of splendid olive oil to the soil, to the many ancient stones that peppered the fields, the sun and the light, and the pleasant breeze that made the trees dance in the fields. This great natural habitat was the best for the olive tree to grow, prosper and yield the best stuff on Earth.

There are three major categories of olive oil:

- Extra virgin olive oil (first press)
- 100% olive oil (second press)
- Other oils that require treatment or refinement

Extra virgin olive oil, from the first (cold) press of the olives, is the highest quality olive oil. It is the most digestible, has great flavor, a wonderful bouquet, and a rich golden color. It's filled with vitamins and Omega-3 fatty acids, and also has the lowest acid content (1%).

My grandparents taught me that to maintain the quality, flavor and color of the oil, it is best to store it in dark color jugs in a cool, dark place to prevent oxidation, preserve the taste *ta3m* and increase shelf life.

Today science interfered and began to label, treat, purify and process olive oil to produce the varying degrees of olive oil in terms of color, flavor and taste.

Olives Olives are the small nut-like fruit of an olive tree mostly grown in the Mediterranean. The flesh (pulp) surrounding the pit (seed) can be as much as 30% oil. There are numerous shapes, types, sizes and colors of olives with varying degrees of oil in their flesh. Raw olives are extremely unpalatable and sometimes very bitter. Olives are cured and moderately stored in salt brine, olive oil brine, and sometimes with lemon, hot peppers and even spices like thyme and oregano. Such technique allows for reducing or removing the bitterness of the olive. On average, only about 20% of the olives are prepared and used in such fashion for stuffing, marinating and cooking. On balance, the remaining 80% of the olive harvest is used for making and producing olive oil.

As the olive matures, it reaches its maximum potential for olive oil content. After harvest, we used to load them up in sacks, strap them on horses or mules and bring them down to the press. We would wait our turn to clean the loads of olives from debris then get them loaded to be crushed. The crushed mixture of olive, pits and sometimes leaves is ground into a very fine paste which is then pressed in order to squeeze the liquid "juice" mixture (oil and water).

An ancient stone olive press used during biblical times.

DISCUSSION ON RED MEAT: LAMB

It is no wonder that lamb (e.g. sheep, goats) is the most popular meat in the Mediterranean. I guess you could say that if Adam and Eve were a meat eating couple, then you could bet that their first meat was grilled lamb over an open fire in the woods somewhere in Eden's garden and perhaps an apple was stuffed in its mouth as a decorative item or a way to seduce Adam to try and eat the other cooked parts of this animal. You see, these folks were very fragile and perhaps had their own economic issues to deal with (e.g., starting the human race on a budget, feeding all the animals (except those that made good eats), the harvest . . . you know, the rest of it, including staying alive from all those snakes and reptiles). On a serious note, sheep, goats, (let's refer to them as lamb), were among man's first animals that were domesticated for a variety of reasons. You see, these animals, "lamb," were very useful and provided their masters with meat, milk, fur "textile" and more. The meat of these animals was very desirable throughout history. Their diet was very simple but abundant, and they survived on food in and around the pastures including shrubs, trees and scrublands. Those are among some of the reasons why "lamb" meat, or what's known as grass-fed lamb, is such a great treat and tender meat and with delicate flavors.

Weeks after arriving in this country, I learned that "lamb" meat was not readily available. So my dad would make these "arrangements" with local farmers to buy and process the meats as we were used to buying and cooking back home. I have to admit that I enjoyed the excitement of the trip to select the lamb and make the rest of the arrangements… you know what I mean… to secure and process the young lamb, just like the way we grew up learning from my grandfather as well as the community in general.

The lack of popularity of eating lamb was and still is, to some degree, surprising to me. Most people gravitate towards large cuts of meat ("beef") which generally has a higher content of fat than lamb. Lamb meat is significantly lower in fat than beef. Proper cooking of the lamb is extremely important. Typically, lamb should be cooked at a lower temperature and depends greatly on the method of cooking. (See the following discussions.) However, for the purpose of this introduction, you must know that "young lamb" or what is referred to as spring lamb is very tender. Either dry or wet heat cooking methods are used depending upon the type of cut or part of the animal's body being prepared.

The one lesson we should learn when purchasing lamb meat is to know the difference between the young "spring lamb" and that of the older lamb referred to as "mutton," which is older and "tougher" meat. Also, imported lamb is typically raised on grass, and produced using younger lamb, compared to lamb in the United States which is usually raised and processed on commercial feed lots in many parts of the country. However, my dad found that grass fed lamb raised on small farms are easily found anywhere in the country.

As meat eaters, humans are faced with an increasing moral dilemma and ethical arguments with regards to eating meat. As we grow culturally sophisticated, both sides of the arguments extend beyond just the consumption of meat for nutritional value and its prominent presence and significant place in our lives, culture and tradition. The U.S. consumes approximately one-third of the world's meat. For us foodies or chefs/cooks, the day to day questions are less philosophical or for that matter, ethical. Rather, it is the question of quality of meat and how it was raised, "living conditions," and certainly the meat production. This is a too important and significant question to be answered adequately in just one chapter. There are several important research findings that suggest that the use of hormones, antibiotics and other chemicals in animals may find their way into the human body and influence our health.

Today, to many people, living conditions, crowding, mass production and the "artificial" nature of processing meat is unacceptable. The challenge to producers and consumers is to insist that animals are treated humanely and that their brief existence is improved by taking into account their natural instincts and animal nature. A small portion of the industry and a modest number of farms are increasingly moving toward the old fashioned and more traditional methods for raising animals. Most consumers do not mind the modest increase in cost for quality meat products, knowing that animal welfare was also accommodated.

Grass-fed livestock, humane treatment of the animal, and the traditional method of slaughter results in a better-tasting and certainly more tender and milder meats. What is known as Halal meat requires exactly such methods. The traditional method of slaughter goes back for centuries, which is to lift the head of the animal backward, slit the throat, drain its blood by hanging it upside down by the hind legs, skinning it, and carving it properly for the desired cuts of meat. Often, a passage or a prayer is read prior to the sacrifice of the animal and the gift of food it provided.

While I am not a big meat eater, meat has still found its way into my dietary life, to some degree. For example, lamb was the prominent red meat in our diet growing up, whereas in this country (USA), beef dominates, followed by pork and chicken. Regardless of your favorite type of red meat, it is very important that you know your preferred meat cuts for that preferred dish. Most food markets or butchers have expert butchers, chefs and other wide varieties of cuts, sizes, and grading of the quality of the meat. That does not excuse you from knowing the type of cut and quality you should purchase for the type of cooking method or procedure you wish to follow. The following will shed some light on this subject from a practical and pragmatic point of view. So let me start with USDA definition of quality cuts available for you in the market. This would range from prime (top quality), choice, and second tier good, standard, to select (commercial quality). You will find these designations listed on your product label, or in brochures available in your favorite meat market.

Storing meat depends largely on the size of the cut and the date it was packaged. Large cuts should be wrapped loosely to allow for air to circulate and could be refrigerated up to 4-5 days. Smaller cuts and processed cuts should be wrapped loosely and should be used two days from the date it was processed. Freezing meats should be done after repackaging and wrapping well to avoid freezer burn.

Meat is a muscle. The more frequently an animal uses the muscle, the tougher the meat will be. The preferred method of cooking tougher cuts of meat is slow and low heat, such as the wet method of cooking, e.g., stew. On the other hand the muscle that is infrequently used will be most tender and full of flavor. These cuts, typically from younger animals, require attention, quick marinade or dry cooking, e.g., grilling; they require less cooking but a great deal of care.

Cooking meat correctly depends greatly on the type of cut it is and therefore the cooking method employed. Here is a quick reference of the various cooking methods as they should be used for the proper cuts of meat.

Dry Methods

Roasting This is dry heat cooking method which may be used for very tender cuts of meat, and by placing the fatty side up in a roasting pan. Cuts with the bone still in the meat will cook faster. Large cuts, like roasts, will continue to cook even after oven cooking time is finished. You should allow time for resting before cutting. Juices and drippings from roasting meats could be used for sauces, gravies and soups.

Broiling Is another form of dry heat cooking method which is mainly used for thin cuts of steaks and chops. Typically the meat is placed 3–4 inches from the heat source on a pan with dripping grid. Thicker cuts like a steak are best on the grill for direct heat, great flavor, smoky taste, and desired doneness.

Pan Searing (Pan Broiling) May be considered another form of dry heat method, except you must use a heavy skillet (cast iron is preferred). This method requires frequent turning and draining of liquid to avoid poaching and to maintain a sizzle. The pan is then deglazed with stock, wine or cream. The resulting liquid can be used to make soups, sauces or stock. Onions, mushrooms and leek may be used.

Wet Methods

Braising Is what is referred to as the wet or moist method of cooking. This method may require the browning of the meat (in a heavy skillet on high heat, turning several times). Browning results in better color and enhances flavor. This method employs the low and slow technique, e.g., stewing, and much of the ingredients are in cooking liquid (stock, wine or oil) for the length of time on the stove or in an oven. Briskets, pot roasts and ribs would be an example.

Sauté Is a quick and light method of cooking by browning or glazing meat in a saucepan using smaller pieces of meat and turning from time to time, without crowding to avoid steaming, as a pool of liquid emerges. Same as in pan broiling you may deglaze the pan for sauce and more flavors.

Stir Fry This method uses a skillet or a wok on high heat, small pieces of vegetables and meat thinly sliced or chopped, constant stirring to avoid over cooking, and the liquids or stock is added at the end for the finishing touch.

Boiling This is used for tougher parts or cuts of the meat where seasoning, vinegar, wine or beer, as well as vegetables such as carrots, onions, leek, celery and garlic are used to add or infuse flavor during the lengthy simmering period of cooking. An example of this is fresh brisket and corned beef.

For the purpose of this discussion, I will treat lamb as the meat of choice and will present many of my favorite dishes to share with you. Lamb was mostly the choice of meat available in the market and in my mom's kitchen. There was a continuous supply of lamb (spring lamb) from March through the summer and perhaps as early as fall. This was the best time to buy genuine tender spring lamb. The older the lamb (mutton) is, the tougher the meat. It has the tendency to be fatty and is not in demand as the spring lamb is. Meat from the older lamb is generally marinated, braised, broiled, and slow roasted and used for stews.

Some of the recipes in the chapters to follow, like kibbee, kabobs and others, use young lamb meat as the preferred choice. While lamb is used extensively in these recipes, beef may be substituted in many, if not all.

While all parts of the lamb are used in many of the Middle Eastern dishes, I will only refer to those that would be palatable to those of us in this audience that are not as adventurous. In any reference to the lamb meat, I will refer to it by part name, such as: leg of lamb, breast, shoulder, shank, etc.

An onion shared with a friend tastes like roast lamb.

DISCUSSION ON RICE

With hundreds of varieties, rice is perhaps second to wheat in terms of how widely cultivated it is, as well as how prominent it is found in this and other world cuisines.

Rice is a great source of carbohydrates and is used in almost every cuisine in the world. In feeding a large family in the Middle East, rice to us is what potatoes are to the Irish people. Rice is cooked with almost every major meal and has made its way into many dishes like vegetables, meat, fish, soups, and stuffings. It is inexpensive, versatile, and simple to prepare, yet easily overcooked. Typically, rice is classified by the grain length (e.g., long-grain rice or short-grain rice). This usually determines the best way the rice should be cooked and which to use for sweet and savory applications.

Long-grain rice is used for most dishes. Long-grain rice (both white and brown), for example, makes a great pilaf and absorbs the juices and stock of the meal you are cooking. Long-grain rice, when it cooks, grows fatter compared to basmati rice, which grows longer and has a very fragrant, nutty flavor. Herbs and spices alter the aroma and taste of cooked rice.

On the other hand, short-grain rice like risotto rice (known as Italian rice) is best used for longer cooking times such as risotto and vegetable dishes, rice pudding, and other sweet applications such as filling for pie and other desserts.

Brown rice, wild rice, black rice, Chinese rice, and other varieties of rice are a major staple and important ingredients in Mediterranean cuisine. Enjoy rice in whatever method or application for its delightful taste and versatility. Since rice is starchy and could result in a sticky texture, it is beneficial to rinse most long-grain rice (white rice, basmati, jasmine) before cooking. I find it is not necessary to rinse short grain rice (e.g., Italian risotto). Cooking methods also vary depending on the variety you are using. Consult with the cooking instructions found on the packaging of the rice. This short description of the most familiar rice varieties is provided as a reminder of the important features and cooking methods for rice.

DISCUSSION ON SALT

Salt is considered one of the simplest and most widely used ingredients in every cuisine throughout the world. For the most part, it has no odor but comes in different colors.

For almost 20 years in my business, and even when I was just enjoying cooking for my family and friends, I always used sea salt on everything I was cooking. Now, for the past four years, as I started to offer cooking classes to interested customers and in-home catering, the question about salt always comes up. The questions varied: what type of salt do I prefer to use? What are the different types of salts out there? What are the differences in taste? Here is an attempt to explain most of that to you. First, you must understand where I stand on the whole question of using salt. I have always advocated that salt is one of the three (Saturated Fats, Sugar and Salt) parts of the axis of evil affecting your heart and overall health. So my advice is to use salt less in your cooking and eating. Please use other substitutes as much as you can; trade good fats for bad ones. So, be warned of those three Weapons of Body Destruction (WBD). With this background, let's talk about the A-salt weapon.

There are two sources of salts. First, the mined type (rock salt) that comes from underground deposits from around the globe. Second, the harvested type (sea salt) that generally comes from evaporated seawater and dried water ponds. By definition, salt is chemically known as sodium chloride, made up of two elements, sodium and chlorine. Salt is widely used as a flavoring agent during cooking, as well as a condiment normally served on the side. Other uses include preserving meat, fish, and vegetables. Other flavored salts are also available and used in a variety of food and drink preparations (e.g., celery salt, rubbing, hickory salt). I highly recommend that you avoid such varieties due to lack of benefits and high sodium content.

The flavor of salts largely depends on the type and level of minerals present in the soil of the source. For the trained eye or tongue, there are noticeable and perhaps a wide range of flavor and color differences between sea salt and mined salt. On the other hand, there are minor differences between the specific type of salts from different regions of the world and the water bodies they come from.

While there are only two sources of salt, there are three types of salt:

Kosher salt This salt is rather coarse with mostly random-sized crystals and should be free of additives. Famous chefs and great kitchens always have this on hand. This salt is my first choice. It has a fresh clean taste without a mineral aftertaste and is known for superior flavor. Kosher salt can come from mined or harvested sources. It gets its name from the Koshering process.

Sea salt This salt is harvested in many regions of the world, for example: French gray salt, Maldon salt from England, red salt and black salt from Hawaii. The colors of the salts are due to the environment they are harvested from (e.g., red clay or black lava deposits). These types of salts are more expensive compared to the mined salts due to the labor-intensive process to harvest them. It is considered the best tasting.

Table salt This is the mined variety and is harvested from the various above-ground or underground mines around the world. Typically, it is processed, fortified with iodine (sodium iodide) and other additives, and ground fine. When using this salt, you will notice it is saltier and it weighs more than the sea salt for the same unit of measure. It also has a greater amount of sodium.

In closing, when it comes to salt, use less of it, adopt an herb, and befriend a favorite spice to bring out the taste in your cooking. So here's to your healthy eating!

The pot always reveals its contents.

DISCUSSION ON SUGAR

Sugar is an extraordinary food with many different sources and forms with varying degrees of sweetness. We enjoy the sweetness of sugar first from our mother's milk as infants and later from the wide array of popular and sugar-rich foods. Today, on average, we consume in excess of 150 pounds of sugar per person per year. This level of consumption is due to sugar availability, low cost, variety and versatility, and use in the modern kitchen. For many of the good and sweet things in life, sugar is present in so many of the foods we eat. It is NOT all that sweet or healthy. As the creative manufacturing use and inventiveness of this basic ingredient's taste sensation grows, sugar (in many of its forms) contributes both directly and indirectly to several of today's diseases including diabetes, tooth decay, and obesity. It is easy to consume a lot of sugar, because it is found in processed form in many of our manufactured foods without even realizing it.

When discussing sugar, we need to compare its basic molecules (simple vs. complex), which affect the degree of sweetness, and the wide array of uses and influences sugar has in cooking, baking, and medicinal applications.

Typical natural sources of sugar come from cane, beet, corn, and honey. In recent years, major developments in sugar processing and manufacturing made it possible to develop sugar substitutes that duplicate or mimic the sweetness and perhaps the characteristics of sugar with somewhat minimal negative effects on body weight and blood sugar levels.

There are several types of sugar. The following is a brief description of each and how they differ.

Glucose A simple sugar and most commonly found in fruit, honey, and corn syrup. It is less sweet than table sugar and doesn't dissolve easily in water.

Fructose Is found in many of the same sources as glucose. It is sweeter than glucose and dissolves very well in water. Our bodies metabolize this sugar slower than glucose, which contributes to a slower rise in blood glucose levels.

Sucrose Is the table sugar we consume daily. It is the combination of one molecule each of fructose and glucose. It is mainly extracted from sugar canes and beet stems. It is sweeter than glucose but takes second place to fructose in sweetness.

Lactose Is the sugar found in dairy (milk). It is the combination of glucose and galactose.

We receive energy from the sugar we consume, but sugars are considered the third ranking source of calories and provide us with loads of "empty" calories. As we consume more of these empty calories, we then consume less of the other much-needed nutrients that come from plant foods that are more essential and beneficial to our general and long-term health. It has been documented that foods rich in sugar replace essential foods that are good for you and foods rich in sugar also contribute greatly to obesity, diabetes, and other health-related problems.

We should not be overly surprised at the volume of sugar we consume, considering that advanced technologies in processed food incorporate refined sugar into many products we eat at every meal. It is easy to consume a great deal of sugar without even realizing it.

Sugars are absorbed and digested at different rates, depending upon the type of sugar. Basically, the slower the absorption and digestion, the more gradual the infusion of sugar is into our bloodstream. This type of sugar is healthier, because our blood sugar does not spike up quickly. Other sugar types that increase the blood-sugar levels rapidly cause increased secretion of insulin, which is needed to regulate the level of sugar in our blood.

Such frequent fluctuation and rapid changes of blood-sugar levels stress our bodies, and that is considered unhealthy. Consulting with your doctor is very important in this regard.

Frequent changes in insulin levels also deter the release of growth hormones, which, in turn, affects our body's immune system. In addition, it has been shown that insulin promotes the storage of fat deposits in our bloodstream. So if you eat lots of sugar-laced food and drinks, you are headed for increased weight gain and other negative health consequences. Other research has cited that there are over 150 bad or negative consequences of great sugar consumption that affect our health.

An important and necessary nutrient, carbohydrates like fruits and vegetables, bread, potatoes, and also sugar, are main sources of energy. One teaspoon of sugar is four grams and equals 16 calories. As mentioned before, sugar consumed in large quantities will lead to weight gain and other health issues.

Sugar is found in many food products and is, or should be, listed on the food labels. Due to the many forms and variations, you should recognize what forms of sugar are present in your food. Consult the nutritional facts on any product you purchase for more information.

Based on the 2005 Dietary Guidelines for Americans, it is recommended that no more than 8 teaspoons of sugar (32 total grams) per day should be consumed for an adult on a 2000 calorie per day diet. One teaspoon of sugar equals one sugar packet. Most sugars that we consume from natural sources are basically considered good sugar. However, sources of bad sugar come in a variety of food types, packages, colors, and styles.

Here are some examples:

- Pancake syrup: ¼ cup = 8 tsp sugar
- Soda: 44 oz = 37 tsp sugar
- Snapple lemon iced tea: 16 oz = 11.5 tsp sugar
- Frozen yogurt: 8 oz = 8.5 tsp sugar
- Chocolate cake: 1 slice = 13 tsp sugar
- McDonald's vanilla milkshake: 21 oz = 24 tsp sugar

Today, many sugar substitutes and varieties are available and considered safe and are now used in formulating food and beverage alternatives. The following is a list types of sugars used.

- Asparatame
- Evaporated cane juice syrup
- High-fructose corn syrup
- Maltodextrin
- Oligofructose
- Polydextrose
- Sucralose

My general advice is to consume even less sugar than what is normally recommended. There are many ways to reduce your consumption of sugar. As you strive to implement those steps, you should always consult with your physician to avoid any unnecessary complications or deprive your system of needed nutrients and energy sources.

Life is two days: one is sweet, the other is bitter.

DISCUSSION ON THE EGG

Ah! The egg is the most basic, most versatile of foods (scrambled, fried, poached, boiled) that has played a significant role in most human food. Loaded with lean protein, it is readily available, inexpensive, and delicious. The egg is very limited in variety, but does come in different sizes. The variety of egg dishes differ based on the origin. You can say the French mastered the egg, its use, and multiple applications in all aspects of cooking and baking. The French have created more egg-based dishes than any other Mediterranean country. Eggs are cooked and enjoyed in just about every way possible. These are some of the uses: soups, sauces, salads, baking, and simply fried, boiled, poached, and even raw. On the Middle Eastern table, we certainly enjoyed the egg on every occasion at every meal in many different dishes. The egg is used throughout the region and in other Mediterranean cuisine and served at breakfast, lunch, and dinner, including the Mezza appetizers and tapas bars. So for example, the Spanish make thick omelets layered with a variety of vegetables, seafood, and spices, which are special treats at any time throughout the day. Vegetable omelets include leeks, potatoes, artichokes, spinach, roasted peppers, olives, and feta cheese, which are just a sample of some of the possibilities. On the other hand, should you enjoy meat like bacon, prosciutto, chicken, or even salmon, then you are in for a delightful surprise, whether you enjoy them with scrambled eggs, or in an omelet or a frittata, which is an open-faced omelet. The frittata is a specialty of the Spanish and the Italians. It is very important in meals for all occasions.

Shopping for eggs is not difficult, however, there are different colored shells and a variety of sizes to choose from (small, medium, and large). First the color of the shell depends largely on the hen's breed. You can, in fact, match the color of the egg shell to that of the hen's ear color. Eggs, regardless of color, taste wonderful. A fresh egg has a deep, golden-colored yolk that is well rounded and plump, not flat, and the white appears as two layers. On the other hand, a two-week-old egg would have a much flatter yolk and little definition between the two white layers. An old trick shown to me by my grandmother is the water test. A fresh egg will sink to the bottom of a glass of water, whereas the older egg will float to the top of the water. When deciding on the size of the eggs to use, generally most cooks and recipes use large eggs for most applications.

Grade A eggs versus grade AA eggs are similar in quality and freshness, with very little distinguishable difference. Eggs should be stored in a cold storage space to keep fresh. I use only hen's eggs in the recipes in this book, but I am sure you're aware of the many other types of birds, farmed and wild, such as quail, duck, and goose. Eggs are enjoyed around the world in many different cuisines.

For me, eggs demand slow, even cooking, preferably in olive oil, regardless of the cooking method. So enjoy the egg every time you cook it. Explore the various uses, applications, and taste regardless of the cooking method you employ. The egg, if separated (yolk and white), offers great applications from soups to desserts and toppings for sweet and savory dishes. Now that's the power of the wholesome egg.

The egg has built in it all the ingredients that make it the most complete and powerful food we know and have. It contains a great source of amino acids, polyunsaturated fatty acid, several minerals, a large number of vitamins, and it is rich in antioxidants.

The egg has been the source of much debate regarding the high level of cholesterol found in it. While that is true, it is the essential component for the development of millions of embryonic cells before hatching. Also, the level of cholesterol may vary based on different breeds, as well as the hen's diet. Recent studies and research have shown that the blood cholesterol is raised more from saturated-fat consumption than the consumption of cholesterol itself. That's because the fat in the egg (yolk) is mostly unsaturated fat compared to red meat.

Finally, please respect the egg and treat it with love by handling it safely and ensuring its quality from initial storage to cooking. Cook eggs gently, properly, and any delicious way you know how.

You can't cook your eggs with wind.

DISCUSSION ON MAKING SOUPS

One of the most important ingredients in any soup is the stock that you use as your (broth) base. The second most important ingredient is how fresh your main components of the soup are. To me, soups start with a great stock. To make a stock, you have to begin with some basic ingredients relative to the type of stock you are making. The following are some quick ideas and ingredients for making some terrific and simple stock. Most stocks can be made ahead of time and, in fact, can be frozen in small amounts (e.g., an ice cube tray) to be used at the time of need. So let's take a look at the different types of stocks we can make.

Chicken One can use a sweet onion or leeks, carrots, celery, bay leaves, thyme, garlic, peppercorn, a spring or two of parsley, and water. Depending on the amounts and how robust the stock is desired to be, then the quantities would vary. Start by using approximately 1 cup of leeks, carrots, celery, 2–3 bay leaves, 12 peppercorns, a teaspoon of thyme, and 3–4 cloves of garlic to approximately 3–4 quarts of water. Bring to a boil, let simmer, and then cool. Chicken scraps could also be used for added flavor. If making a turkey stock, then you would use turkey scraps to add flavor.

Fish One can use a sweet onion (e.g., Vidalia onion), leeks, carrots, celery, a light mushroom (e.g., an oyster mushroom), springs of parsley, bay leaves, white peppercorns, garlic, and water. Use the same quantities as described above in the chicken stock. Fish scraps could also be added for increased flavor.

Vegetable You could use Spanish onions, leeks, carrots, celery, parsley, tomato, bay leaves, thyme, rosemary, black peppercorn, garlic, and water. Other vegetable scraps could be added for additional and varying flavors.

Meat For the most robust flavors in making meat stocks (e.g., beef, veal, lamb), use the bones of different parts of the animal, onions, leeks, carrots, celery, tomato, parsley, bay leaves, peppercorn, red wine, and water.

General Note When making any of these stocks, if you roast the main ingredients before boiling them with herbs and spices, the result will be more intense, deeper-colored flavors that would add a special *ta3m* to your soup, sauce, or stock. Personally, if I have the time, I always roast the main ingredients first for a good 15–30 minutes at 300°F.

DISCUSSION ON BEVERAGES

With the vast cultural and religious compositions of the countries all across the Mediterranean, the beverage of choice can be literally defined by ethnicity, religion, and cultural history. One must understand alcoholic drinks, wine, beer, Arack (Greek ouzo) and other spirits are forbidden or outlawed in public areas in mostly Muslim countries of the Middle East.

I can in good conscience say that, despite all the cultural or religious restrictions from government limitations on public consumption of alcohol, alcohol is being consumed by many across the Mediterranean region in varying degrees.

Iced water, coffee, and tea top the list. Discussions on water and wine follow. They will shed some light on use and preferences.

Cinnamon Hot Tea

This fragrant and satisfying tea is served throughout the eastern Mediterranean and usually as the beverage of choice in the afternoon with light snacks, fruits, and nuts. Also, ground walnuts or toasted almonds are used as topping. I remember when I was very young, the ladies from the neighborhood would get together for a treat in the afternoon and share last-minute anecdotes before the spouses returned home after a long day in the field.

This tea was also served as a treat or a thank-you for visiting guests and for carrying gifts and well wishes to the family after the birth of a child.

Card players, chess players, backgammon players, dice throwers, and pipe-smoking high rollers would have such a drink as a treat to celebrate their friendships and perhaps to toast the winner as they sip on sweet and fragrant tea and chew on the nuts as consolation for their loss.

Sweet Minted Tea

Where alcoholic drinks are not allowed, such as in public, nonalcoholic drinks—both hot and cold—take front and center, even in those countries with hotter climates. The type of beverage varies by country and region and is influenced by culture and religion. All kinds of fresh fruit drinks, syrup-infused drinks, sweet minted teas, strong black coffees, and even yogurt drinks are among the favorites.

Sweet minted tea is brewed using green China tea and fresh spearmint. Typically, it is very light in color and sweetened. Traditionally, it is served in a heavily designed teapot with matching sugar bowl and ornately painted miniature glasses. Try this variation: Add a boiled variety of spices like cinnamon, anise seeds, and nutmeg, then serve with crushed pine nuts, walnuts, almonds, and a little sugar. Coconut is another wonderful addition. Enjoy!

INGREDIENTS

3 cups water
1–2 tbsp green tea
3 tbsp sugar
A few fresh mint leaves

DIRECTIONS

Bring water to a boil. Add the tea and sugar. Remove from heat then add mint leaves. Let stand for 1 minute then serve hot. Serves 4.

Arabic Coffee

Ah, coffee! I remember the aroma of the coffee being roasted in the open markets and sold as if it's going out of style. Hand roasting not only took place in the coffee houses, but also at individual homes. My grandfather used a long-handled cast-iron roasting pan with an attached, flattened spoon long enough to reach the roasting beans to stir and constantly release their addictive aroma. You have not had coffee unless you have had it roasted for you by hand, ground, then boiled to perfection for that ultimate cup of coffee. The experience of drinking coffee starts with the brewing pot, the urn used for serving it, as well as the crafty and various designer-looking cups used to serve it. That's what I call the best cup of coffee to yearn for. So whether you are at the market, at home, or attending whatever occasion, engagement, wedding, graduation, the birth of a child, a holiday, or visiting for a "Sahra" (a gathering to socialize), coffee is essential. All of these occasions, visits, or events are accented with indulgence in drinking coffee or sweet minted tea, fresh fruit, and snacks. The ultimate hospitality of a Middle Eastern home is having coffee "on" and serving it throughout the day. Have you heard of "Coffee Arabica," or the Origin of the Bean? Of course, it is the Middle East where coffee was originally discovered. In these parts of the world, coffee, with its multiple ways of roasting, brewing, and serving, is drunk in liters from early in the morning to the late hours of the night. Farmers are early risers but are customarily to bed as late as midnight.

Remember that after enjoying the midday meal, an afternoon nap or "siesta" helps out a lot. Now coffee is the preferred drink of all generations across the new homeland, America. My mom and dad always had coffee brewing and their constant and warm hospitality, which they showered on everyone, was and continues to be the most gratifying gesture to me. Much of this generosity was the hallmark, the gracious gestures, of my grandparents before them. To this day, I carry on the same kind of hospitality both at home and at my restaurant. Often, my friends, and even my own kids (today's generation), ask if this is necessary or needed, but not because the kids, unlike my parents and siblings, are unaware of this. Perhaps it's because less importance or value is placed on such things. One could argue that it's generational or due to the differences in the value systems or customary traditions of the time we live in. It is heartwarming, however, that as our own kids are exposed more to this, in the long run, they will become more appreciative of this unconditional gift of sharing or giving and return to the wonderful, interesting, and most gratifying gesture of giving for the sake of peace, love, and friendship.

INGREDIENTS

1 tsp coffee
1 cup water

DIRECTIONS

Bring water to boil (with sugar if desired). Add coffee; notice coffee will begin to foam and creamy bubbles start to form. Turn heat down and perk for a short minute. Pour coffee into cups and spoon some of the foam topping each cup.

Arabic coffee is ground very fine compared to the American or French versions. It is very similar to espresso grounds. Unlike espresso, however, it is traditionally sweetened with sugar or honey and spiced with whole or ground cardamom. So how strong do you like it?

Arabic coffee can be ground with cardamom or without. In fact, specialty stores stock both types of ground Arabic coffee, vacuum sealed for freshness and taste.

The original, unsweetened coffee Ala Arabica, also known as Bedouin style, normally is kept on a stove with coffee grounds added to the liquid as needed. This version of coffee is served in small cups without handles, and poured sparingly, about a fifth of the cup in capacity and sipped briefly or taken with a shot of whisky.

Coffee drinkers and coffee houses, much like today, were becoming the main gathering center for socializing and politicking, smoking the water pipe, and perhaps awaiting the fate or fortune the "cup" will yield. OK, let me explain. Unlike here, the women did not really participate in this public assembly of coffee drinking, sweet fragrant tobacco smoking, and/or card playing with politically destitute fellows. Women gathered at homes where they had sweet minted tea and baklava, and not much smoking took place or was permitted. Women like conversation about courtship, about their absent husbands and brothers, or potential young suitors for some lucky, young girl coming of age. If you were superstitious or a disbeliever, then you would avoid such gatherings. To some, it was the hope for that first inkling of what fate might bring you. Let me explain further.

There was always a woman advanced in age who was invariably the chosen one to "read" the fortune from your coffee cup. Never mind horoscopes, tarot cards, or fortune cookies. Arabs love coffee, fairy tales, hand gestures, and the reading of the coffee cup. After finishing your sweetened coffee, the sediments of coffee (the sludge left in the bottom of your cup) hold the secrets and the keys that became your destiny. The "Chosen One" is able to read the various patterns that develop from turning your coffee cup upside down into your saucer after a little shake and swirl. Of course, as a believer or a skeptic, you always enjoyed the story, the prediction, the revealed secret, and the laughter you shared with your family and friends. Yet ... as a believer, don't ever underestimate the power of a good cup of coffee with friends which may translate to good karma—lots of luck!

DISCUSSION ON WATER

Ah, water! Right about now, I long for a drink of that water from my childhood that was carried from the well at the bottom of the hill and crated in army-like containers, straddling the mule and sloshing around in harmony to the step of the animal. As a kid, I used to look forward to going on what then seemed like a small journey when in reality was a short five-minute walk to get water. Everything seemed far, and it seemed to be a little expedition to discover water. We arrived sometimes at this ancient central well with others getting their share of this clear, delicious water. Lowering the rope with a bucket tied to its end, it would splash on the surface of the water then tilt enough for water to begin to fill and overtake the empty space of this magical vessel. The bucket is drawn up slowly as it spills and splashes, dropping some of its fill back into the well. The rain-like echo fills the airy space of the well as if inviting the bucket back for another try. The smell, the sound, the feeling, the taste of the water, and the delight in the experience conjures a favorite memory. Water was served before, during, and after every meal time. The reason is the sure interpretation and understanding that it is where life originated. It is revered and is considered a blessed source of life, both at home and church, in celebrating a newborn, at weddings, Sunday ceremonies, and celebrating the living as the dead are buried. Water was the drink and the sacrament and the ointment for sins and the sinful. Make no mistake; it was used with reverence and virtue.

In the old days, we did not have the government (e.g., Environmental Protection Agency) overlooking the safety of our water. We had Mother Nature supplying us with the purest and least harmful. In the USA, there is always the debate about the safety of our water supply and what are acceptable levels of toxins present in our water (e.g., bacteria, lead, etc.). The idea of bottled water mushroomed as a big business, generating tons of profit for companies. It was thought to be the solution to our drinking water problems and, in fact, turned out the other way. Much of the bottled waters, including name brands, are tapped municipal water. Many tests have been taken, and it is reported that many name-brand bottled waters purchased and tasted from many states contain several contaminants including bacteria, caffeine, fertilizers, and radioactive materials. These findings were reported in October 2008. AP reports and even the FDA's own survey found approximately a third of more than 50 brands tested were tainted with less-than-acceptable levels of bacteria, and approximately a quarter of the bottling companies had less-than-average manufacturing practices. This is not by any means considered a huge health risk, however, you should always consider the source of the water you drink.

Drinking water before and during your meal is a healthy habit and a good thing. I have always encouraged people to do so. Don't take your water for granted. You should always strive to know the source. You must understand the water in order to drink and cook with pure, nontoxic, refreshing water.

Let's talk about water "footprint," or the total amount of water used to produce a product, grow a plant or vegetable (like celery), raise a cow, or transport a product from one end of the country to the other. I asked one of my sons about the impact on his water footprint of a 15-minute shower versus a 5-minute shower! With water as a scarce resource, this is one place we can start conserving. And did you know it takes approximately one gallon of water to produce, ship, and store a single 16-ounce bottle of water? That's just not acceptable, not to mention all the trash generated by those empty bottles. Conserve, conserve, conserve!

Any water in the desert will do.

GRAPES, WINE, AND LOTS OF SPIRIT

This is not about the science of grape growing, wine making, or the history thereof. Grape vines and wine making are ancient, perhaps before history and writing began. Why, you say? Because it makes sense now and made good sense then. You see, wild grapes thrived throughout the region. Historic events, discoveries, and even sketches on paintings of offerings to the Gods from the pharaohs to the Greek Gods all depicted the gift of grapes and wine making.

It is no surprise that wine throughout history within the various cultures of the Mediterranean region played an important role in daily life, even perhaps defining the social fabric. Very much like olive oil, wine played a crucial part in the diet of the Mediterranean region, both in cooking and as a social favorite as a signature drink for the hospitable host.

As we all know, wine today plays a great part in the main meal in much of the region. I can assure you that to this day, wine and wine making for personal or commercial production and consumption remain an important aspect of the daily lives of the habitants of the region.

Today, red wine is considered a healthful ingredient as part of the Mediterranean diet. It is no wonder that following in their footsteps, based on much research, wine is now considered a great benefit to heart health. This is something that, due to lifestyle or due to inventiveness or need—perhaps an accident—wine is a great discovery. Regardless, here we are. I always toast my cooking class participants with a glass of wine stating, "Here's to your health." I guess I am following the steps of my own great grandparents with great pride in my job. A word of precaution. It is great to enjoy wine with your food, but be careful to not overdo it.

As a general rule, our wines were made to be consumed and not to be sold commercially. The white wine always tasted fresh and fruity. The color was slightly pale or a bit cloudy, yet tasted great. The red wines, on the other hand, were slightly heavier, richer, and more robust with great grape taste. Hardly any preservatives or purifications were used, yet the great taste of your own wine with homemade rich, soft, cheese, freshly baked bread, olives, and fruit, was a treat to look forward to. Most of the wine we made growing up was produced for consumption, so long-term storage or aging of the wine was not imperative. Most of the wine that we made was red; there was very little white.

As a young adult, of legal age, of course, even as an aspiring professional, I always enjoyed the taste of wine over many other beverages, regardless of the setting. At home when I cooked and entertained, I always preferred the wine of choice with everything I served. You can bet it was more fun to select the right kind of wine for that dinner or occasion than the other hard stuff. As I was growing up, my brother and I were very familiar with making wine from "scratch," or is it "stomp"? By the time we were seven years old, my grandparents employed us as the "expert grape crushers" as we hopped, jumped, and danced to crush the grapes for that special wine that was harvested. Boy, I tell you, those were fun-filled memories, and I enjoyed the special feeling, sticky as it was, where the kid-clan not only had fun, but also contributed to the family in terms of making it, bottling it, and sometimes bartering with it.

There are so many different varieties of grapes in numerous climates, types of soil, and even blends of grapes. My attempt here is to explore in simple terms what it meant (means) to grow grapes, harvest them, and produce that favorite-tasting wine that perhaps took a lifetime to explore, perfect, and enjoy.

The world of wine is huge and involves many profiles of wine from many regions of the entire world. It can be overwhelming, sometimes intimidating, resulting in an uncomfortable feeling, enough to stick to what is familiar to you and shy away from wonderful varieties of wines and tastes. The literature is enormous, ranging on all fronts of wine growing, making, buying, storing, and how to order your best selections at a restaurant.

Learning how to explore and develop your ability to evaluate what I call see (appearance), smell (the scents or aromas), and taste (*ta3m*), the flavors and finish of the wine is imperative for any wine enthusiast. Of course, for the enjoyment of wine, the range for appearance, scents, and flavor is as wide as enjoying a chilled chardonnay from a plastic cup to indulging in an aged Bordeaux from a fancy designer glass. In fact, that's how wide the spectrum is. I fall somewhere in between, and I have to admit, I am still learning about and enjoying new wines whenever I can. What we are dealing with here is both an art and a science, compounded by the variety of grapes and their origins.

Labels on wine bottles are the key to many important pieces of information about the wine including the origin (vineyard), type of grape used, the year produced, and the winemaker.

Serving good wines from a real glass is a must. Always avoid thick or colored glasses; use larger clear and tall-shaped glasses for white wines and a rounder glass for red wines. The size of the glass is important in that it should hold four to five ounces of wine, allowing for aeration and maintaining proper temperature for either type. All wines have personality and character, like people. Treat them with gentle love and care.

I love to cook, and I love wine, and sometimes I even put wine in my cooking. Okay, seriously now, as a chef/restaurateur, I would have a predetermined menu, then think about what wine would go well with the meal. On the other hand, if you are a serious wine enthusiast, most definitely you decide what type of wine you would like to drink, identifying type and flavor, and then you would decide what food will be served. In both cases, both chefs and wine enthusiasts will intuitively know, sense, and even taste what and how those flavors would pair well together. So in seeking the pleasure of enjoying a good wine with your great meal, develop a deep sense of flavors, tastes, and smells.

Chicken

B'Stilla

Prep time: 35 minutes
Ready in: 90 minutes
Serves: 10

WOW! Get ready to sink your fingers and your teeth in such an authentic dish with great flavors, aromas and taste. This is one taste on this Moroccan dish.

Nutritional Information

Serving Size: ⅒ recipe • Calories 408, Total Fat 26g, Saturated Fat 6g, Cholesterol 178mg, Sodium 188mg, Total Carbohydrates 20g, Dietary Fiber 3g, Protein 22g

■ INGREDIENTS

4 tbsp blended olive oil and butter
4 lb squab or chicken (with livers and giblets, optional)
1 cup onion, chopped
4 tbsp fresh cilantro or coriander
2 tbsp Italian parsley
1 tsp each ginger and cumin
½ tsp each cayenne, turmeric, cinnamon
⅛ tsp saffron threads, crushed
1 cup water
2 tbsp lemon juice (optional)
8 eggs
4 tsp olive oil (unsalted) for browning almonds
1 cup slivered blanched almonds
2 tbsp sugar
½ tsp cinnamon
12 sheets filo
Blended olive oil with equal portions of oil and melted butter for brushing

■ DIRECTIONS

In a heavy skillet, heat ¼ cup of blended olive oil; brown birds, remove, pull meat off bone, and set aside. Sauté onions (and liver and giblets if using). Add spices and water; bring to a boil. Reduce liquid to 1¾ cups. Add lemon juice. Beat eggs, stir into pan while on low heat. In a separate pan, brown almonds, drain, add sugar and cinnamon.

Layer 8 sheets filo and brush with butter and blended olive oil; spread half the almonds, half the egg mix, poultry, rest of egg mix, rest of almonds; top with rest of filo.

Bake for 20 minutes, drain and flip. Bake 10–15 minutes, flip again. Bake 5 minutes. Sprinkle with powdered sugar and decorate with cinnamon. Serve hot.

Note: Of course in Morocco, the tradition is to use no utensils and you have to break the crushed filo with your fingers. Then OH!! The first encounter with the escaping steam is the ultimate way to begin. Remember, no pain, no gain. So enjoy this very delightful dish. Serve with couscous or orzo pilaf.

This recipe is high in fat and cholesterol content. Savor the taste, and enjoy in moderation.

CHICKEN CACCIATORE

Prep time: 20 minutes
Ready in: 45 minutes
Serves: 6

This is a variation on a classical Italian dish. The combination of the fresh herbs, vegetables and cheese is a great way to enjoy the fresh harvest in a hearty dish that gets better as it lasts.

Nutritional Information

Serving Size: ⅙ recipe • Calories 282, Total Fat 12g, Saturated Fat 2g, Cholesterol 66mg, Sodium 229mg, Total Carbohydrates 14g, Dietary Fiber 4g, Protein 29g

■ INGREDIENTS

4 tbsp olive oil
1½ lb skinless chicken breast cubed
  (may substitute tofu)
1 large onion cubed
2 cups of sliced mushrooms
1 red pepper cubed
1 green pepper cubed
½ cup white wine (red wine is often used
  as a substitute)
3–4 cloves garlic
1 tsp basil
1 tsp oregano
1 tsp thyme
2 bay leaves
4 cups tomato (fresh, whole peeled in cans)
2 tbsp Parmesan cheese
Black pepper to taste
Kosher sea salt to taste (optional)

■ DIRECTIONS

Heat large skillet and add 2 tbsp oil. Cook chicken pieces until cooked through and set aside. Heat skillet and add 2 tbsp oil. Add onions and mushrooms; cook 3 minutes. Add peppers; cook and stir well. Add wine and garlic; cook and stir for 3 minutes. Add basil, oregano, thyme, and bay leaves. Add tomatoes. Let simmer for 8 to 10 minutes. Add Parmesan cheese and stir. Add salt and pepper to taste. Serve over pasta.

Note: If you like this spicier, you may add 3 pinches of cayenne pepper or crushed hot pepper flakes. May substitute tofu for chicken or use brown rice for pasta. Garlic smashed red skin potatoes make a great side dish.

CHICKEN DIJON

Prep time: 25 minutes
Ready in: 45 minutes
Serves: 8

This delightful and flavorful dish is an excellent variation for a main chicken dish—sautéed not deep fried.

Nutritional Information

Serving Size: ⅛ recipe • Calories 201, Total Fat 8g, Saturated Fat 2g, Cholesterol 76mg, Sodium 194mg, Total Carbohydrates 1g, Dietary Fiber 0g, Protein 30g

■ INGREDIENTS

3 tbsp olive oil
3 tbsp Dijon mustard
6 (6–8 oz) skinless chicken breasts, cut into strips
¼ cup grated Parmesan/Romano cheese blend
additional olive oil for cooking

■ DIRECTIONS

Mix oil, mustard and whisk well. Coat chicken pieces in Dijon mixture. Dredge chicken pieces in the cheese blend. Preheat skillet with olive oil. Place coated chicken pieces in skillet. Sauté chicken for 2 minutes on each side then rotate. Continue until golden brown. Remove, let rest, then serve.

Note: Possible dipping sauces may include: honey mustard, roasted tomato pesto, basil pesto, or leave it to your imagination. Also, you could let cool, cut into small pieces and toss with a salad or steamed vegetables. Toasted sesame noodles as a garnish are also a nice touch.

CHICKEN DIJONNAISE

Prep time: 25 minutes
Ready in: 45 minutes
Serves: 8

The addition of mayonnaise and seasoned breadcrumbs and baked instead of pan sautéed makes this dish a delightful alternative.

Nutritional Information

Serving Size: ⅛ recipe • Calories 286, Total Fat 16g, Saturated Fat 4g, Cholesterol 82mg, Sodium 315mg, Total Carbohydrates 5g, Dietary Fiber 0g, Protein 29g

■ INGREDIENTS

6 (6–8 oz) chicken breasts (skinless and boneless)
1 tbsp butter (optional)
3 tbsp olive oil (100%) or a blend of canola and olive oil
¾ cup mayonnaise (the light variety)
3 tbsp Dijon mustard
¼ cup Parmesan cheese
¼ cup unsalted yellow cornmeal

■ DIRECTIONS

Pound chicken breast slightly at the thick part. Sauté chicken (may cut into smaller strips) in the oil (and butter if you are using it) until cooked through. Preheat oven to 350°–375°. Place chicken on sheet pan.

Combine mayo, mustard, cheese. Spread evenly over chicken to cover. Sprinkle with little more cheese and the crumbs. Cook 10–12 minutes until golden brown.

Note: This is a wonderful version of chicken with mustard. You may increase the heat by adding a few drops of hot pepper sauce. I have tried this with boneless pork chops and I thought it was really good. You know, the other white meat. Serve with a cabbage salad with raisins, or salad with a light dressing. Cornmeal crumbs give a little more crunch than bread crumbs.

Chicken Salad

Prep time: 20 minutes
Ready in: 40 minutes
Serves: 8

Not your typical chicken salad. The addition of sweet and savory tastes create a great depth in flavor.

Nutritional Information

Serving Size: ⅛ recipe • Calories 329, Total Fat 16g, Saturated Fat 2g, Cholesterol 70mg, Sodium 299mg, Total Carbohydrates 22g, Dietary Fiber 1g, Protein 24g

■ INGREDIENTS

3 cups diced, cooked chicken breast
3 tbsp fresh lemon juice
1 cup light mayonnaise
¼ tsp sea salt
1 tsp dry mustard
1 tsp curry powder
1½ cups seedless grapes
1 cup drained pineapple pieces
⅓ cup sliced almonds, toasted
⅔ cup water chestnuts, dried

■ DIRECTIONS

Toss chicken with lemon juice in a large bowl. Cover and refrigerate for 1 hour. Combine mayonnaise, salt, mustard and curry powder in small bowl. Add grapes, pineapples, almonds and water chestnuts to chicken and toss lightly. Blend in mayonnaise mixture and toss well.

Note: If you are adventurous like me, you may want to try this with small shrimp for another great summer, light salad dinner. Garnish with shredded carrots or sweet peas for a great presentation.

EVERYTHING JAMBALAYA

Prep time: 40 minutes
Ready in: 75 minutes
Serves: 8

This is a great variation on a Spanish style dish that yields great flavor.

Nutritional Information

Serving Size: ⅛ recipe • Calories 300, Total Fat 13g, Saturated Fat 5g, Cholesterol 95mg, Sodium 813mg, Total Carbohydrates 24g, Dietary Fiber 39g, Protein 22g

■ INGREDIENTS

1 tsp extra virgin olive oil
1 pat unsalted butter
1 lb boneless, skinless chicken thighs or breast meat, diced
½ lb andouille, chorizo, or linguica sausage, diced
1 medium onion, chopped
2 ribs celery from the heart of the stalk, chopped
1 green bell pepper, seeded and chopped
1 bay leaf, fresh or dried
1 tsp cayenne pepper
2–3 tbsp flour
4 oz sundried tomatoes, roughly chopped
2 cups low-sodium chicken broth (1 cup if cooked rice is used)
1 cup white enriched rice, uncooked, or 2 cups cooked rice
1 tsp ground cumin
1 tsp hot chili powder
1 tbsp paprika
1 tbsp Tabasco sauce (hot sauce)
1 tbsp Worcestershire sauce
¾ lb medium shrimp, peeled and deveined (tails on)
Black pepper to taste
2 tbsp fresh thyme leaves, chopped
4 scallions, sliced thin

■ DIRECTIONS

Heat a large, deep skillet over medium high heat. Add oil to pan and melt butter into it. Add chicken and brown 2 minutes, then rotate. Add sausage and cook 2 minutes more. Add onion, celery, pepper, bay leaf and cayenne. Sauté vegetables until tender—about 3–5 minutes. Sprinkle flour over vegetables and meat and cook a minute more. Add tomatoes and broth to pan and combine ingredients well. Add rice by spreading over entire pot. Season with cumin, chili, paprika, Tabasco and Worcestershire. Scatter shrimp into pot and cook until shrimp are pink and firm and sauce thickens a bit—about 5 minutes. Season with thyme, salt and pepper to your taste. Sprinkle with chopped scallions, and serve.

Note: One option is to cook the rice separately and then add it towards the end of the cooking procedure. If cooked rice is used, then the amount of broth needs to be reduced by about a cup. If raw rice is used, wait 8–10 minutes before adding shrimp so the rice has time to cook. Notice that the rice will settle at the bottom of the pan as it cooks. Therefore, the level of heat should be monitored to avoid overcooking or burning.

GRILLED CHICKEN FAJITA SALAD

Prep time: 20 minutes
Ready in: 30 minutes
Serves: 8

This is a simple, straightforward and fun dish to make with your family.

Nutritional Information

Serving Size: ⅛ recipe • Calories 170, Total Fat 5g, Saturated Fat 1g, Cholesterol 37mg, Sodium 137mg, Total Carbohydrates 16g, Dietary Fiber 4g, Protein 19g

■ INGREDIENTS

1 lb grilled skinless/boneless chicken breast (or sliced roast beef, or sliced turkey)
1 tbsp taco seasoning
3 tsp extra virgin olive oil
1 red pepper, sliced
1 green pepper, sliced
1 head romaine lettuce, chopped
4–5 ripe tomatoes, chopped
½ cup red onion, diced
3–4 bunches of scallions, chopped
½ cup fresh cilantro
Juice of 1 lime
¼ cup shredded cheddar cheese

■ DIRECTIONS

Toss chicken with taco seasoning. Heat 1 tsp oil and add peppers, cooking until soft (3–4 minutes or until lightly caramelized). Add chicken and bring up to temp. Cook chicken until done/no longer pink. Mix lettuce, tomato, onion, scallions and cilantro in a bowl. Drizzle with 1 tsp olive oil and lime juice. Top with chicken and peppers. Serve chilled or warm; sprinkle with cheddar cheese at time of serving. Use baked pita chips to garnish (optional).

Note: Make sure that taco seasoning is low in sodium, and avoid adding more salt.

Grilled Chicken Kabob Aloha

Prep time: 20 minutes
Ready in: 35 minutes
Serves: 10

Grilling is, without question, the number one way of cooking in my old home. It's healthy and it offers great options. Here we add a little spice and sweetness to the mix.

Nutritional Information

Serving Size: ¹/₁₀ recipe • Calories 82, Total Fat 1g, Saturated Fat 0g, Cholesterol 32mg, Sodium 271mg, Total Carbohydrates 4g, Dietary Fiber 1g, Protein 13g

■ INGREDIENTS

3 skinless/boneless chicken breasts
    (1–1½ lb)
2 tbsp of chopped cilantro
1 tbsp fresh ginger shaved
2 tsp chopped garlic
1 tsp chopped hot peppers
1 tsp zesty vinaigrette dressing or lemon
    juice
2 tsp each of cumin, coriander, and black
    pepper
1 green bell pepper
1 red bell pepper
1 cup cubed fresh pineapple
Season with 2 pinches of black pepper
    and salt each

■ DIRECTIONS

Place cut-up chicken in a bowl and add chopped cilantro, ginger, garlic, hot pepper, zesty dressing, cumin, coriander, salt and pepper then toss. Let marinate for 15–30 minutes in fridge or 10 minutes at room temperature. Use 10-inch bamboo shoots for skewers (metal skewers optional). Alternate chicken, peppers, and pineapple on skewers. Place kabobs on grill, turn and rotate every 3–4 minutes until chicken is cooked through.

Note: Jalapeño peppers or dried chilies may be used for extra heat in the marinade. You also can substitute Ahi tuna or swordfish in place of the chicken.

GRILLED TUSCANY CHICKEN

Prep time: 15 minutes
Ready in: 35 minutes
Serves: 8

Free-range chicken is really great for this. Ask your butcher to trim and cut two whole chickens in half, or as many as you need for your guests. The more, the better!

Nutritional Information

Serving Size: ⅛ recipe • Calories 117, Total Fat 10g, Saturated Fat 2g, Cholesterol 14mg, Sodium 27mg, Total Carbohydrates 2g, Dietary Fiber 0g, Protein 4g

■ INGREDIENTS

2 whole chickens, cut in half
2 tbsp chopped garlic
¼ cup olive oil
¼ cup lemon juice
1 tsp each of thyme, rosemary, sage, and oregano
Zest of 1 lemon
3 pinches paprika
Salt and pepper
Hot chili pepper (optional)

■ DIRECTIONS

Clean and rinse the chicken well with very cold water, then pat dry. In a small mixing bowl, combine all ingredients except chicken. Rub the chicken with the mixture, coating well, then set aside for at least one hour before grilling.

Grill the chicken, skin side down first over medium high heat. Grill each side for 4–5 minutes, then turn, repeatedly brushing and basting as you turn to the other side. Continue for 20–25 minutes on low to medium heat.

You can check if done by twisting the leg (the chicken's leg, not yours). It should move easily in its socket; or, cook until internal temperature gets to 170°.

Place the chicken on the lower heat side of grill; baste as needed to avoid burning and drying then close the cover till until done.

Remember, white meat cooks faster than dark meat. Let cool for 5–10 minutes before cutting and serving. Serve with lemon wedges.

Note: Other serving suggestions: grill fresh sweet corn in the husk, portobello mushrooms, speared plum tomatoes, even sliced red onions. YUM! Until next time, happy and safe grilling. Remember you're really playing with fire.

MOROCCAN CHICKEN

Prep time: 25 minutes
Ready in: 65 minutes
Serves: 15

This is a great variation on a traditional Moroccan dish. It is typically made with a whole or half chicken. Also, the livers and giblets are incorporated into the dish. This recipe does not go that direction.

Nutritional Information

Serving Size: ⅟₁₅ recipe • Calories 401, Total Fat 16g, Saturated Fat 3g, Cholesterol 143mg, Sodium 488mg, Total Carbohydrates 10g, Dietary Fiber 3g, Protein 54g

■ INGREDIENTS

9–10 oz skinless chicken breasts (5–6 lb)
½ cup whole wheat flour seasoned with a few pinches of cinnamon, white pepper, and cumin
3 onions, julienned
4 lemons, sliced into half moons
1 tsp each of cumin, curry, cinnamon, ginger, white pepper, and paprika
1 tbsp of basil chopped or 1 tsp of dry basil
2 tbsp chopped garlic
½ cup lemon juice
½ cup olive oil
1 cup green olives with brine

■ DIRECTIONS

Clean chicken breast of all traces of fat. Dredge chicken in flour mixture. In a large skillet, sauté floured chicken 2–3 minutes on each side. Place in bottom of baking pan. In a bowl, mix remaining ingredients and pour over chicken, spreading evenly. Let sit for 1–2 hours. Bake in oven at 300° for 1¼ hours, uncovered. Remove, let cool, and serve.

Note: You may separate the chicken from the sauce for serving purposes. Also, if you have access to preserved lemons and saffron, those will add great depth, color and taste. Use zest of a lemon as garnish. This is great with Moroccan couscous and glazed carrots.

Moroccan Chicken with Tomato

Prep time: 25 minutes
Ready in: 65 minutes
Serves: 10

As a slight variation on the original, you may use grape tomatoes for olives or lemons and use dry wine in place of olive brine to reduce the salt level of the dish.

Nutritional Information

Serving Size: 1/10 recipe • Calories 271, Total Fat 12g, Saturated Fat 2g, Cholesterol 76mg, Sodium 417mg, Total Carbohydrates 12g, Dietary Fiber 3g, Protein 30g

■ INGREDIENTS

4 tbsp olive oil
2 lb chicken breast cut into strips
1/2 cup whole wheat flour
2 onions sliced
4–6 cloves of garlic chopped
1 cup green olives, pitted (with brine)
2 lemons sliced (half moon)
2 pinches pepper
10 pinches cumin
10 pinches coriander
6 pinches curry
8 pinches cinnamon
6 pinches ginger
8 pinches basil
8 pinches paprika
1/2 cup olive brine or dry wine
1/2 cup lemon juice

■ DIRECTIONS

In a large skillet, heat oil. Dredge chicken in flour until coated well. Sauté chicken, remove and place in a baking dish or pan. Add onions. Add garlic, olives, lemons (or tomatoes), and spices and mix well. Add olive juice (brine), and lemon juice on top of chicken. Place pan in preheated oven and bake for 30–40 minutes at 325°.

Note: You may follow the same procedure and substitute shrimp or a hearty fish like tuna. Grape tomatoes can be substituted for olives or lemons. Serve on top of pasta or couscous.

POMEGRANATE CHICKEN

Prep time: 15 minutes
Ready in: 45 minutes
Serves: 8

This is a fabulous way to knock chicken outside the box. Use fresh pomegranate juice (now readily available) for best results.

Nutritional Information

Serving Size: ⅛ recipe • Calories 523, Total Fat 20g, Saturated Fat 5g, Cholesterol 143mg, Sodium 263mg, Total Carbohydrates 30g, Dietary Fiber 4g, Protein 54g

■ INGREDIENTS

16 oz pomegranate juice
2 cups chicken stock (low fat)
1 cup barley
3 tbsp olive oil
½ cup onions (shallot), chopped
1–2 jalapeño peppers, diced
8 chicken breasts (with bone)
4–6 pinches sea salt
4–6 pinches black pepper
½ cup chopped parsley

■ DIRECTIONS

Preheat oven to 375°. Reduce pomegranate juice until it thickens, and set aside. In a separate saucepan, bring chicken stock to boil. Add barley and cook until tender.

In another pan, sauté shallots and jalapeños in oil. Add the cooked barley and keep warm. Season chicken with a little salt and pepper and roast 15–20 minutes until cooked through. Serve with barley, drizzle chicken with glaze, garnish with parsley.

Note: A little honey, lemon, and cinnamon stick could be added to pomegranate juice for a greater flavor. You may substitute lentils for barley. You may also add chopped walnuts to the pomegranate juice for a crunchy texture and flavor or just sprinkle over chicken. Remove skin prior to serving for even healthier results. If pomegranates are not available, try using cranberries or Craisins.

Roasted Cornish Hen with Garlic Pesto

Prep time: 15 minutes
Ready in: 45 minutes
Serves: 8

Ah!! Comfort food! Wholesome, healthy food with robust flavors made in the coziest place in town. Where else but in your own home?? To me, the fall season evokes the whole idea of "back to basics" and cooking comfort food for the love of food, enjoying and sharing with family and friends.

Nutritional Information

Serving Size: ⅛ recipe • Calories 418, Total Fat 31g, Saturated Fat 8g, Cholesterol 168mg, Sodium 233mg, Total Carbohydrates 4g, Dietary Fiber 1g, Protein 30g

■ INGREDIENTS

4 (1 lb) Cornish hens
8 whole cloves garlic
½ cup shallots
1 cup fresh basil, chopped
½ cup chopped parsley
¼ cup extra virgin olive oil
4 pinches of salt and pepper per hen

■ DIRECTIONS

Rinse and pat dry hens. Lightly salt and pepper each bird, inside and out. In a food processor combine garlic, shallots, basil, parsley, olive oil until smooth. Rub hens generously with the garlic mixture inside, outside and under the skin. Place hens in shallow roasting pan with breast side facing up. Place ¼ cup water in the bottom of pan. Baste as needed (2–3) times during cooking. Roast in 325° oven uncovered for 45 minutes, or until hens test done. Remove and let rest 5–10 minutes before cutting. Serve with your favorite vegetables and stuffing sides.

Note: Try the following as sides: roasted mashed garlic red skin potatoes; wild mushroom and wild rice pilaf; glazed baby carrots; pearl onions and peas; rice, nut, and raisin stuffing. Roast chicken substitute—follow recipe above with 2 two-pound chickens cut in half.

YOGURT CHICKEN

Prep time: 10 minutes
Ready in: 35 minutes
Serves: 8

Simple yet has rich flavors and goes very well with aromatic rices like jasmine or basmati rice. See note below for further flavors.

Nutritional Information

Serving Size: ⅛ recipe • Calories 196, Total Fat 15g, Saturated Fat 3g, Cholesterol 16mg, Sodium 146mg, Total Carbohydrates 8g, Dietary Fiber 1g, Protein 8g

■ INGREDIENTS

½ cup vegetable oil
2 medium onions, cleaned and chopped
12 cloves of garlic, chopped
4 dried red chilies (or fresh when available)
1 fresh ginger, grated (the size of a walnut)
2½ lb boneless, skinless chicken breast, cut into
    2-inch strips
1½ cups low fat yogurt
8 pinches of salt
8 pinches white pepper

■ DIRECTIONS

In a large skillet, sauté onion, garlic, red chilies and fresh ginger for 3–5 minutes. Add chicken and continue to sauté until chicken is tender and begins to brown (5–6 minutes). Add yogurt, stir well and simmer on low heat for 8–10 minutes. Remove from heat. Add salt and pepper, stir mixture and cover.

Note: You may add turmeric, saffron or cumin for additional depth in flavor. I have also added whole cardamom for a unique Indian-like taste. Serve with Basmati rice, lentils or spinach korma.

Dairy

ARABIC CHEESE

Prep time: 45 minutes
Ready in: 8–10 hours
Makes: 8 ounces

In the Mediterranean region, goat's milk is more abundant and available than cow's milk. Therefore, you will find dairy products to be made from goat's milk. I have made this cheese with cow's milk and sheep's milk. The taste is not the same, but it is still very good.

Nutritional Information

Serving Size: ⅛ recipe • Calories 163, Total Fat 13g, Saturated Fat 9g, Cholesterol 35mg, Sodium 231mg, Total Carbohydrates 1g, Dietary Fiber 0g, Protein 10g

■ INGREDIENTS

1 gallon goat's milk (see Note)
2 junket tablets (see Note)

■ DIRECTIONS

Bring milk to a scald (180°) then remove from heat, let cool to 110°–115°. Mix junket tablets into one cup of the warm milk then add to remaining milk. Mix well and set aside for 15–20 minutes. Stir again, set and allow to cool for 10 minutes. The cheese should be noticeably settled at the bottom of the pot. Pour into a cheesecloth-lined colander, pressing with your hand to extract excess liquid and cheese becomes solid. Divide the cheese into 4–5 balls by rolling, cupping, squeezing, and forming into disc-like shapes, firm and spongy. Pack into salt brine to preserve, or cut into small wedges and serve with pita, olives and cut up fresh vegetables for a great appetizer or snack.

Note: We sometimes make this with other milk types (cow, sheep) depending on availability or the desired taste.

Junket tablets are a sweet, mild-flavored rennin, which coagulates hot milk to form soft a pudding-like texture, which ultimately makes a firm, spongy, white cheese.

LABAN
(MIDDLE EASTERN YOGURT)

Prep time: 30 minutes
Ready in: 10–12 hours
Serves: 4

For centuries, this mixture of milk (boiled) and a starter culture (yogurt) are the basic two ingredients in making yogurt. This recipe, handed down in the family for generations, is simple yet profound in terms of how it reveals the versatility of the product as well as the person who makes it. There has been a lot of research in support of the health benefits attributed to yogurt. Among these benefits is improved digestion and how yogurt aids in controlling some diets. The following is a simple recipe that would produce the best results.

Nutritional Information

Serving Size: ¼ recipe • Calories 143, Total Fat 5g, Saturated Fat 3g, Cholesterol 20mg, Sodium 151mg, Total Carbohydrates 14g, Dietary Fiber 0g, Protein 10g

■ INGREDIENTS

4 tbsp prepared low-fat yogurt (starter culture)
3 tbsp warm milk
1 quart milk (2% or whole milk)

■ DIRECTIONS

Mix warm milk with yogurt, set aside and allow to reach room temperature. Bring milk to a scald (180°). Remove from heat, let cool to 110°–115° (My mother used to apply the finger test to check for temperature; she inserted the tip of a finger into the milk and counted to ten to determine if the temperature in the milk was just right). Add yogurt mixture to the warm milk, stir well. Wrap with large quilt and place in a warm place for 5–6 hours. When mixture becomes semisolid like a pudding, uncover, refrigerate, and serve. The degree of sweetness or tartness of the yogurt is dependent on the starter culture used. You may save some of the new Laban (yogurt) to be used as culture for future batches. Yogurt may be used as salad dressing or over rice pilaf, and may be brought to a boil for sauces used with lamb kibbee balls, chicken, and fish dishes.

Note: Low-fat yogurt could be made by using 2% or skim milk following the same method. Grainy or coarse texture of yogurt may result due to higher temperature of milk. You may process yogurt, then use to make Laban cheese. See recipe for Laban cheese balls.

Laban Cheese Balls

Prep time: 10 minutes
Ready in: 2–3 days
Makes: 15 balls

These hardened cheese yogurt balls will last for a long time and may be enjoyed at room temperature. After laban is made, or perhaps you have an abundance of it left over, the following is a step you can take to make hardened laban cheese. These simple steps will yield yet another variation of this great dish.

Nutritional Information

Serving Size: ¹⁄₁₅ recipe • Calories 204, Total Fat 18g, Saturated Fat 4g, Cholesterol 11mg, Sodium 74mg, Total Carbohydrates 7g, Dietary Fiber 0g, Protein 5g

■ INGREDIENTS

4–5 lb laban
2–3 cups extra virgin olive oil
Thyme, oregano

■ DIRECTIONS

Place the laban in a cheesecloth. Tie it and squeeze out excess water. Let the cheese cloth hang over a sink or container for 2–3 days. Mix the cheese by squeezing the cloth to incorporate the middle and outer portion of cheese to drain any remaining moisture—it should be similar to cream cheese in texture and consistency. Make small balls, a little smaller than a golf ball. Lay on a tray and refrigerate covered for 4–6 hours. Once hardened or dry, place balls in a pickling glass jar and cover with olive oil. Add spices, seal and keep soaked for 1–2 weeks in a cool place. After that, they are ready to serve and are best at room temperature.

Note: Salt may be added to extract more moisture if the Laban is a little soft, but remember this will increase the sodium content. Let it drain longer for better results. This variety lasts longer covered with olive oil. Serve with warm pita bread, olives, and hot peppers. Also, Zaatar spice may be used for dipping.

Desserts

Almond Peach Crepes

Prep time: 15 minutes
Ready in: 25 minutes
Serves: 8

Crepes are popular in France. The riper the peaches, the better. Toasted almonds would elevate the taste a notch for breakfast, brunch or snack.

Nutritional Information

Serving Size: ⅛ recipe • Calories 274, Total Fat 15g, Saturated Fat 4g, Cholesterol 60mg, Sodium 68mg, Total Carbohydrates 30g, Dietary Fiber 3g, Protein 8g

■ INGREDIENTS

8 (6-inch) crepes (see below)
¾ cup blanched slivered almonds, toasted
4–5 fresh peaches, peeled and pitted
2 tbsp lemon juice
3 tbsp packed brown sugar
⅛ tsp ground ginger
¾ cup sour cream or fat-free Greek yogurt

Crepes:

2 eggs
1 cup flour
1¼ cups milk
1 tbsp vegetable oil
1 pinch sea salt

■ DIRECTIONS

For Crepes: Combine all ingredients in a food processor and blend until smooth. Refrigerate batter at least ½ hour. Heat crepe pan and brush lightly with butter. Take pan from heat; pour in 2 tbsp or enough batter to cover bottom, swirling pan to distribute batter evenly. Cook over medium heat about a minute or until the edges loosen, the top is dry and underneath is golden brown. Invert crepe on towel to cool. Repeat.

Chop ½ cup of the almonds. Chop 3 peaches. Slice remaining peaches into 10 thin wedges; brush with lemon juice. Toss chopped peaches with lemon juice. Add brown sugar, chopped almonds and ginger. Drain.

Place 1 crepe on serving platter and spread with 2 tbsp sour cream. Spoon over ¼ cup of the peach mixture; top with another crepe. Arrange 5 of the reserved peach slices in spoke-shape on top. Sprinkle with 2 tbsp of the remaining almonds. Complete second crepe stack using same procedure. Serve immediately.

Note: Crepes may be prepped and stacked beforehand, wrapped in clean towel, placed in plastic bag and kept in refrigerator for 1 to 2 days.

Avocado Smoothie

Prep time: 5 minutes
Ready in: 10 minutes
Serves: 6

OK! This is not your average—maybe—predictable smoothie but hey, what are you waiting for?

Nutritional Information

Serving Size: ⅙ recipe • Calories 231, Total Fat 9g, Saturated Fat 4g, Cholesterol 18mg, Sodium 100mg, Total Carbohydrates 33g, Dietary Fiber 2g, Protein 6g

■ INGREDIENTS

1 ripe avocado
1 cup milk (skim or 1% recommended)
1 cup sweetened condensed milk
Pinch of sea salt
2–2½ cups of ice

■ DIRECTIONS

Combine first four ingredients in a blender. Add ice. Start blender, mixing slowly. Pulse until very smooth. Serve chilled, garnish with lime or fruit.

Note: A ripe avocado is a must. For this one, you should indulge at least one time a season. Avocado is a great source of protein, carbohydrates and other nutrients. It also contains good fat.

BAKED BRIE EN CROUTE

Prep time: 10 minutes
Ready in: 20 minutes
Serves: 8

Dazzle your guests with this simple but classy gourmet dish. OK, it's that good. Take ownership and get good at it—it's amazing. Just remember, this is a "once in a great while" treat!

Nutritional Information

Serving Size: ⅛ recipe • Calories 370, Total Fat 23g, Saturated Fat 8g, Cholesterol 42mg, Sodium 292mg, Total Carbohydrates 31g, Dietary Fiber 1g, Protein 12g

■ INGREDIENTS

3 (4-oz) brie
1 puff pastry shell
1 cup brown sugar
1 cup walnuts (crushed or small pieces)
1 egg wash (see notes)

■ DIRECTIONS

Cut each brie into 2 halves (discs). Cut puff pastry into 6 equal squares (4-inch x 4-inch squares). Place equal portions of brown sugar in center of each pastry square. Place equal amounts of walnuts on top of sugar. Place each brie half with outside down on top of sugar and walnuts. Begin to fold the edges of pastry inward toward the center topping the brie. Brush with egg wash to ensure good seal. Cup your hands over folded edges and press firmly. Place each packet upside down on baking sheet. Brush with egg wash. Bake in preheated oven 390°–400° for 8–10 minutes or until golden brown. Remove and serve hot with fruit slices or berries.

Note: Serve and enjoy as an appetizer, desert or snack. Fruit or fruit glazes may be used to garnish for great presentation.

Egg wash is made by mixing 1 egg yolk or egg white with an equal amount of water or milk. It is used to brush over baked goods before baking to give a glossy, golden finish when baking is complete. The recipe's nutrient content is based on an egg wash made of egg white mixed with water.

BAKLAVA

Prep time: 40 minutes
Ready in: 60 minutes
Serves: 10

All together now—say "BAKLAVA!" No matter how you say it, it is a sweet, decadent dessert. It doesn't matter where the origin of baklava is. So go ahead and take credit for this dessert.

Nutritional Information

Serving Size: 1/10 recipe • Calories 726, Total Fat 53g, Saturated Fat 16g, Cholesterol 55mg, Sodium 220mg, Total Carbohydrates 60g, Dietary Fiber 4g, Protein 10g

■ INGREDIENTS

1/2 lb drawn butter (unsalted)
1 lb chopped walnuts (pistachio nuts may be substituted)
1 1/2 cups sugar
2–3 tsp orange flower water
1 tsp crushed mahlab (optional) (see Note)
1 1/2 cups water
1 lb filo dough
Melted butter for brushing
Juice from 1/2 lemon

■ DIRECTIONS

Filling: Mix butter, walnuts, 1/2 cup sugar, 1–2 tsp orange flower water, and mahlab well; refrigerate and let set a while. Can be done a day ahead of time. Combine remaining sugar and water together, bringing to a boil until it reaches string stage* (don't stir frequently). Set the syrup aside to cool until baklava is baked.

Divide filo dough in half. Brush a 9 by 13 inch pan with butter. Place filling on layers and drizzle top with some melted butter. Layer the remaining sheets of dough as before. Do not butter top sheet. Cut the pastry into square/triangle/diamond shapes. Place in a 375° preheated oven and bake for 35–45 minutes or until golden brown.

Remove from oven. Immediately add the lemon juice and 1 tsp. orange flower water to cooled sugar syrup and pour over hot baklava. Set aside for 15–20 minutes, and then serve warm.

Note: Mahlab is an aromatic spice that comes from a wild cherry seed. Find it in Asian or specialty stores.

*While boiling the sugar and water, avoid stirring after sugar dissolves. It should reduce by half until it reaches string stage; it will have the consistency of honey. When lifting a spoon up and away from the pot, a string of syrup pours off the spoon.

BREAD PUDDING

Prep time: 20 minutes
Ready in: 45 minutes
Serves: 20

Whiskey was not added or utilized when serving underage guests; it was served with a different sauce made with marmalade and confectioner's sugar.

Nutritional Information

Serving Size: ½₀ recipe • Calories 444, Total Fat 11g, Saturated Fat 6g, Cholesterol 105mg, Sodium 451mg, Total Carbohydrates 76g, Dietary Fiber 2g, Protein 10g

■ INGREDIENTS

2 loaves crusty bread
1 quart skim milk and 1 quart whole milk
2 tbsp butter
6 eggs
3 cups granulated sugar
4 tbsp vanilla extract
2 cups raisins

Sauce:

8 tbsp butter
8 tbsp confectioner's sugar
3 eggs
¼ cup whiskey

■ DIRECTIONS

Break up bread into a large mixing bowl. Add milk and let it soak for ½ hour. Preheat oven to 350°. Butter a baking pan with little butter. In a mixing bowl, mix and beat eggs, sugar, and vanilla extract. Add egg mixture and raisins to bread bowl and mix well. Scoop into baking pan, bake for 45 minutes or until golden brown. Let cool.

Sauce may be made in advance. Melt butter over double boiler; add confectioner's sugar and mix until well incorporated. Remove from heat. Lightly beat 3 eggs and whisk with whiskey until frothy. Whisk well into the sugar mixture and let reach room temperature. Serve on top of pudding.

Note: You may serve individual portions, drizzled with sauce and heated for a great caramelized taste and color. The whiskey sauce is simply heavenly. If you lack time, use a scoop of ice cream.

CHOCOLATE CREPES

Prep time: 15 minutes
Ready in: 75 minutes
Serves: 10

A quick way to have a dessert vessel that is ready for your choice of filling.

Nutritional Information

Serving Size: 1/10 recipe • Calories 110, Total Fat 4g, Saturated Fat 2g, Cholesterol 71mg, Sodium 228mg, Total Carbohydrates 14g, Dietary Fiber 1g, Protein 4g

■ INGREDIENTS

3 eggs
1 cup flour
2 tbsp sugar
2 tbsp cocoa
1 1/4 cups low-fat/reduced-fat buttermilk (if you don't have buttermilk use regular milk and add 1 tbsp fresh lemon juice)
2 tbsp melted butter

■ DIRECTIONS

Put all the ingredients in your blender, blend 1 minute. Scrape down the sides, blend a few seconds more or until smooth. Refrigerate 1 hour. Heat a skillet and add a little butter. Pour crepe mixture (like pancakes) to form very light and round wafers. Flip over once after small air bubbles form. Remove and set aside to cool. Fill with pudding, fresh fruit, and other tasty treats.

Note: Should you desire plain crepes, eliminate the cocoa, add 1/2 tsp vanilla extract, and follow the same procedure.

CHOCOLATE GANACHE

Prep time: 5 minutes
Ready in: 15 minutes
Serves: 4

Don't have time for a great dessert, but love chocolate? Try this one. Indulge yourself every once in a while.

Nutritional Information

Serving Size: ¼ recipe • Calories 742, Total Fat 56g, Saturated Fat 34g, Cholesterol 82mg, Sodium 35mg, Total Carbohydrates 72g, Dietary Fiber 7g, Protein 6g

■ INGREDIENTS

1 lb chocolate semi-sweet chips
1 cup heavy cream

■ DIRECTIONS

Combine ingredients in a microwavable container. Heat one minute at a time in microwave; whip well until smooth. Stir after each time to incorporate well. Serve cold with any dessert as a topping.

Note: The traditional way to make ganache is a little labor intensive. This procedure is simpler and the results are better controlled for a greater taste.

CHOCOLATE LAVA CAKE

Prep time: 15 minutes
Ready in: 35 minutes
Serves: 10

OK! When it comes to baking, butter is a must even if you use butter lower in cholesterol or trans fats. Of course I know everyone enjoys chocolate from time to time.

Nutritional Information

Serving Size: ¹⁄₁₀ recipe • Calories 761, Total Fat 49g, Saturated Fat 30g, Cholesterol 197mg, Sodium 294mg, Total Carbohydrates 73g, Dietary Fiber 3g, Protein 11g

■ INGREDIENTS

2 cups butter (melted)
6 cups flour
6 oz semisweet chocolate chips
4 oz heavy cream
4 eggs (4 yolks, 2 whites, at room temperature)
4 tbsp sugar
Pinch of salt
Fresh strawberry/mint for garnish

■ DIRECTIONS

Preheat oven to 425°–450°. Lightly butter and flour custard cups (¾ size). Combine the melted butter and flour until well incorporated. Set aside. Melt chocolate with cream over double boiler; remove and let cool. Beat egg yolks and 3 tbsp sugar and fold into flour mixture. Fold in ⅔ of chocolate mixture. Beat egg whites, 1 tbsp sugar and a pinch of salt until stiff peaks form. Fold egg white into chocolate mix in three portion additions. Divide equally into cups and bake for 10 minutes until done, let cool. Make a hole in the center top of each cake. Take remaining ⅓ of chocolate mixture and spoon into center of each cake. Heat each cake to melt the chocolate filled center and serve.

Note: This dessert is much simpler than it sounds, although care and a little technique will make the results much more rewarding.

CHOCOLATE SPICE CAKE

Prep time: 15 minutes
Ready in: 40 minutes
Serves: 12

The combination of cloves and cinnamon add to the zesty, spicy flavor of this cake.

Nutritional Information

Serving Size: 1/12 recipe • Calories 246, Total Fat 8g, Saturated Fat 5g, Cholesterol 20mg, Sodium 261mg, Total Carbohydrates 42g, Dietary Fiber 2g, Protein 3g

■ INGREDIENTS

1 1/2 cups water at room temperature
1 cup sugar
1 cup chopped, pitted fresh dates
1/4 lb butter (no trans fats) at room temperature
3/4 tsp ground cinnamon
1/2 tsp ground cloves
2 tbsp cocoa powder
2 tsp baking soda
3 tbsp cold water
1 tsp vanilla extract
2 cups all purpose flour

■ DIRECTIONS

Combine 1 1/2 cups water, sugar, dates, butter, cinnamon, cloves, and cocoa in a saucepan and simmer 8–10 minutes; let cool completely. Dissolve baking soda in 3 tbsp water, then add vanilla. Add baking soda/water/vanilla into first step mixture. Sift flour and add to mixture. Pour into a 9-inch buttered and floured Bundt cake pan. Bake at 350° for 35–40 minutes. Test with a toothpick for moisture. Let rest, and serve at room temperature or warm.

Note: Check your baking oven and adjust time and temperature to ensure minimal crusting or overbaking the edges of the cake.

DATE AND NUT TART

Prep time: 25 minutes
Ready in: 45 minutes
Serves: 10

Dates and nuts, nuts and dates!
Oh my, count me in! What a great
combination! Buttery, nutty, chewy,
and one of a kind. Celebrated for
major holidays, it is no doubt one
of the favorites for any occasion.

Nutritional Information

Serving Size: ¹⁄₁₀ recipe • Calories 380, Total Fat 24g, Saturated Fat 11g, Cholesterol 84mg, Sodium 129mg, Total Carbohydrates 36g, Dietary Fiber 3g, Protein 7g

■ INGREDIENTS

Dough:

1½–2 cups flour
6 tbsp butter, softened
1 egg, beaten
1 tbsp cold water

Filling:

8 tbsp butter
½ cup powdered sugar
1 egg, beaten
1 cup ground nuts (almonds and/or
  walnuts)
2 tbsp flour
2 tbsp orange water (rose water
  substitute)
1 orange rind, grated
12–15 pitted fresh dates (cut in half)
2 tbsp apricot jam

■ DIRECTIONS

Preheat oven to 325°. Mix dough ingredients in a small bowl. Make filling by incorporating butter, powdered sugar, egg, ground nuts, flour, 1 tsp orange water, and orange rind. Press dough into buttered 9-inch round pie or cake pan and spread filling evenly over dough. Arrange dates in a circle over filling. Bake 20–25 minutes. Brush with mixture of apricot jam and remaining orange water.

Note: Mom used cast iron pans to press the dough into and then filled the center, topping it off with a fun design using dates and sometimes figs. Regardless, you will definitely enjoy.

Date Mamool

Prep time: 30 minutes
Ready in: 55 minutes
Serves: 10

Fresh dates offer such a delicious filling for a cookie or a tart. Treated simply, they burst into flavor upon heating.

Nutritional Information

Serving Size: ⅒ recipe • Calories 556, Total Fat 29g, Saturated Fat 12g, Cholesterol 49mg, Sodium 76mg, Total Carbohydrates 70g, Dietary Fiber 6g, Protein 9g

■ INGREDIENTS

Dough:

1 cup semolina
2 cups all purpose flour
⅓ tsp salt
2 tbsp vegetable oil
1 cup unsalted butter
½ cup cold water

Filling:

1 lb pitted dates
1 cup walnuts, chopped
2 tbsp all natural raspberry preserves
½ tbsp orange marmalade or Mistki (optional)
½ tsp cinnamon
Confectioner's sugar for sprinkling
Cinnamon for sprinkling

■ DIRECTIONS

Dough:

Combine semolina, flour, salt, oil and butter until mixture becomes crumbly and then slowly add cold water and mix well until mixture turns smooth and doughy. Let stand for 10–15 minutes.

Filling:

In a saucepan, put the dates in and add water enough to cover. Cook over low heat for 15–20 minutes until dates are soft. Puree the dates to a paste and leave on low heat to cook for 5 minutes or until mixture becomes thicker. Stir to avoid sticking. Add walnuts, preserves, marmalade and ½ tsp cinnamon. Roll dough like meatballs into 1-inch balls. Using your finger, open a hole in center and spoon date mixture. Fold the dough to close and then press into a cookie mold by flattening gently. Tap mold to remove cookies. Place on a baking sheet and bake in a pre-heated oven at 350° for 20–25 minutes. Sprinkle each with confectioner's sugar or cinnamon and let stand to cool. Serve.

Note: This is one of the most desired desserts during the holidays. You may find the wooden cookie molds in import stores. These special molds have decorative designs that leave imprints on the cookie upon pressing the dough into the mold.

FRUIT SKEWERS

Prep time: 15 minutes
Ready in: 35 minutes
Serves: 8

Fruit kabobs you say? Yes. A cool way to enjoy the fruit harvest in season and have the kids involved in the fun.

Nutritional Information

Serving Size: ⅛ recipe • Calories 182, Total Fat 5g, Saturated Fat 4g, Cholesterol 1mg, Sodium 68mg, Total Carbohydrates 34g, Dietary Fiber 4g, Protein 4g

■ INGREDIENTS

2 cups pineapple, or ½ pineapple
1 (16 oz.) container strawberries
½ pint green grapes
½ pint red grapes
½ pint blueberries
1 pint blackberries
Skewers
½ bag shredded coconut
1 pint vanilla yogurt, nonfat
Honey

■ DIRECTIONS

Cube pineapple and slice strawberries. Take grapes off vine. Skewer fruit, alternating. Roll skewers in shredded coconut. Use vanilla yogurt as a dip. Drizzle with honey.

Note: I also have a great variation, like aged balsamic vinegar for dipping. It is delightful and robust. A fruit coulis may also be used. To make coulis, use 4 oz of raspberries and strawberries. Add 2 tsp of confectioner's sugar and blend in the food processor (you may remove tiny seeds of the fruits prior to mixing). Then add 1 tsp of orange liqueur for flavor.

Golden Saffron Cake

Prep time: 20 minutes
Ready in: 50 minutes
Serves: 10

This is a relatively easy cake to make and with all the ingredients available, in 20 minutes it will yield a moist and vibrant yellow color cake.

Nutritional Information

Serving Size: 1/10 recipe • Calories 236, Total Fat 3g, Saturated Fat 1g, Cholesterol 3mg, Sodium 136mg, Total Carbohydrates 51g, Dietary Fiber 0g, Protein 3g

■ INGREDIENTS

1 tbsp butter, softened
⅔ cup non-fat milk
1 tsp saffron threads
1⅓ cups cake flour
1¾ cups sugar
1 tsp baking powder
½ tsp baking soda
¼ cup frozen non-fat egg substitute, thawed
2 tbsp rose water
1½ tsp vanilla
¾ cup water
1 tbsp chopped pistachio nuts

■ DIRECTIONS

Brush 9-inch baking pan with butter. Combine 2 tbsp non-fat milk and saffron threads in small saucepan. Heat and stir to simmer. Remove from heat. Sift together cake flour, 1 cup sugar, baking powder and baking soda. Stir together saffron mixture, remaining non-fat milk, egg substitute, rose water and 1 tsp vanilla. Quickly stir into dry ingredients just until blended. Pour into prepared 10-inch baking pan. Bake at 375° about 30 minutes or until toothpick inserted in center comes out clean. Let cool for 5 minutes.

Combine remaining ¾ cup sugar and water in small saucepan. Heat to simmering. Simmer 5 minutes. Stir in remaining ½ tsp vanilla. With a skewer, poke holes evenly over entire surface of cake. Spoon syrup evenly over top of cake. Sprinkle with pistachios. Cut into diamond-shaped pieces.

Note: Serve with strong, unsweetened coffee. You may use a spring-form pan for easy removal of the cake.

HARVEST APPLE PIE

Prep time: 15 minutes
Ready in: 45 minutes
Serves: 8

Of course grandmother's pie was the best, but why? It's filled with freshness, tenderness and lots of love and care in every step. With all the variation of this classical treat, I invite you to try this one. Add just enough cinnamon and dried fruit so that it's a twist for the whole crowd to enjoy.

Nutritional Information

Serving Size: ⅛ recipe • Calories 455, Total Fat 20g, Saturated Fat 13g, Cholesterol 53mg, Sodium 181mg, Total Carbohydrates 67g, Dietary Fiber 3g, Protein 4g

■ INGREDIENTS

Pastry:

2 cups all-purpose flour
⅛ tsp salt (4 pinches)
¾ cup shortening (no trans fats) or butter
5–6 tbsp chilled water (milk may be used)

Filling:

⅔ cup sugar (10–11 tbsp)
2 tbsp all-purpose flour
¾ tsp ground cinnamon
½ tsp ground nutmeg
8 Granny Smith apples, peeled, cored, and sliced
¼ cup dried Craisins or raisins or sliced dried apricots
2 tbsp softened butter
2 tsp 2% or skim milk
2 tsp sugar

■ DIRECTIONS

For pastry shell, stir together flour and salt in a bowl. Add small pieces of butter into the flour mixture. Sprinkle 1 tbsp of cold water at a time over mixture, and gently fold with a fork until the dough is soft and moist. Cut dough in half and form each into a ball. Flatten 1 ball of dough on a floured surface. Then roll out the dough from the center to the outside edge, to form a 12-inch circle. Put pastry into a 9-inch pie plate. Be careful not to break it. Roll out the second ball of dough to a 12-inch circle to top the pie; set aside.

For filling, mix together sugar (⅔ cup), flour, cinnamon, and nutmeg in a large bowl. Add apples, dried fruit, and 2 tbsp softened butter. Toss well to coat. Put apple mixture into pastry pie plate. Trim the bottom pastry to the size of pie plate. Place top pastry over filling, trim, and poke holes to allow steam to escape. Press top crust to seal and flute as desired. Brush top crust with milk and sprinkle lightly with 2 tsp sugar. Cover edge of pie with foil to prevent browning. Bake in a 375° oven for 25 minutes or until top is golden brown. Cool, serve and enjoy.

Note: This could be served hot or at room temperature with any of your favorite toppings. This is considered a treat. Enjoy and repeat once in a while.

KATAIFI

Prep time: 25 minutes
Ready in: 55 minutes
Serves: 10

This is one dessert that is a variation on the classical dish using shredded wheat, which is harder to work with. However, this alternative would do just fine.

Nutritional Information

Serving Size: ⅒ recipe • Calories 749, Total Fat 17g, Saturated Fat 10g, Cholesterol 93mg, Sodium 201mg, Total Carbohydrates 142g, Dietary Fiber 2g, Protein 16g

■ INGREDIENTS

Couscous:

2 cups couscous (uncooked)
½ cup unsalted butter at room
     temperature OR butter/canola oil blend
1 pinch saffron
2 cups boiling water
2 eggs beaten
1 pinch of salt

Filling:

2 cups ricotta cheese, part skim
6 oz shredded mozzarella, part skim
2 cups honey
½ cup water
1 tsp orange flower water (or extract)
Options: chocolate or coconut extract

Syrup:

2 cups honey
2 tbsp water
1 pinch saffron
Cinnamon for dusting

■ DIRECTIONS

Place couscous, butter (or butter blend) and a pinch of saffron in a large bowl; pour most of the water into the bowl, and stir until blended. Cover bowl with a plate and allow to steam for a few minutes. Mix with a fork and add more water if it seems dry. Add two beaten eggs and a pinch of salt to the couscous; cover and set aside. Mix ricotta, mozzarella and honey thoroughly. Add orange flower water and mix.

Butter a 9-inch x 9-inch baking pan. Pour half of couscous mix into baking dish; level and pat down tightly. Spread the cheese filling on the couscous. Level and pat firmly. As an option, you may sprinkle chopped almonds or pistachios on the filling. Add the remaining couscous on top of the cheese filling, spreading lightly. Put additional chopped nuts on top. Place in a preheated 375° oven for 30–40 minutes, turning to brown evenly. While the cake is cooking, prepare the syrup. Combine all ingredients in a saucepan and simmer, stirring periodically until thickened.

After removing cake from oven, drizzle the syrup on top, spreading evenly. Serve immediately, or allow to sit and let the syrup seep into the cake. Serve with cinnamon sprinkled on top.

Note: Hey, what can I say? Enjoy!

RICE PUDDING

Prep time: 15 minutes
Ready in: 60 minutes
Serves: 10

There are all kinds of rice puddings in the Mediterranean region. Rice pudding is one of the favorite desserts in the Mediterranean and even in our restaurant. It is a sweet, tasty treat.

Nutritional Information

Serving Size: 1/10 recipe • Calories 484, Total Fat 6g, Saturated Fat 4g, Cholesterol 24mg, Sodium 213mg, Total Carbohydrates 92g, Dietary Fiber 1g, Protein 15g

■ INGREDIENTS

1 lb of short grain rice (risotto)
3 quarts milk
1 pint of sugar (2 cups)
2–4 tsp vanilla
3 tsp rose water
4 pinches salt

■ DIRECTIONS

Put rice in plenty of boiling water for 4–5 minutes and stir. Drain rice. Combine rice and all ingredients in a saucepan and bring to a boil, stirring. Let simmer over a very gentle low heat for 30–45 minutes. May add more milk until the rice is creamy and all milk is absorbed. Check for sweetness. Honey may be added at serving time.

Note: You may serve hot or cold, drizzled with honey, cinnamon, toasted almonds, or chopped pistachio nuts.

Semolina Cake

Prep time: 20 minutes
Ready in: 50 minutes
Serves: 12

When I was growing up, every time you went to the market this was a must-have treat for all the children and adults alike. It is easy to make, and uses familiar and available ingredients. This sweet delight goes perfectly with dark, rich Arabic coffee.

Nutritional Information

Serving Size: ¹⁄₁₂ recipe • Calories 438, Total Fat 25g, Saturated Fat 6g, Cholesterol 73mg, Sodium 23mg, Total Carbohydrates 52g, Dietary Fiber 3g, Protein 7g

■ INGREDIENTS

Cake:

½ cup softened butter (unsalted)
½ cup powdered sugar
1 tbsp orange flower water
3 tbsp orange juice
3 eggs
1 cup semolina flour
2 tsp baking powder
1 cup ground hazelnuts

Syrup:

2 cups sugar
3 cups water
3 cinnamon sticks
4 tbsp lemon juice
4 tbsp orange flower water
½ cup each pine nuts and blanched
    almonds for topping
½ cup ground, roasted hazelnuts
    for topping
1 orange rind, grated, for garnish

■ DIRECTIONS

Preheat oven to 375°. Butter the bottom of an 8-inch x 10-inch baking dish and line with parchment paper. In a mixing bowl, lightly cream the butter, then add the sugar, orange water, orange juice, eggs, semolina, baking powder and hazelnuts. Mix well until smooth. Spoon into the baking pan, level and smooth the surface. Bake for 20 minutes until golden brown. Let cool.

To make the syrup, place sugar and water in a saucepan, add cinnamon sticks, and heat gently on medium heat. Bring to boil and reduce by half until thick. Remove cinnamon sticks. Add lemon juice and orange water. Pour half the syrup over cake until absorbed. Upturn the cake and cut into squares or triangles. Pour the rest of the syrup on top and serve. Garnish with pine nuts, almonds and roasted hazelnuts.

Note: You can make the syrup thicker by reducing it further. Also, you may toast the pine nuts and almonds for a great, toasty taste. Orange peel may be used for garnish. Enjoy with coffee.

Sour Cream Vanilla Cake

Prep time: 20 minutes
Ready in: 60 minutes
Serves: 8

This is a soft, creamy and sweet cake that has a personality and a zesty, orange flavor.

Nutritional Information

Serving Size: ⅛ recipe • Calories 610, Total Fat 24g, Saturated Fat 14g, Cholesterol 185mg, Sodium 281mg, Total Carbohydrates 91g, Dietary Fiber 1g, Protein 9g

■ INGREDIENTS

Cake:

6 oz soft butter (unsalted)
2 cups sugar
5 large eggs or 1 cup egg substitute
2 tsp vanilla
Zest of 1 lemon or orange (optional)
12 oz flour
½ tsp baking soda
½ tsp salt
1 cup reduced-fat sour cream

Glaze:

3 tbsp lemon juice or orange juice
    or combination
¼ cup sugar
2–3 tbsp poppy seeds (optional)

■ DIRECTIONS

Cake:

Grease and flour 10-inch Bundt pan. Beat butter, sugar, eggs, vanilla and zest in a mixer. Mix flour, baking soda, salt into a bowl, fold into the egg mixture, add sour cream. Bake at 350° in a convection oven for 45–50 minutes. Test with a toothpick. Remove from pan to wire rack.

Glaze:

Whisk together juice, sugar and poppy seeds (optional) together. Brush on top of cake while hot.

Note: To finish, sprinkle some grated semisweet chocolate on top and serve.

Strawberry Banana Yogurt Freeze

Prep time: 10 minutes
Ready in: 25 minutes
Serves: 4

In a hurry for a quick dessert, shake or sweet treat? This one might just do it.

Nutritional Information

Serving Size: ¼ recipe • Calories 136, Total Fat 1g, Saturated Fat 0g, Cholesterol 1mg, Sodium 65mg, Total Carbohydrates 32g, Dietary Fiber 6g, Protein 3g

■ INGREDIENTS

¾ lb fresh strawberries, sliced
½ lb bananas, sliced and frozen
½ tsp vanilla
1 cup plain non-fat yogurt

■ DIRECTIONS

Place all ingredients in a food processor or blender and blend until smooth. Serve immediately or place in freezer and let thaw 10 minutes before blending again and serving. Using crushed ice adds to the texture of this treat.

Note: Enjoy a wide variety of your favorite fruits. Berries will make surprising alternatives.

STREUSEL CRUMB

Prep time: 10 minutes
Ready in: 25 minutes
Serves: 8

An easy topping for a multitude of desserts, pies and even ice cream.

Nutritional Information

Serving Size: ⅛ recipe • Calories 431, Total Fat 17g, Saturated Fat 11g, Cholesterol 45mg, Sodium 146mg, Total Carbohydrates 68g, Dietary Fiber 1g, Protein 3g

■ INGREDIENTS

2 cups sugar
1½ cups flour
2 tsp cinnamon
1 tsp nutmeg
2 pinches of sea salt
6 oz melted butter

■ DIRECTIONS

Mix dry ingredients, then add melted butter. Incorporate by using a fork till evenly mixed. Let stand a few minutes before using; crumble over fruit pie. Bake at 375° until fruit is tender.

Note: As a fruit pie or cake topping, this crumb will go a long way to impress even the best bakers out there. This is also good with ice cream or fruit. You may substitute crushed nuts like walnuts, almonds, and pecans in place of flour, and use as a topping for custard, pumpkin pie, and cheesecakes.

Tiramisu

Prep time: 20 minutes
Ready in: 35 minutes
Serves: 10

A classic Mediterranean dessert that combines the creaminess of Mascarpone, the flavor of vanilla and rum and the intensity of espresso coffee to perfectly round off a Mediterranean feast.

Nutritional Information

Serving Size: 1/10 recipe • Calories 381, Total Fat 21g, Saturated Fat 12g, Cholesterol 176mg, Sodium 116mg, Total Carbohydrates 35g, Dietary Fiber 0g, Protein 10g

■ INGREDIENTS

18 oz mascarpone
3 egg yolks
3 cups cream
1½ cups caster (powdered) sugar
1 tbsp vanilla
Ladyfingers, 1 store package (2–3 per cup)
4 tbsp rum
4–5 espresso coffee servings, enough to soak lady fingers (8–10 oz)

■ DIRECTIONS

Beat mascarpone slightly (overbeating will curdle the mascarpone). Gradually add yolks; beat and scrape down. Add cream, sugar and vanilla and beat. Place ladyfingers around inside of plastic cups, 2–3 ladyfingers per cup. Mix together rum and espresso; sprinkle lady fingers with this mixture. Pour filling into center of cups, to fill up. Top with whipped cream and garnish with chocolate shavings. Serve chilled.

Note: There are several variations of ingredients, techniques, and even ways of serving this dish. I have used Turkish or Arabic coffee in place of espresso, and Kahlua in place of rum. This cup presentation makes for easy serving. Enjoy!

TRADITIONAL PUMPKIN PIE

Prep time: 15 minutes
Ready in: 55 minutes
Serves: 8

A classic holiday recipe that utilizes the convenience of canned pumpkin and premade pie shell.

Nutritional Information

Serving Size: ⅛ recipe • Calories 274, Total Fat 8g, Saturated Fat 2g, Cholesterol 82mg, Sodium 211mg, Total Carbohydrates 47g, Dietary Fiber 5g, Protein 6g

■ INGREDIENTS

1 purchased 9-inch pie crust
    (6 oz. crust)
1 (15-oz) can pumpkin
⅔ cup sugar
1 tsp ground cinnamon
½ tsp ground ginger
½ tsp ground nutmeg
3 large slightly beaten eggs
1 (5-oz) can (⅔ cup) evaporated
    non-fat milk
½ cup non-fat milk

■ DIRECTIONS

Unwrap the pie shell and place in a pie plate. For filling, combine pumpkin, sugar, cinnamon, ginger, and nutmeg in a mixing bowl. Add eggs. Whisk lightly with a fork until combined well. Stir in evaporated milk and milk; mix until smooth. Pour filling into pie shell, then place the pie plate on the oven rack. Cover edge of the pie with foil to prevent overbrowning. Bake in a 375° oven for 20 minutes. Remove foil. Bake about 15 minutes more or until a toothpick inserted near the center comes out clean. Let cool and refrigerate within 2 hours.

Note: To make your own pastry shell, see recipe for single pastry pie shell. Also, light brown sugar may be substituted for regular sugar.

White Vanilla Ganache

Prep time: 10 minutes
Ready in: 20 minutes
Makes: 8 cups

Similar to chocolate ganache, it is simple, and easy to make when in a hurry.

Nutritional Information

Serving Size: ⅛ recipe • Calories 900, Total Fat 88g, Saturated Fat 55g, Cholesterol 326mg, Sodium 140mg, Total Carbohydrates 24g, Dietary Fiber 0g, Protein 6g

■ INGREDIENTS

2 quarts heavy cream
½ cup powdered sugar
2 tbsp vanilla
1 packet unflavored gelatin

■ DIRECTIONS

Mix ingredients together until well incorporated and gelatin is dissolved. Microwave for 5 minutes. Transfer into a double boiler. Whisk briskly until smooth and silky. Use to garnish or plate desserts.

Note: See chocolate ganache recipe for more information.

DIPS AND SPREADS

BABAGHANOOJ

Prep time: 20 minutes
Ready in: 35 minutes
Serves: 8

Creamy, garlicky, or lemony, how do you like it? Also, you may prepare this without chickpeas for a more intense eggplant taste.

Nutritional Information

Serving Size: ⅛ recipe • Calories 112, Total Fat 8g, Saturated Fat 1g, Cholesterol 0mg, Sodium 98mg, Total Carbohydrates 10g, Dietary Fiber 3g, Protein 3g

■ INGREDIENTS

1 medium eggplant cut in half, grilled or roasted
½ cup chickpeas (reserve liquid)
¼ cup tahini
4 pinches cumin
4 pinches lemon rock or citric acid
4 cloves of garlic, chopped
4 pinches salt
4 pinches white pepper
Water or chickpea liquid
2 tbsp extra virgin olive oil
Sliced lemon and parsley for garnish

■ DIRECTIONS

Roast or grill eggplant with skin until soft; let cool. Coarsely chop eggplant with skin. Put in processor with chickpeas, tahini, cumin, lemon rock, garlic, olive oil, salt, and pepper. Process until smooth and creamy. Add liquid as desired to achieve a proper consistency. Serve garnished with oil, lemon slices, and parsley.

Note: Serve with pickled olives, chopped parsley or coriander, and toasted pita. I have used this as a spread and even condiment for sandwiches and wraps. You may also peel off the eggplant skin.

Lemon rock, also known as citric acid or sour salt (no sodium), has a strong, sour, and very tart taste, like lemon-lime. Found in Asian or specialty import stores.

HOT PEPPER HUMMUS

Prep time: 20 minutes
Ready in: 30 minutes
Serves: 8

Next to kabobs, hummus is the most known food in the Middle East. I avoid the stuff you buy from the market because it is generally not well flavored. Here is a simple recipe that you will do much better yourself.

Nutritional Information

Serving Size: ⅛ recipe • Calories 169, Total Fat 10g, Saturated Fat 1g, Cholesterol 0mg, Sodium 217mg, Total Carbohydrates 17g, Dietary Fiber 4g, Protein 5g

■ INGREDIENTS

2 cups (or 12-oz. can) garbanzo beans (chickpeas), cooked and drained
¼ cup (3 oz) tahini paste
Juice of 1 lemon
1–2 tbsp garlic, chopped
2–5 tbsp fresh hot cherry peppers, crushed
2–4 pinches of sea salt
½ tsp black pepper
½ tsp cumin powder
½ tsp cayenne pepper powder (more or less to taste)
2 tbsp extra virgin olive oil
Lemon slices and parsley for garnish

■ DIRECTIONS

If using canned chickpeas, drain half of liquid from can of chickpeas and reserve remainder. Combine chickpeas and remaining liquid with rest of ingredients in a food processor, blending at least 5 minutes, adding additional liquid (or water) as needed to achieve a smooth consistency. Add additional spices like sumac to taste. Serve on a round plate; garnish with olive oil, sliced lemon, and parsley.

Note: Roasting the peppers (hot or sweet peppers) will elevate the *ta3m* and texture of the hummus.

HUMMUS BI-TAHINI

Prep time: 15 minutes
Ready in: 30 minutes
Serves: 10

This is one of the most-consumed spreads in the Middle East. The blending of the chickpeas with garlic, tahini, and lemon makes a delicious and healthy appetizer or dip for vegetables and pita bread.

Nutritional Information

Serving Size: 1/10 recipe • Calories 179, Total Fat 10g, Saturated Fat 1g, Cholesterol 0mg, Sodium 267mg, Total Carbohydrates 19g, Dietary Fiber 4g, Protein 6g

■ INGREDIENTS

3 cups garbanzo beans (chickpeas), cooked and drained
½ cup tahini paste
3–4 cloves chopped garlic
4 pinches white pepper
3–4 pinches kosher salt
6 pinches lemon rock (or citric acid)
6 pinches cumin
½ cup bean juice (or water)
2 tbsp extra virgin olive oil
Sliced lemon and parsley for garnish

■ DIRECTIONS

Combine beans, tahini paste, garlic, pepper, salt, lemon rock, and cumin in food processor. Run for 3–5 minutes; add water or bean juice; process until you achieve a smooth consistency. Place on a serving plate or bowl. Garnish with olive oil, sliced lemon, and parsley.

Note: Various other ingredients can be added (toasted pine nuts or pomegranate seeds) as garnish. Serve with pickles, turnips, olives, hot peppers and of course warm pita. Cayenne pepper is also often used for garnish and taste as well. Canned chickpeas, if used, must be drained and rinsed thoroughly. If dried chickpeas are used, allow for 24 hours of soaking. Then they must be boiled for a good 30 minutes, then simmered for another 30–45 minutes until soft.

YOGURT CREAM

Prep time: 20 minutes
Ready in: 120 minutes
Serves: 8

You may make your yogurt cream or you may purchase it ready-made. Making it yourself allows you to sweeten it to your own taste.

Nutritional Information

Serving Size: ⅛ recipe • Calories 48, Total Fat 1g, Saturated Fat 1g, Cholesterol 4mg, Sodium 43mg, Total Carbohydrates 7g, Dietary Fiber 0g, Protein 3g

■ INGREDIENTS

2 cups plain, low-fat, or non-fat yogurt
Cheesecloth or heavy-duty paper towels
1 tsp vanilla
Honey or maple syrup to taste

■ DIRECTIONS

Place yogurt in cheesecloth or paper towels in colander over a bowl and let drain for 2–3 hours. Remove yogurt from cheesecloth. Mix drained yogurt with vanilla and sweetener. Keep chilled. It keeps for several days. Serve on top of fresh fruit with powdered cocoa or cinnamon.

Note: A simple and unique topping compared to whipped cream. Add chocolate or raspberry sauce and lightly mix to make a great swirly topping. It can also be used as a dipping sauce for chocolate cookies, strawberries, and other citrus-type fruit.

Eggs

Breakfast Egg Bake

Prep time: 15 minutes
Ready in: 60 minutes
Serves: 8

This dish is a good way to incorporate various ingredients into an egg casserole which may be made in advance and served several times.

Nutritional Information

Serving Size: ⅛ recipe • Calories 250, Total Fat 11g, Saturated Fat 5g, Cholesterol 195mg, Sodium 411mg, Total Carbohydrates 11g, Dietary Fiber 1g, Protein 14g

■ INGREDIENTS

6 slices of whole wheat or grain bread
6 slices of ham, diced or 6 links of
    sausage, cooked and chopped
1 heaping cup of cheddar or Swiss
    cheese
8 eggs
2 cups milk or half and half
1 tsp dry mustard powder or ½ tsp
    yellow mustard

■ DIRECTIONS

Cover the bottom of a 9" x 13" inch baking dish with the bread. Cover with ham or sausage and then cheese. Beat eggs with milk, salt and mustard, and pour over layers. Cover and refrigerate overnight. Bake at 350° for 45 minutes. Remove, let rest, and serve with salad, pastries and fruit for a delicious brunch.

Note: For vegetarians, you may substitute a variety of vegetables for the meat. Sautéing the vegetables briefly with onion and garlic in some olive oil will enhance the flavors greatly.

Onion and Gorgonzola Frittata

Prep time: 20 minutes
Ready in: 45 minutes
Serves: 7

This is such an easy and fun dish to make. You can get the family involved in the preparation, especially around the holidays or as breakfast in bed for mom and dad on their special day.

Nutritional Information

Serving Size: ½ recipe • Calories 204, Total Fat 13g, Saturated Fat 5g, Cholesterol 285mg, Sodium 264mg, Total Carbohydrates 10g, Dietary Fiber 1g, Protein 12g

■ INGREDIENTS

1 tbsp olive oil
1 tbsp butter
2 cups diced potatoes
1 medium Vidalia onion (sliced)
1 tbsp thyme
8–10 eggs, beaten
½ cup milk (2%)
Sea salt and pepper to taste
½ cup gorgonzola cheese (crumbled)

■ DIRECTIONS

In a large skillet, heat olive oil and butter over medium heat. Add potatoes, sliced onion, and thyme and stir. Cook the onions and potatoes for 10–15 minutes or until golden brown. In a bowl, mix eggs, milk, salt and pepper until frothy. Pour the egg mixture over onions and potatoes, cover. Cook the frittata for 5–6 minutes or until it is almost set. Sprinkle the gorgonzola cheese over the frittata. Finish in oven 15–20 minutes at 350°–375°. Let rest and serve.

Note: You may substitute green onion and you may add fresh chopped spinach. I love this dish with fruit salad or a hearty salad and light dressing.

Pesto, Goat Cheese, and Tomato Quiche

Prep time: 20 minutes
Ready in: 40 minutes
Serves: 8

This is a delightful and versatile dish where many alternative ingredients would work well.

Nutritional Information

Serving Size: ⅛ recipe • Calories 499, Total Fat 32g, Saturated Fat 12g, Cholesterol 277mg, Sodium 583mg, Total Carbohydrates 39g, Dietary Fiber 1g, Protein 14g

■ INGREDIENTS

½ cup pesto
1 9-inch pie crust unbaked
½ cup goat cheese or feta, crumbled
½ cup half and half or cream
10 eggs
½ cup all purpose flour
Sea salt and pepper to taste (optional)
12–16 sundried tomatoes, cut into thin
    strips

■ DIRECTIONS

Preheat oven to 325°. Spread pesto evenly on bottom of crust. Sprinkle goat cheese over pesto. Beat half and half, eggs, and flour. Season with salt and pepper. Pour egg mixture over cheese in pie crust. Arrange sundried tomato strips on top. Bake 20–30 minutes until golden.

Note: Basil pesto or parsley and mint pesto work well with this dish. Beating the egg whites separately then mixing the yolks creates an air puffed quiche. Try using puff pastry instead of a pie crust.

Proscuitto Ham Frittata with Green Onion

Prep time: 20 minutes
Ready in: 35 minutes
Serves: 8

The Italians cook this for any occasion. Lightly cooking the scallions preserves their tender flavor. Sprinkle more on top of the finished frittata.

Nutritional Information

Serving Size: ⅛ recipe • Calories 208, Total Fat 15g, Saturated Fat 4g, Cholesterol 229mg, Sodium 592mg, Total Carbohydrates 2g, Dietary Fiber 0g, Protein 17g

■ INGREDIENTS

3 tbsp extra virgin olive oil
1 bunch trimmed and sliced scallions
¼ lb proscuitto sliced thin and cut small
8 eggs
¼ cup milk (or half and half)
¼ cup grated cheese (Parmesan or
　　romano)
4 pinches black pepper
4 cups chopped spinach (arugula or
　　spring mix)
¼ cup goat cheese, feta cheese, or
　　blue cheese for topping

■ DIRECTIONS

Preheat oven to 325°. Heat oil, cook scallions 2–3 minutes. Add the prosciutto, continue to cook for 2 minutes. Whisk eggs. Add milk, cheese and pepper to the egg. Pour egg mixture to skillet and mix well. Let cook for 3–5 minutes. Remove and cook 10–15 minutes in preheated oven. May also cook in pan over stove and flip based on your flipping skills for 4–6 minutes in skillet. Cut; serve over bed of spinach. Sprinkle with cheese.

Note: May substitute honey smoked ham or cooked bacon. Also, arugula or spring mix may be used as a partner to this dish.

Spinach and Cheese Casserole

Prep time: 20 minutes
Ready in: 35 minutes
Serves: 12

Easy to execute, yet delivers the best alternative to working with filo dough.

Nutritional Information

Serving Size: ¹⁄₁₂ recipe • Calories 208, Total Fat 12g, Saturated Fat 6g, Cholesterol 64mg, Sodium 329mg, Total Carbohydrates 16g, Dietary Fiber 2g, Protein 11g

■ INGREDIENTS

3 tbsp oil/butter blend
3 10-oz bags fresh spinach
1 cup sharp cheddar cheese
1 cup feta cheese
1 cup Monterey Jack cheese
1½ –2 cups flour
2 cups skim milk
2 eggs
1 tsp low sodium baking powder
4 tsp Dijon mustard
6 pinches salt
6 pinches pepper
6 pinches nutmeg
6 pinches cayenne pepper

■ DIRECTIONS

Preheat oven to 350°. Coat baking dish with oil and butter. Coarsely chop spinach and place in pan. Spread cheese evenly over spinach. Combine flour, milk, eggs, baking powder, mustard and spices, and pour over spinach. Bake 20–30 minutes at 350° until top is golden brown. Let stand for 5 minutes, then serve.

Note: You may use frozen spinach, but you need to thaw and drain the excess liquid.

Squash-Spinach-feta Frittata

Prep time: 25 minutes
Ready in: 40 minutes
Serves: 10

Yellow squash and fresh spinach make great partners in this dish.

Nutritional Information

Serving Size: 1/10 recipe • Calories 257, Total Fat 19g, Saturated Fat 8g, Cholesterol 243mg, Sodium 393mg, Total Carbohydrates 9g, Dietary Fiber 1g, Protein 12g

■ INGREDIENTS

5 oz fresh spinach
4 tbsp olive oil
½ lb potatoes peeled and chopped or sliced thin
5 cups sliced squash
2 tbsp butter
½ lb feta cheese
½ cup cheddar cheese
10 eggs lightly beaten
Onion, shallots, or green onions

■ DIRECTIONS

Steam spinach until wilted; drain well. Cook potato in cast iron skillet or pan with 2 tbsp of oil until soft (5 minutes). Add squash and stir to incorporate. Cook for 5 minutes. Set aside. Melt the butter in the same skillet over medium heat and add 2 tbsp of olive oil. Add spinach, feta, cheddar, potato mixture, and eggs. Stir and cook until slightly thickened. The eggs should be moist yet firm. Top with sliced onion, remove from heat. Place skillet in oven at 375° and bake for 5–10 minutes or until brown on top. Let rest for 5 minutes and serve.

Note: An awesome combination of vegetables and egg in the form of a frittata. Using an oven-safe skillet or pan is important for finishing the dish in an oven.

ZUCCHINI FRITTATA

Prep time: 25 minutes
Ready in: 40 minutes
Serves: 6

In season, zucchini fresh from the garden has that special and delicious taste. In this dish, we make an Italian or Spanish style frittata.

Nutritional Information

Serving Size: ⅙ recipe • Calories 173, Total Fat 15g, Saturated Fat 5g, Cholesterol 226mg, Sodium 221mg, Total Carbohydrates 3g, Dietary Fiber 0g, Protein 8g

■ INGREDIENTS

3 cups water
2 pinches of sea salt
1 shallot, diced
1 medium zucchini, unpeeled and diced
3 tbsp milk (low fat or skim)
⅓ cup Parmesan cheese, grated
1 tsp lemon zest
6 eggs
2 tbsp butter
2 tbsp olive oil

■ DIRECTIONS

Bring the water with a pinch of salt to a boil. Blanch the zucchini by dropping it into the boiling water for 2 minutes. Remove the zucchini and drain in a colander to cool. In a large skillet, heat one tbsp of olive oil over medium heat. Add the shallot and cook until translucent. Remove from heat and set aside. Put the zucchini, Parmesan cheese and lemon zest in a bowl. Mix well. In another bowl, lightly beat the eggs with the milk. Add the eggs into the zucchini mixture. Add the cooked shallot. Melt the butter in the skillet and add one tbsp olive oil over medium heat. Add the egg-zucchini mixture to the skillet and cook over medium heat for 3 minutes. The eggs should still be moist but firm. Place the skillet under the broiler or in an oven for 3–5 minutes until brown on top. Serve at once.

Note: You can make a different selection of cheese for this dish from sharp to mild or creamy. Breadcrumbs may be added for flavor and firm frittata.

fish

Asparagus Salmon Scramble

Prep time: 25 minutes
Ready in: 35 minutes
Serves: 12

A more interesting and inviting look than an omelet or quiche. It takes a little preparation but it is worth it. You may change toppings and cheese for variation on taste and flavor.

Nutritional Information

Serving Size: ¹⁄₁₂ recipe • Calories 245, Total Fat 16g, Saturated Fat 7g, Cholesterol 306mg, Sodium 782mg, Total Carbohydrates 5g, Dietary Fiber 1g, Protein 21g

■ INGREDIENTS

1 puff pastry sheet cut into 6 4" x 4"
   squares, rolled out to 6" x 6" squares
1 lb asparagus cut 1-inch long
18 eggs
½ cup skim milk
2 cups Havarti cheese shredded
¾ lb smoked salmon filet
Fresh dill springs, chopped

■ DIRECTIONS

Pull corners and sides of pastry squares to make purses. Par bake (enough time for the puff pastry to take form and harden a bit) puff pastry and set aside. Cook asparagus for 3–4 minutes in boiling water, then cool. Beat the eggs with milk, and cook (soft scramble for 2 minutes); fold in cheese. Portion out eggs, salmon and asparagus equal to the number of servings. Place eggs, asparagus and smoked salmon in each square of puffed pastry. Place on a baking sheet and bake in a preheated oven at 350° for 3–5 minutes until pastry turns golden brown and egg, salmon and cheese are hot. Serve hot.

Note: May serve with potatoes, green salad or steamed vegetables. May garnish with fresh dill and top with crème fraiche or sour cream. Use this method for other types of fish and also use whole eggs.

Baked Cajun Tuna Steak

Prep time: 10 minutes
Ready in: 30 minutes
Serves: 8

When it comes to hot and spicy food, one thing I love to eat is Ahi tuna encrusted with special Cajun spices, cooked medium rare with the right side dishes like rice and vegetables.

Nutritional Information

Serving Size: ⅛ recipe • Calories 223, Total Fat 12g, Saturated Fat 2g, Cholesterol 43mg, Sodium 116mg, Total Carbohydrates 0g, Dietary Fiber 0g, Protein 26g

■ INGREDIENTS

4 8-oz fresh tuna steaks, ½-inch-thick
   (or 8 4-oz)
1 cup low-sodium Cajun spice mix
¼ cup olive oil

■ DIRECTIONS

Rinse tuna if needed and pat dry with paper towels (may cut tuna in half if large portion). Lightly rub steaks with olive oil and smother steaks on all sides with generous amounts of spice mix. Place steaks in baking dish brushed with olive oil to prevent sticking. Bake in preheated oven for 10 minutes. Turn over and continue cooking for another 10 minutes or until flesh is firm yet tender. Serve garnished with lemon wedges and parsley or a red pepper sauce (cool) or something sweet to offset the heat of the spice.

Notes: The degree of hotness is a matter of taste. Smoked hot paprika may be used to add depth to the taste. You may pan sear the tuna steaks after encrusting them with the spice and cook 2–3 minutes on each side in a skillet with olive on high heat.

There are many blends for Cajun seasoning. Each reflects the chef's style which brings out how bold and zesty the flavors might be. In general, these ingredients may include granulated garlic, onion powder, white pepper, hot chili powder, paprika (hot or smoked), mustard powder, oregano, thyme, and sea salt. The art in blending these ingredients and quantities, for the most part, is in your hands. So go ahead make this taste differently each time and make it the way you like it, but you'll have to share your perfect blend with me. Enjoy!

Whole Filet of Baked Fish Casserole

Prep time: 20 minutes
Ready in: 45 minutes
Serves: 10

Generally, the best tasting fish is the absolutely freshest fish. This recipe brings out the delicate flavor of fish.

Nutritional Information

Serving Size: ¹⁄₁₀ recipe • Calories 282, Total Fat 13g, Saturated Fat 3g, Cholesterol 52mg, Sodium 74mg, Total Carbohydrates 8g, Dietary Fiber 2g, Protein 33g

■ INGREDIENTS

1 full fresh filet of fish, 3–4 lb (tuna, salmon, haddock or swordfish steak)
1½ chopped red onions
3–4 tsp fresh garlic, chopped
1–2 bay leaves
1 32-oz whole peeled tomato (chopped)
¼ cup fresh lemon juice (2 lemons)
½ cup orange juice
Zest of an orange
4 tbsp extra virgin olive oil
6 pinches each of oregano, thyme, basil, and black pepper
Parsley and about 2 tbsp grated Romano cheese for garnish

■ DIRECTIONS

Preheat oven to 325°. Place cleaned fish in baking dish. Combine onions, garlic, bay leaf, chopped tomato, lemon juice, orange juice, orange zest, and extra virgin olive oil in a saucepan and cook for 3–5 minutes. Add spices and black pepper, stir. Pour sauce mixture over fish and bake for 15–25 minutes. May add parsley and cheese prior to cooking or after. Serve hot with wedges of lemon.

Note: Firm steak-like fish, which can stand baking for a longer period of time, is the best choice for this dish. Fish like sole and tilapia, because they don't require a long amount of time to bake, do not hold up as well in this dish. You may add capers, black olives, roasted red peppers, or artichokes.

Baked Fish Tahini

Prep time: 20 minutes
Ready in: 45 minutes
Serves: 8

Baked fish and tahini sauce are a natural pair and taste great together. The best fish to select is the hearty type like swordfish, cod, haddock or tuna. Whole fish or steaks are appropriate.

Nutritional Information

Serving Size: ⅛ recipe • Calories 315, Total Fat 20g, Saturated Fat 3g, Cholesterol 44mg, Sodium 173mg, Total Carbohydrates 11g, Dietary Fiber 4g, Protein 26g

■ INGREDIENTS

Fish

4 tbsp olive oil
2–2½ lbs. fresh fish
4 pinches each of salt and black pepper
4–6 garlic cloves, crushed
2 lemons, sliced
1 large white onion, sliced
2 large ripe tomatoes, sliced or wedged
1 tbsp each crushed red pepper, fresh
    thyme, parsley, rosemary, and dill

Tahini Sauce

½ cup tahini
2 garlic cloves, crushed
4 tbsp lemon juice
1 tsp cumin
1 tsp white pepper

■ DIRECTIONS

Preheat oven to 395° and oil the bottom of a casserole dish. Prepare the fish. If using a whole fish, scaled and cleaned, make several (3–4) diagonal cuts on each side of the fish. Rub salt and pepper (crushed) over the fish. If using a whole fish, place some garlic and lemon slices into the cuts and cavity of the fish. Layer the remaining garlic, lemons, tomatoes, onions, and some of the herbs in the casserole pan. Place the fish on top and then bake for 25–30 minutes. Place tahini sauce ingredients in a mixing bowl and whisk until smooth. Cook for 3 minutes and serve on the side. Serve the fish topped with the cooked onions, tomatoes, lemons and garnish with herbs.

Note: Should you choose fish steaks, reduce cooking time and temperature accordingly. Also, you may remove fish from casserole or keep fish in, top with tahini, and bake 3–4 minutes. Garnish with fresh parsley, herbs and toasted pine nuts.

Baked Salmon with Scallions and Yogurt

Prep time: 20 minutes
Ready in: 30 minutes
Serves: 8

Baked salmon with the light flavor of soy and caramelized or wilted spring onions is a good simple way to enjoy salmon or the fish of your choice.

Nutritional Information

Serving Size: ⅛ recipe • Calories 241, Total Fat 10g, Saturated Fat 2g, Cholesterol 83mg, Sodium 117mg, Total Carbohydrates 4g, Dietary Fiber 0g, Protein 31g

■ INGREDIENTS

1 cup plain, non-fat/low-fat yogurt (thick Greek yogurt works well)
½ cup cucumber (seeded, peeled, diced)
4 pinches dill (fresh is better, dry is good)
1 tsp horseradish
2 tsp brown mustard
1 tsp honey
6 salmon fillets (5–8 oz)
1 tsp sesame oil (toasted sesame for bolder flavor)
½ tsp soy sauce (low sodium) or juice of ½ lemon
One bunch scallions cut into ¼-inch dice

■ DIRECTIONS

Strain yogurt. Combine with cucumber, dill, horseradish, mustard and honey; set aside. Preheat oven to 375°. Spray tray with good oil. Place salmon on tray; brush salmon with sesame oil and soy or lemon juice. Wilt scallions in a skillet with a drop of olive oil or in hot water for one minute. Place scallions on top of salmon. Bake 8–10 minutes at 375° until fish flakes, then remove and let sit. Serve with yogurt sauce or a Greek yogurt on the side.

Note: Feta cheese and chopped Kalamata olives would add great taste and flavor in place of soy and sesame oil. Try halibut for a more firm, rich and hearty taste.

BAKED TUNA STEAK CASSEROLE

Prep time: 15 minutes
Ready in: 35 minutes
Serves: 8

I like this dish and its robust tuna flavor. It's unique and easy to do in a short amount of time.

Nutritional Information

Serving Size: ⅛ recipe • Calories 207, Total Fat 5g, Saturated Fat 1g, Cholesterol 57mg, Sodium 55mg, Total Carbohydrates 9g, Dietary Fiber 2g, Protein 31g

■ INGREDIENTS

1 cup chopped onions
2 tbsp extra virgin olive oil
1 32-oz can tomatoes, whole, peeled, with all juices
1 bay leaf
2 tbsp minced garlic
¼ cup lemon juice (juice of 2 lemons)
¼ cup orange juice (juice of 1 orange)
1 tsp each orange zest, fennel seed, oregano, thyme, basil, black pepper
6 6-oz tuna steaks, cut into 1- to 2-inch cubes

■ DIRECTIONS

Preheat oven to 350°. Combine all ingredients in a baking pan, mix well, and cover. Bake for 20–25 minutes (until fish is cooked through). Serve over pasta, rice or couscous. Can substitute swordfish, mahi mahi, or other fish.

Note: This dish was meant for a hearty fish like tuna and swordfish. If you cook like me, then I would use it with raw shrimp (big boys) or even lobster meat. In this case, I would sauté the onions, add other ingredients, top the fish of choice, then bake for 10 minutes and add your favorite cheese.

FISH IN ZESTY ORANGE SAUCE

Prep time: 20 minutes
Ready in: 25 minutes
Serves: 6

Awesome, zesty and delicious. Seafood stock from shrimp, lobster or a combination with chicken or veal will add to the intensity of the flavor.

Nutritional Information

Serving Size: ⅙ recipe • Calories 270, Total Fat 17g, Saturated Fat 10g, Cholesterol 64mg, Sodium 280mg, Total Carbohydrates 7g, Dietary Fiber 1g, Protein 17g

■ INGREDIENTS

2 oranges
1 lb thick boneless fish steak or filet, such
    as grouper, halibut, or fresh cod, cut in
    tapas-size (small) portions
All purpose flour for dusting
8 tbsp butter
4 tbsp orange liqueur, such as Cointreau,
    or Grand Marnier
4 tbsp fresh orange juice
½ cup chicken broth
2 tbsp chopped parsley

■ DIRECTIONS

Cut the orange rinds (orange part only) in julienne strips. Clean the oranges of all white skin, divide them into clean sections, and set aside. Dust the fish pieces well with flour. Heat 6 tbsp of the butter in a skillet, add the fish, and sauté until golden on both sides and cooked through. Remove fish from pan and set aside. To the same skillet, add the liqueur, orange juice, orange strips, broth and remaining 2 tbsp of butter, simmering for 5 minutes, covered. Serve the fish, garnished with parsley, with orange sauce and oranges sections on the side.

Note: Pan-seared scallops or shrimp may be used. Lemon and lime may be introduced to add to the citric flavor of the dish.

GRILLED SHRIMP

Prep time: 10 minutes
Ready in: 15 minutes
Serves: 8

This simple dressing or marinade is well suited for the shrimp (large prawns).

Nutritional Information

Serving Size: ⅛ recipe • Calories 167, Total Fat 7g, Saturated Fat 1g, Cholesterol 170mg, Sodium 178mg, Total Carbohydrates 2g, Dietary Fiber 0g, Protein 23g

■ INGREDIENTS

2 lb large shrimp or prawns, cleaned, peeled, with tail on (12–15/lb)
3 tbsp extra virgin olive oil
Juice of one lemon
½ tsp paprika
Pinch of dry dill
Salt and pepper to taste

■ DIRECTIONS

Place the olive oil, lemon juice, paprika, dill in mixing bowl, whisk well. Add salt and pepper to taste. Mix in shrimp, cover for one hour in refrigerator. Drain excess marinade to avoid flaming, grill shrimp (skewers) for 2 minutes and turn. Don't overcook. Enjoy over mixed greens salad or serve with steamed or grilled vegetables (asparagus, red bell pepper, fennel or eggplant dish).

Note: You can provide a parsley pesto sauce for dipping or as part of a pasta dish. Serve as an appetizer with sweet or savory sauces.

GRILLED SWORDFISH WITH PUTTANESCA SAUCE

Prep time: 25 minutes
Ready in: 35 minutes
Serves: 8

This dish is one of my favorites to make, because it is simple and quick but yet has that great flavor and robust color. Trust me, you will impress your significant other or you will dazzle your friends. It's sensational!

Nutritional Information

Serving Size: ⅛ recipe • Calories 332, Total Fat 21g, Saturated Fat 4g, Cholesterol 49mg, Sodium 421mg, Total Carbohydrates 9g, Dietary Fiber 2g, Protein 27g

■ INGREDIENTS

Swordfish Marinade

1 cup of plain fat free yogurt
1 tbsp of sour cream
1 tsp of chopped garlic (2–3 cloves)
2 pinches of freshly ground black pepper
2 pinches of dry dill or freshly chopped
4 8-oz swordfish steaks, cut 1 to 1½ inches thick. Fresh cut is best.

Puttanesca Sauce (Lady of the Night)

½ cup extra virgin olive oil
1 medium onion finely chopped
2 tsp of freshly chopped garlic (4–5 cloves)
4 cups of whole peeled plum tomatoes crushed or chopped
¾ cup pitted Kalamata olives (whole, you can chop if you like)
2 oz anchovy fillets with oil, chopped (optional)
3 or 4 tbsp of drained capers (2-oz jar)
2 pinches of freshly ground black pepper
Parsley for garnish

■ DIRECTIONS

In a medium sized bowl, mix all ingredients for marinade well. Add the swordfish steaks, turn until well coated in the marinade. Preheat your grill on medium high. Clean your grill well with a cloth and a little oil. Place steaks on hot grill and cook for 3–4 minute each side, or enough to just cook through. Turn the steaks once to avoid sticking. Put on a serving pan. To make the sauce, place the olive oil in a large, heavy, sauté pan over medium heat. Add the onions and garlic and cook until soft. Add tomatoes, olives, anchovies, capers, and pepper, and cook for 5 minutes. Reduce heat to low and simmer uncovered for 10 minutes or until your steaks are ready, stirring occasionally. Take a smell of heaven from time to time. Serve on your favorite pasta, something thin and long, you choose. Garnish with parsley. You may add 1 pinch of cayenne pepper (hey, how hot do you like it?)

Note: You can also grill some of your favorite vegetables as you are grilling the swordfish steaks.

GRILLED TUSCANY SHRIMP KABOB

Prep time: 15 minutes
Ready in: 20 minutes
Serves: 6

The heat wave is back! Don't despair and don't you be cooking indoors; there will be plenty of time for that in a few months . . . so keep on grilling and enjoying the flavor of the outdoors. Here is a recipe to hold you over until next time.

Nutritional Information

Serving Size: ⅙ recipe • Calories 223, Total Fat 10g, Saturated Fat 1g, Cholesterol 227mg, Sodium 237mg, Total Carbohydrates 2g, Dietary Fiber 0g, Protein 30g

■ INGREDIENTS

2 lb shrimp or prawns—the larger the
    better (12 shrimp/lb)
Juice of one lemon
3 tbsp olive oil
½ tsp paprika
Pinch of dry or fresh dill
Salt and pepper to taste

■ DIRECTIONS

Clean, peel and devein shrimp, keeping the tail on. For a quick marinade, combine lemon juice, oil, paprika, dill, salt, and pepper, then whisk all together. Mix together with the shrimp and cover for ½ hour in the refrigerator. Thread shrimp on skewers. Drain excess marinade to avoid flaming. Grill shrimp skewers, turning every two minutes or until shrimp turns pinkish in color. Don't overcook. Enjoy over a mixed greens salad or steamed vegetables. Serve with lemon wedges.

Note: Grill summer squash, asparagus, and red bell pepper brushed with same marinade. Serve along with the shrimp. A light starch dish like couscous and even grilled heads of romaine lettuce (cut in half the long way) with olive oil and lemon juice would go well with this.

HERB ROASTED SALMON

Prep time: 10 minutes
Ready in: 25 minutes
Serves: 10

This is one of the simplest dishes to prepare. Making your own herb blend is easy and fun too.

Nutritional Information

Serving Size: ¹⁄₁₀ recipe • Calories 262, Total Fat 12g, Saturated Fat 2g, Cholesterol 99mg, Sodium 80mg, Total Carbohydrates 0g, Dietary Fiber 0g, Protein 36g

■ INGREDIENTS

3–4 lb fresh salmon filet trimmed and cut into 6-oz portions
Olive oil in a spray bottle
2 tbsp blended herbs (rosemary, thyme, basil, oregano) in equal portions
1 tbsp fresh dill, chopped
Paprika for sprinkling

■ DIRECTIONS

Oil a roasting pan and place salmon with skin down. Spray salmon with olive oil. Encrust or sprinkle with the herbs and dill. Sprinkle with a few pinches of paprika. Roast in a preheated oven at 375° for 8–10 minutes. Serve hot or cold.

Note: This dish is healthy enough by itself for a light lunch, or over a bed of fresh or wilted spinach with a little lemon juice, chopped tomatoes and peppers. It goes well with salad, steamed vegetables over pasta, or rice pilaf. Experimenting with blending spices is lots of fun, and you may discover just the right formula to suit your taste buds.

Mediterranean Baked Fish

Prep time: 20 minutes
Ready in: 35 minutes
Serves: 8

As part of Heart Healthy cooking, we stress the use of food and recipes that are high in Omega-3 Fatty Acids and lower in fat and salt. This recipe is one example of such food. It is simple and great tasting, done in few minutes.

Nutritional Information

Serving Size: ⅛ recipe • Calories 189, Total Fat 7g, Saturated Fat 1g, Cholesterol 54mg, Sodium 96mg, Total Carbohydrates 5g, Dietary Fiber 1g, Protein 22g

■ INGREDIENTS

3 tbsp extra virgin olive oil
1 cup sliced onion
1 tsp chopped garlic
1 can whole Roma tomatoes, peeled, in juices
Juice of one lemon
Juice of one orange
1 tsp orange water or the peel of an orange, grated
1 cup dry white wine
4 pinches each basil, oregano, dill, and thyme
1 tsp or 5 pinches of ground fennel seed
White pepper to taste
2 lb Dover sole filets (sole, tilapia or flounder can be used)

■ DIRECTIONS

Start with a large hot skillet. Heat the oil and then sauté the onions and garlic until tender. Add the rest of the ingredients except the fish. On medium heat, cook for 10–15 minutes and stir well. In a baking dish, line the fish on the bottom of the pan, pouring the sauce to cover. Bake for 15 minutes at 350°–375° to ensure the fish is cooked through. Serve over bed of fresh spinach with couscous and steamed vegetables.

Note: Add fresh fennel and chopped cilantro to the fish as it bakes to deepen the taste of the dish and add a great new texture and flavor.

SALMON FILET WITH TOASTED PINE NUTS

Prep time: 20 minutes
Ready in: 30 minutes
Serves: 6

You will enjoy this healthy meal in less than a half hour. It is zesty and has a great, nutty taste.

Nutritional Information

Serving Size: ⅙ recipe • Calories 457, Total Fat 33g, Saturated Fat 8g, Cholesterol 113mg, Sodium 132mg, Total Carbohydrates 4g, Dietary Fiber 1g, Protein 35g

■ INGREDIENTS

6 6-oz fresh salmon filet, patted dry
½ cup of equal parts of butter and 100% olive oil
4 tbsp red wine
4 tbsp fresh lemon juice (½ lemon)
4 tbsp fresh chives or scallions, chopped
4 cloves garlic, chopped
4 tbsp cilantro or parsley, chopped
⅓ cup pine nuts

■ DIRECTIONS

Combine the oil mixture, wine, lemon juice, scallions, garlic, and cilantro in a mixing bowl. Place the salmon filet in a sheet pan, pour the mixture over the salmon, let stand in refrigerator for half hour then sprinkle with the pine nuts. Place in a preheated oven (350°) for 10 minutes or till done. Place on a serving plate, garnish with lemon, and serve with your favorite seasonal vegetable.

Note: This recipe could be used over lighter fish (such as tilapia) or even a small chicken breast with slight time and temperature changes (for chicken, cook for 12–15 minutes). One alternative is to grill the fish or chicken first, then brush with the oil mixture. The pine nuts can be pan roasted till golden brown then added to the top of the dish upon serving.

SALMON WITH YOGURT-DILL SAUCE

Prep time: 15 minutes
Ready in: 25 minutes
Serves: 8

If not using cilantro-tomato sauce or tahini sauce, many of the cuisines in the region would use a yogurt sauce to baste the fish, then bake it. This is one variation.

Nutritional Information

Serving Size: ⅛ recipe • Calories 351, Total Fat 20g, Saturated Fat 3g, Cholesterol 103mg, Sodium 355mg, Total Carbohydrates 5g, Dietary Fiber 0g, Protein 35g

■ INGREDIENTS

1 3–4 lb salmon filet
1 cup plain, non-fat yogurt
1 cup light mayonnaise
2 pinches parsley, chopped
2 pinches scallions, chopped
2 pinches fresh dill (if using dry dill,
    mix with 1 tbsp chives)
2 pinches each sea salt and pepper
1 tsp lemon juice (½ lemon)
2 tsp capers, drained (optional)

■ DIRECTIONS

Thoroughly mix all ingredients except fish in a bowl. Refrigerate. Preheat oven to 350°. Cut salmon filet into 2- to 3-inch strips. Pat dry salmon with a paper towel. Heat oil in a sauté pan on medium heat. Place salmon in the heated pan on flesh side (with skin up) and sear for 2 minutes. Flip to skin side and sear an additional 2 minutes. Flip to the skin side for 2 minutes. Place in a baking dish skin down. Drizzle or spoon the yogurt sauce over the salmon. Put in oven for 6–8 minutes. Place on a serving dish and serve with chopped parsley or dill.

Note: This recipe reminds me of some treasured time visiting family friends of the old days, although at times we used other types of fish. Serve with rice pilaf and lemon wedges.

Sea Bass in Wine

Prep time: 25 minutes
Ready in: 35 minutes
Serves: 8

Sea bass is a versatile fish and has few bones, firm flesh, and delicate flavor. The method in this recipe lends itself well to cooking the bass.

Nutritional Information

Serving Size: ⅛ recipe • Calories 250, Total Fat 10g, Saturated Fat 2g, Cholesterol 46mg, Sodium 238mg, Total Carbohydrates 14g, Dietary Fiber 3g, Protein 23g

■ INGREDIENTS

¼ cup extra virgin olive oil
1 onion cut in rings
2 stalks celery, sliced
2 scallions, chopped
¼ cup parsley, chopped
2 tomatoes, sliced and cut into half moons
4 cloves garlic, chopped
2 lb sea bass filet (1 fish)
Sea salt and pepper to taste, or 8 pinches
    of each
2 tbsp oregano
½ cup lemon juice
1 cup dry, white wine
½ cup bread crumbs (or crushed crackers)
2 lemons, sliced and cut into half moons

■ DIRECTIONS

Preheat oven to 350°–375°. Sauté onion, celery, scallions, parsley, tomato, garlic, salt and pepper for 5 minutes. Brush baking pan with olive oil. Place fish in bottom of baking pan and sprinkle with sea salt, pepper and oregano. Add lemon juice and wine, and top with prepared vegetables. Sprinkle breadcrumbs on top, evenly covering the fish. Layer in lemon slices and bake until lightly browned and the fish is firm to the touch (about 20–25 minutes).

Note: All types of fish (whole) may be prepared in this method. Serve with a hearty salad, some boiled potatoes and sautéed green beans with fennel and onion in olive oil.

SHRIMP CREOLE

Prep time: 25 minutes
Ready in: 40 minutes
Serves: 10

You like spicy shrimp (Spanish dish) done the way of New Orleans?! This is another variation on a classic dish. Enjoy!

Nutritional Information

Serving Size: 1/10 recipe • Calories 360, Total Fat 23g, Saturated Fat 8g, Cholesterol 24mg, Sodium 407mg, Total Carbohydrates 36g, Dietary Fiber 8g, Protein 10g

■ INGREDIENTS

½ cup butter (unsalted)
½ cup light olive oil
½ cup flour
6 cups finely chopped onions
5–6 cups of finely diced celery
5 cups diced green peppers
3 tbsp freshly crushed garlic
1 tbsp fresh thyme
8 bay leaves
1 tbsp chili powder
1 tsp cayenne pepper
½ tsp smoked paprika
60 oz tomato puree or crushed tomato
White pepper to taste
⅛ tsp kosher sea salt
1½ tsp sugar
1 tsp hot sauce (e.g., Tabasco)
1 tsp Worcestershire sauce
8 cups low-sodium chicken broth
4 lbs. cleaned and deveined shrimp

■ DIRECTIONS

Melt the butter and oil and add the flour to make a roux. Stir constantly until it browns; make sure it doesn't burn. Set aside. Sauté the onions, celery, green peppers, and garlic and stir 3–5 minutes. Add thyme, bay leaves, chili powder, cayenne pepper and paprika; stir to mix. Add the tomato puree and stir well. Season with white pepper and salt and add sugar and let simmer for 3–5 minutes. Add hot sauce and the Worcestershire sauce and stir. Add the chicken stock and shrimp; bring to boil, and let simmer 5 minutes. Adjust seasonings for taste.

Note: This dish can be made as hot as you please.

Shrimp Scampi

Prep time: 15 minutes
Ready in: 30 minutes
Serves: 8

Scampi is normally served with pasta. However, this recipe and technique are so easy and simple to do, that it can be served as an appetizer or as a main entrée. This is heart healthy!

Nutritional Information

Serving Size: ⅛ recipe • Calories 350, Total Fat 20g, Saturated Fat 3g, Cholesterol 170mg, Sodium 170mg, Total Carbohydrates 17g, Dietary Fiber 3g, Protein 26g

■ INGREDIENTS

2 lb shrimp (18–20 pieces)
5 oz olive oil
6 garlic cloves, sliced
2 tbsp lemon juice
5–6 tbsp chopped parsley
4 tablespoons of your favorite herb (basil, oregano, thyme, or a blend)
2 garlic cloves, chopped
1 lb whole wheat pasta, cooked, drained

■ DIRECTIONS

Clean shrimp, remove shells. Heat olive oil in sauce pan. Add sliced garlic. Sauté for 2–3 minutes. Add shrimp, lemon juice, and most of the parsley. Add the herbs. Cook slowly over low heat until shrimp turn pink, approximately 5 minutes. Add chopped garlic and toss. Serve your cooked and drained pasta in the middle of a large bowl. Add shrimp around the edge of the bowl. Garnish with the rest of the parsley. Enjoy!

Note: You may also garnish with lemon slices and cheeses on the side. Other options to be served with this would be clams or mussels. Add to pan with shrimp, cover until shells open and the shrimp are cooked through.

SWORDFISH AND OLIVES

Prep time: 15 minutes
Ready in: 25 minutes
Serves: 8

A variation on the original Moroccan chicken dish with a little Italian twist, adding tomato, lemon, wine, and basil.

Nutritional Information

Serving Size: ⅛ recipe • Calories 193, Total Fat 11g, Saturated Fat 2g, Cholesterol 27mg, Sodium 396mg, Total Carbohydrates 6g, Dietary Fiber 2g, Protein 15g

■ INGREDIENTS

3 tbsp olive oil
1–1½ lb swordfish, whole steaks or cubed
4 pinches of sea salt (optional)
4 pinches of black pepper
1 onion sliced
¾ cup olives (whole, green, cut etc.)
2–3 cloves of garlic (2 tsp chopped garlic)
1 lb cherry tomatoes (halved)
½ cup dry white wine
Juice of ½ lemon
6 leaves of basil
½ cup chopped parsley (may substitute cilantro or Thai basil) for garnish

■ DIRECTIONS

Heat saucepan with 2–3 tbsp olive oil. Sauté swordfish for 2 minutes on each side and remove from saucepan (3–4 minutes). Use same saucepan to sauté onion, olives, garlic and tomato (5 minutes). Return swordfish chunks to pan and mix. Add wine, lemon juice, and basil and stir. Add sea salt and black pepper. Simmer for 2–3 minutes and serve.

Note: Serve over risotto, couscous pasta, vegetable orzo, rice pilaf, or a bed of spinach. I suggest the use of a hearty fish like swordfish or ahi tuna. Chicken and even pork would go well with the sauce you are creating.

Swordfish in Saffron Sauce

Prep time: 25 minutes
Ready in: 35 minutes
Serves: 6

This chunky fish stew looks awesome against the rich and spicy tomato sauce served over plain couscous.

Nutritional Information

Serving Size: ⅙ recipe • Calories 258, Total Fat 11g, Saturated Fat 2g, Cholesterol 58mg, Sodium 201mg, Total Carbohydrates 6g, Dietary Fiber 2g, Protein 31g

■ INGREDIENTS

2 tbsp olive oil
4 tbsp white onion, finely chopped
4 cloves garlic, minced
1 green bell pepper, chopped
1–2 ripe tomatoes, chopped
2 bay leaves
2 tbsp brandy, preferably Spanish brandy or cognac
½ cup chicken broth
2 pinches sea salt
4 pinches freshly ground pepper
4–6 pinches nutmeg
Several strands Spanish saffron
1 2-lb swordfish or mahi mahi in 1½-inch cubes

■ DIRECTIONS

Heat the oil in a shallow sauté pan and sauté the onion, garlic and green pepper until softened. Add the tomato and bay leaf and cook for a minute. Stir in the brandy, chicken broth, salt, pepper, nutmeg and saffron. (May be prepared ahead.) Add the fish, cover, and cook for 10 minutes until fish and vegetables are tender.

Note: This is great and is as good as it gets. Serve with Israeli couscous or on a bed of rice and beans.

GRAINS
AND
LEGUMES

BASMATI RICE PILAF

Prep time: 10 minutes
Ready in: 15 minutes
Serves: 8

This rice dish can be prepared as a vegetarian (vegan) dish or with chicken or beef stock. This is starchy rice; you may rinse before cooking.

Nutritional Information

Serving Size: ⅛ recipe • Calories 309, Total Fat 7g, Saturated Fat 1g, Cholesterol 0mg, Sodium 76mg, Total Carbohydrates 55g, Dietary Fiber 3g, Protein 5g

■ INGREDIENTS

2–3 tbsp canola/olive oil blend
½ large chopped onion
3 cups brown basmati rice (imported is best)
6 pinches caraway seeds
6 pinches salt/kosher sea salt
6 pinches white pepper
6 pinches turmeric or saffron strands
5 cups water, vegetable* or chicken* stock

■ DIRECTIONS

Sauté onion in oil blend. Add rice and stir 1 minute. Add spices. Add stock/water. Bring mixture to a gentle boil; cover until all liquid is absorbed. Remove from heat and let cool. Spray with oil and stir with a fork to avoid clumping. Serve as a side with any dish like fish, lamb, chicken or beef.

Note: Unlike other rice, basmati rice grows longer, not fatter, as it cooks. Avoid heavy stirring; stir only once or twice while in liquid. For best results, once most of liquid is absorbed, remove from heat and partially cover until ready to serve.

*Vegetable or chicken stock will increase sodium level.

Brown Rice and Sautéed Vegetables

Prep time: 20 minutes
Ready in: 30 minutes
Serves: 9

In a hurry? Here's something easy to prepare yet healthy. It's great the next day.

Nutritional Information

Serving Size: ⅑ recipe • Calories 371, Total Fat 6g, Saturated Fat 1g, Cholesterol 0mg, Sodium 281mg, Total Carbohydrates 72g, Dietary Fiber 5g, Protein 8g

■ INGREDIENTS

2 tbsp olive oil
2 cups chopped onion
2 tsp basil (fresh is preferred)
1 cup chopped red pepper
1 cup thinly sliced carrot
4 cups fresh spinach, lightly chopped
1 cup yellow squash, cut in half and
    sliced thin
5–6 cloves garlic, chopped
3 tbsp low-sodium soy sauce
4 pinches sea salt
8 pinches pepper
4 cups cooked brown rice

■ DIRECTIONS

Sauté onion and basil in the olive oil. Add the pepper, carrots, spinach, yellow squash and garlic. Sauté for 3–5 minutes until the vegetables are cooked down. Add soy sauce. Season with salt and pepper. Stir mixture well. Serve on top of cooked, brown rice.

Note: You may substitute orzo or Israeli couscous for the brown rice. Grated cheese, zest of lemon and chopped parsley may be used instead of the soy sauce.

Bulgur Pomegranate Pilaf

Prep time: 15 minutes
Ready in: 20 minutes
Serves: 8

The combination of chewy bulgur wheat, sweet peas, and sour crunch of the pomegranate seeds is a great new taste for a different pilaf. The combination of dried fruit and nuts may be added for a heartier dish.

Nutritional Information

Serving Size: ⅛ recipe • Calories 197, Total Fat 4g, Saturated Fat 1g, Cholesterol 0mg, Sodium 9mg, Total Carbohydrates 36g, Dietary Fiber 9g, Protein 6g

■ INGREDIENTS

2 cups bulgur wheat (dry, No. 3 bulgur)
2 tbsp olive oil
1 red onion, chopped
3 garlic cloves, chopped
3 tsp fresh ginger, grated
2 cups peas (frozen)
Juice of 1 orange
1 cup pomegranate seeds (seeds of
    1 large pomegranate)
Orange zest from 1 orange
1 tsp parsley, chopped

■ DIRECTIONS

Soak bulgur for 5 minutes in enough water to cover; drain well. Heat skillet, add olive oil. Sauté onions, garlic and ginger. Add bulgur, stir for 1 minute. Add peas and orange juice and stir for 2 minutes. Add pomegranate seeds, orange zest and parsley, stir and cook for 1 minute. Remove from heat, fluff with a serving fork and serve.

Note: You may add toasted pine nuts or caramelized onions as a garnish. Barley may be used instead of bulgur wheat. This step may require longer cooking time to ensure the barley is cooked well and tender. No pomegranates available? Use cranberries or Craisins!

Lentil Rice Pilaf with Browned Onions

Prep time: 35 minutes
Ready in: 45 minutes
Serves: 8

The addition of the humble onion, browned and sweet, makes this dish a contemporary art form.

Nutritional Information

Serving Size: ⅛ recipe • Calories 288, Total Fat 7g, Saturated Fat 1g, Cholesterol 0mg, Sodium 6mg, Total Carbohydrates 49g, Dietary Fiber 6g, Protein 9g

■ INGREDIENTS

2 cups lentils, washed and drained
9 cups water
2 cups brown rice, washed and drained
2 large onions, sliced
3 tbsp olive oil

■ DIRECTIONS

Boil the lentils until tender, about 10 minutes. Add rice to the lentils and mix well. Cover pan, bring back to a boil for 10 minutes, then lower heat to medium for 5–10 minutes. Place onions in a non-stick pan with olive oil and sauté slowly until onions are brown or caramelized. Add small amounts of water or a splash as needed to help with the browning. Remove half of the onion and set aside. Add remaining onions to rice and lentil mixture, stirring well. Cover and let simmer until all liquid is absorbed. Garnish with remaining onions. Serve hot with a big green salad and cucumber-yogurt sauce (tzatziki).

Note: Lentils and rice are two important staples of the Mediterranean diet. The addition of chopped, fresh cilantro and even toasted pine nuts elevates this dish to another level.

LENTIL SAUTÉ

Prep time: 20 minutes
Ready in: 35 minutes
Serves: 8

I love lentils. Growing up, it seemed like we had cooked lentils with a variety of spices in so many ways. They are such a good source of plant protein and carbohydrates.

Nutritional Information

Serving Size: ⅛ recipe • Calories 222, Total Fat 6g, Saturated Fat 1g, Cholesterol 1mg, Sodium 109mg, Total Carbohydrates 33g, Dietary Fiber 11g, Protein 11g

■ INGREDIENTS

1 cup chopped fresh onions
1 cup each diced red and green bell peppers
4–6 cloves garlic, chopped
4 cups brown lentils, washed, boiled, and drained
2 tbsp canola or olive oil, or a blend (25/75)
2 cups marinara sauce (low sodium)
¼ tsp each of cumin, curry, coriander, white pepper
Hot pepper or cayenne pepper
6 pinches of salt to taste

■ DIRECTIONS

Sauté onions, peppers, garlic, and lentils in olive oil until tender (5 minutes). Add marinara sauce, cumin, curry, coriander, and white pepper. Cook for 5 minutes and add hot pepper or cayenne pepper and adjust for taste. Add salt if desired.

Note: A handful of chopped, fresh spinach may be added at the end for an interesting contrast in flavor. Also, I have added chickpeas, fresh tomatoes, and cooked rice. Try any of those individually or in combination next time for great variation. Mom always caramelized sliced onions until they were crispy brown and sprinkled them on top with chopped parsley and even toasted pine nuts.

MOROCCAN NUTTY COUSCOUS

Prep time: 25 minutes
Ready in: 35 minutes
Serves: 8

Couscous is well known North African pasta made from semolina wheat flour. It is used as often as we use pasta. Steaming couscous is simple. You could use a couscousiere (2-part pot), or follow this simpler procedure.

Nutritional Information

Serving Size: ⅛ recipe • Calories 424, Total Fat 17g, Saturated Fat 3g, Cholesterol 8mg, Sodium 26mg, Total Carbohydrates 62g, Dietary Fiber 6g, Protein 10g

■ INGREDIENTS

2 cups hot water
1 pinch saffron
2 cups dry couscous
3 tbsp oil
2 tbsp butter
½ cup chopped apricot
½ cup dates, pitted and chopped (6 dates)
½ cup raisins
⅔ cup toasted almonds
⅔ cup pistachios
2 tsp cinnamon
3 tsp powdered sugar (optional)

■ DIRECTIONS

Add saffron to hot water and bring to a boil. Place couscous in a mixing bowl. Pour water over couscous and cover for 5 minutes. Heat oil and butter, stir in apricots, dates, raisins, almonds, and pistachios, reserving some for garnish; cook for 2–3 minutes. Uncover couscous and fluff with a fork. Add dried fruit mixture to couscous and mix well. Put into a baking pan and bake for 10 minutes. Remove from oven, sprinkle almonds, pistachios, cinnamon, and sugar on top and serve.

Note: The versatility of couscous offers so many options for so many dishes including using couscous as a base for roasted seasonal vegetables, grilled meats, like kabobs, fish, and even beans. Orange zest or orange juice may be added for flavor or making the couscous moist.

MUSHROOM COUSCOUS

Prep time: 30 minutes
Ready in: 45 minutes
Serves: 8

This is another great couscous variation using available vegetable and mushroom types.

Nutritional Information

Serving Size: ⅛ recipe • Calories 246, Total Fat 5g, Saturated Fat 1g, Cholesterol 2mg, Sodium 112mg, Total Carbohydrates 41g, Dietary Fiber 4g, Protein 9g

■ INGREDIENTS

2 tbsp olive oil
4 cups sliced mushrooms
1 cup sliced onions
4 cloves garlic, chopped
1 cup diced red pepper
2 cups chicken or vegetable stock
1 pinch saffron
2 cups couscous
Sea salt and pepper to taste

■ DIRECTIONS

In a skillet, heat oil and sauté mushrooms, onions, garlic, and peppers. Bring stock and pinch of saffron to a boil. Place couscous in a mixing bowl. Pour stock over couscous and cover for 5 minutes. Uncover couscous and fluff with a fork. Add sautéed vegetables and mix well. Season with sea salt and pepper. Serve as a side dish or light meal.

Note: Try different types of mushrooms for a different and richer flavor, e.g., shiitake, porcini.

Rice Fritters

Prep time: 20 minutes
Ready in: 30 minutes
Serves: 10

Like miniature vegetable fritters, this pancake-like patty can be served as a great side dish, and it's a good use of leftover rice.

Nutritional Information

Serving Size: ¹/₁₀ recipe • Calories 166, Total Fat 5g, Saturated Fat 1g, Cholesterol 42mg, Sodium 52mg, Total Carbohydrates 27g, Dietary Fiber 1g, Protein 4g

■ INGREDIENTS

2 cups cooked long-grain, brown rice
¼ cup warm water
1½ tsp baking powder
3 pinches salt
4 pinches grated nutmeg
1½ cups flour
2 large eggs and one egg white, beaten
2–4 tbsp vegetable oil
2 tbsp powdered sugar

■ DIRECTIONS

Place rice in a large bowl. Add warm water. Mash with fork until smooth. Add baking powder, salt and nutmeg. Mix well. Add flour and eggs to mixture, folding in and blending well. Heat a skillet with vegetable oil. Spoon rice mixture into oil and cook 2 minutes on each side. Drain on paper towels. Sprinkle with sugar and serve.

Note: May use part oats to enhance flavor and nutritional value. Also, grains like bulgur wheat or barley may be used for great crunchy texture. Whole wheat flour may be used. This is a good rice makeover.

PITA BREAD

Prep time: 20 minutes, plus 30 minutes
holding time
Ready in: 60 minutes
Makes: 10-12 small loaves

When I was a young teenager, I worked in a bakery. One of the benefits was that my mom made the dough every day and then I took it to bake it there. It is the only way to eat pita bread: out of the oven, "puffed," blown up like a balloon. That childhood memory of kneading the dough, let rise, cutting it up, baking it the old fashioned way, is a great memory that I will hold forever.

Nutritional Information

Serving Size: 1/10 recipe • Calories 160, Total Fat 1g, Saturated Fat 0g, Cholesterol 0mg, Sodium 227mg, Total Carbohydrates 35g, Dietary Fiber 1.4g, Protein 5.5g

■ INGREDIENTS

1 cup lukewarm water (95-110°)
1 package rapid rise dried yeast
½ tsp sugar
1 tsp sea salt
6 cups of all-purpose white flour
2 tsp olive oil

■ DIRECTIONS

In a mixing bowl, combine water and yeast, then stir in sugar and salt. Let sit for 5 minutes. You will see bubbles form. Place the flour in a mixing bowl. Add the water and yeast mixture and oil, then work with your hands until the dough is smooth and stiff. Cover the dough and let rest for at least ½ hour. Knead the dough for 10 minutes or until smooth. Cover and let rest again for 1 hour or the dough rises until double the size. On a floured table surface, divide the dough evenly into 10–12 balls. Roll each ball out into an 8-inch round loaf and about ¼- to ½-inch thickness. Preheat oven to 450°-475°. Place flattened dough on preheated baking sheet and bake for 2–3 minutes or until it bubbles or "puffs up." Remove, serve hot or cool to room temperature and freeze.

Note: To ensure that pita puffs up and cooks uniformly, the oven must be hot, and the dough baked on a preheated surface. Temperature and baking time are key. Pita is served hot while it is soft and moist.

Lamb

BAKED KIBBEE-SINEEAH

Prep time: 30 minutes
Ready in: 50 minutes
Serves: 8

Traditionally, this is a mixture of ground lamb and bulgur wheat which is layered, stuffed with cooked lamb and pine nuts, and then baked. It is served all over the eastern region of the Mediterranean, especially in Lebanon. Lean meat ground from the lamb leg is the best choice; however, when lamb is not available, ground lean beef may be used as a substitute. I also have used a mixture of both with equal portions of each. Of course, some adventurous chefs have tried and used other substitutes such as ground chicken, fish and veal. At one catered wedding, one of the main dishes was a vegetarian kibbee (recipe included!).

To simplify, this section will be devoted to making the basis of this popular dish—the kibbee mixture. As I have found over the years, to make the best kibbee, use lean cuts of meat, presoaked number one bulgur wheat, and sweet, white onions.

Nutritional Information

Serving Size: ⅛ recipe • Calories 228, Total Fat 9g, Saturated Fat 4g, Cholesterol 50mg, Sodium 479mg, Total Carbohydrates 19g, Dietary Fiber 4g, Protein 17g

■ INGREDIENTS

1 cup dry bulgur wheat, pre-soaked
3 cups finely minced onions
1 lb ground meat (lamb, beef, etc.)
1 tsp allspice
½ tsp cumin
½ tsp cinnamon
½ tbsp kosher sea salt
½ tsp finely ground pepper
½ tsp finely ground white pepper
Ice water

■ DIRECTIONS

Soak dry bulgur wheat with enough water to cover the wheat. Set aside until all liquid is absorbed. Finely mince the onion; a food processor will do a perfect job. Add ground meat and minced onions into bulgur wheat. Mix in spices, salt and pepper. Knead the mixture very well, adding ice water to keep mixture cool and moist. Refrigerate for one hour, until ready to use. For best result, knead again and make sure it is cool, moist and smooth. Flatten the meat mixture on the bottom of a baking pan and smooth by hand. Score the surface with a knife into square, diamond or triangle shapes. Bake in preheated oven at 375° for 20–25 minutes, or until browned.

Note: Should chicken or fish be used as a substitute, certain spices and seasoning may be needed. I have used ground coriander, chopped parsley, dill and lemon juice (or zest). If the mixture is not doughy, you may add pureed potatoes, cooked chickpeas or cooked rice to achieve desired texture.

BRAISED BRAINS

Prep time: 20 minutes
Ready in: 40 minutes
Serves: 8

I can still remember the delicate and savory taste of this dish from forty years ago. See note.

Nutritional Information

Serving Size: ⅛ recipe • Calories 167, Total Fat 13g, Saturated Fat 4g, Cholesterol 1780mg, Sodium 161mg, Total Carbohydrates 0g, Dietary Fiber 0g, Protein 11g

■ INGREDIENTS

2 lamb brains
1 tbsp vinegar
2 pinches salt
1 tbsp olive oil
2 tbsp butter
2 tbsp parsley, chopped
4 pinches fresh ground pepper

■ DIRECTIONS

Clean brains and wash well. Bring water to a boil, add vinegar and salt. Put brain in boiling water for 10 minutes. Drain and cool. Cut into small pieces. Heat oil and 1 tbsp butter in a saucepan. Add brain, sauté for 5 minutes. Add chopped parsley, the remaining butter, pepper, and serve hot.

Note: There are many variations on the preparation of this dish. It can be boiled, sautéed, or fried, even served in sauces, such as Béchamel sauce. Please know that this is a once in a decade or more treat. It is naturally high in cholesterol and fat. Extreme moderation is a must. I only want to share with you what I enjoyed forty years ago, unless you are in Paris, France, or Beirut, Lebanon.

LAMB CHILI

Prep time: 25 minutes
Ready in: 60 minutes
Serves: 10

This recipe came in first place at one of the chili competitions. So try to work it until you get it just right. Here is my take on it.

Nutritional Information

Serving Size: 1/10 recipe • Calories 186, Total Fat 12g, Saturated Fat 5g, Cholesterol 34mg, Sodium 342mg, Total Carbohydrates 10g, Dietary Fiber 3g, Protein 11g

■ INGREDIENTS

1 tbsp garlic, chopped
½ cup onions, finely chopped
1 lb fresh ground lamb
½ cup tomato puree
16 oz lamb (or chicken) stock
1 tsp sea salt
½ tsp white pepper
½ tsp black pepper
1 cup kidney beans
½ cup red pepper, chopped
2 tbsp chili powder
1 tsp cumin powder
2 cups fresh tomatoes, crushed

■ DIRECTIONS

Sweat garlic, onion and lamb until meat is golden brown and onions and garlic are translucent. Drain excess fat. Add tomato puree, simmer until thick. Add remainder of ingredients. Bring to boil, reduce to a simmer for about 45–50 minutes until thick. Garnish with finely chopped red onion, parsley and nutty rice.

Note: This will keep for a few days. I have used chickpeas as an alternative to kidney beans and still enjoyed the great combination of flavors. Low sodium and low fat stock may be used.

LAMB KABOBS

Prep time: 20 minutes
Ready in: 60 minutes
Serves: 8

This is a great spring and summer grilling dish. If you love lamb like I do, then this is a good way to go. Enjoy in the outdoors for a casual gathering or an elegant dinner for eight.

Nutritional Information

Serving Size: ⅛ recipe • Calories 383, Total Fat 30g, Saturated Fat 10g, Cholesterol 74mg, Sodium 361mg, Total Carbohydrates 7g, Dietary Fiber 2g, Protein 22g

■ INGREDIENTS

Boned leg of lamb (1–2 lb)
2 medium red onions, cut in wedges
2 each red and green peppers, cut in
    cubes or wedges
½ cup extra virgin olive oil
2 tbsp lemon juice
1 tsp crushed rosemary
1 tsp black pepper
1 tsp sea salt
1 tsp crushed thyme
5–6 cloves of crushed garlic

■ DIRECTIONS

Clean, trim and remove fat from the lamb leg. Cut lamb into cubed pieces (approx. 1-inch cubes). Cut onions and peppers into ½-inch square wedges. Combine all other ingredients in a small bowl. Add lamb, onions and peppers. Mix well and cover for one hour. Begin skewering lamb, onions, and peppers in an alternating fashion. Drain excess marinade to avoid flare ups from grill. Grill skewers over medium/high flame, turning every two minutes until meat is cooked.

Note: You may serve over rice, mixed greens, or in pita bread. Enjoy with a cucumber yogurt sauce along with freshly sliced lemon. You got to love it . . . for any season or any reason. Remember, red meat in general was considered a treat rather than a daily occurrence. So enjoy as a treat and festive time.

Lamb Meatballs

Prep time: 15 minutes
Ready in: 30 minutes
Serves: 8

This style meatball, also known as kefta in Arabic or keftedes in Greek, is almost always on the table for a hearty appetizer. It is simple, yet delicious.

Nutritional Information

Serving Size: ⅛ recipe • Calories 344, Total Fat 23g, Saturated Fat 8g, Cholesterol 102mg, Sodium 449mg, Total Carbohydrates 18g, Dietary Fiber 2g, Protein 16g

■ INGREDIENTS

4 cups ground lamb
1 cup onion, chopped fine
1 cup whole wheat breadcrumbs
2 tsp thyme
2 tsp oregano
4 tsp chopped fresh parsley
1 tsp chopped fresh mint
2 eggs, beaten
8 pinches salt
8 pinches black pepper
½ cup flour (whole wheat is preferred)
3 tbsp olive oil

■ DIRECTIONS

In a mixing bowl add meat, onion, breadcrumbs, thyme, oregano, parsley, mint, eggs, salt, and pepper. Mix until well blended. Make meatballs by shaping into golf ball size. Roll in flour and shake off excess. Heat oil in medium sauté pan. Add meatballs, turn until golden brown. Drain excess oil. May add hot tomato sauce and serve with lemon wedges.

Note: After shaping the meatballs, you may bake for 15–20 minutes in a 375° heated oven. Yogurt sauce, tahini sauce, or a simple marinara could make this dish even more luxurious.

MOUSSAKA

Prep time: 30 minutes
Ready in: 55 minutes
Serves: 10

Moussaka is very popular in the Eastern Mediterranean, especially Greece, Lebanon, and Jordan. In fact, many variations exist. So try all of them and enjoy.

Nutritional Information

Serving Size: 1/10 recipe • Calories 288, Total Fat 18g, Saturated Fat 7g, Cholesterol 99mg, Sodium 353mg, Total Carbohydrates 11g, Dietary Fiber 2g, Protein 18g

■ INGREDIENTS

1 large eggplant, peeled and sliced thin, grilled or roasted

Meat sauce

2 tbsp olive oil
½ large onion (or 1 small onion)
1 tbsp garlic chopped
1 cup tomato sauce
2 cups (16 oz) of ground lamb, cooked and drained
¼ cup red wine
¼ tsp black pepper
2 tbsp chopped parsley
½ tsp dry mint or dill
Whites of two eggs beaten (save yolks for topping)

Topping

1 tbsp each of olive oil and butter
3–4 tbsp flour
1 cup 1% milk
1 tsp nutmeg
1 cup Romano/Parmesan cheese blend
2 egg yolks
Nutmeg and cinnamon

■ DIRECTIONS

Meat sauce

Heat oil in saucepan. Sauté onions and garlic until brown. Add tomato sauce and cooked meat, mix well. Sauté for 2–3 minutes. Add wine, salt, pepper, parsley, mint and whites of two eggs.

Topping

Melt oil/butter. Add flour and mix until incorporated to make a paste. Add milk, nutmeg and mix well until thickens. Add egg yolks and whisk. Add cheese and blend well until sauce becomes smooth. Layer half of the eggplant in bottom of pan. Spread meat mixture over eggplant. Layer remaining eggplant on top of meat mixture. Top with creamy cheese sauce. Sprinkle with nutmeg and cinnamon and bake 30–35 minutes at 350°.

Note: The method of treating each component in this dish would likely reduce the amount of oil or grease resulting from the meat, butter or cheese. So it is all about the meat sauce and the cheese sauce topping for the casserole. Higher in fat, it is best to control your portion and serve with lots of green vegetables.

ROASTED LEG OF LAMB

Prep time: 45 minutes
Ready in: 75 minutes
Serves: 12

There is no question in my mind about this; NO meat holds more importance and presence in the Mediterranean diet than LAMB. Lamb was my favorite meat to have for all occasions while growing up on the farm. My grandfather raised the sheep for the meat, of course, but also for the soft, warm, versatile wool.

Nutritional Information

Serving Size: 1⁄12 recipe • Calories 291, Total Fat 14g, Saturated Fat 5g, Cholesterol 119mg, Sodium 314mg, Total Carbohydrates 1g, Dietary Fiber 0g, Protein 39g

■ INGREDIENTS

1 leg of lamb, 5–6 lb
5–8 large cloves of garlic, diced or
    chopped
2 tbsp extra virgin olive oil
1–1½ tsp fresh or dry rosemary
1–1½ tsp fresh or dry thyme
1 tsp sea salt
1 tsp fresh ground pepper

■ DIRECTIONS

Clean and remove excess fat from the leg as necessary. Combine other ingredients in a small bowl and mix well. Rub the mixture all over the lamb and inside the cavity as desired. Preheat the oven to 350°, place the lamb in a roasting pan in the oven and roast for 45 minutes. Lower the temperature to 300° and roast for ½ hour for perfect medium rare or until the lamb is light pink. Let the lamb rest for 15–20 minutes before slicing. Serve with rosemary garlic potatoes, rice pilaf or grilled vegetables topped with goat cheese. Make my mint pesto recipe and serve it on the side. A great and easy side salad dish to make is a tomato, cucumber, red onion and feta cheese salad with light extra virgin olive oil and lemon juice dressing. Serve with a robust red wine and enjoy.

Note: In buying lamb, consider the weight of the leg, because it tells you a lot about the age and tenderness of the lamb (meat). 4–6 lb is a spring lamb, and 7–9 lb or more is a winter lamb. Therefore the more it weighs, the older it is and the less tender the meat will be. You have to love it . . . for any season or any reason. Leg of lamb is also great when crusted with some herbs and seasonings and grilled over indirect heat.

Upside Down Meat and Rice Casserole (Magloobah)

Prep time: 35 minutes
Ready in: 75 minutes
Serves: 12

This dish is, perhaps, the second national dish of the Middle East. I know it was certainly in my mom's kitchen. The aroma and taste of the dish, and the element of surprise, make it magical.

■ INGREDIENTS

½ cup olive oil

2 large onions, sliced

2 lb choice of meat (lamb or chicken), cut into small chunks

½ tsp each ground cumin, coriander, cinnamon, and allspice

¼ tsp each sea salt and fresh ground black pepper

4 cups of chicken stock (low salt/sodium)

1 medium cauliflower, clean, cut into small florets, lightly fried in olive oil until brown, set aside on paper towel to drain

1 large tomato, wedged

1 carrot, cleaned and cut into discs

2 cups of uncooked rice (brown rice optional)

1 medium eggplant cut into ½-inch discs, lightly fried in olive oil until brown, set aside on paper towel to drain

½ cup of pine nuts, lightly roasted

½ bunch of parsley, chopped

Nutritional Information

Serving Size: ¹⁄₁₂ recipe • Calories 333, Total Fat 16g, Saturated Fat 2g, Cholesterol 32mg, Sodium 109mg, Total Carbohydrates 31g, Dietary Fiber 3g, Protein 17g

■ DIRECTIONS

In a saucepan, sauté the onions in oil. Add the meat to the onions and continue to sauté until golden brown. Add the spices and the chicken stock. Cover and bring to a boil, then simmer for 20–30 minutes and set aside. In a large cooking pot, arrange the meat pieces on the bottom. Save the meat broth. Add the cauliflower, tomato, and carrots. Add rice over vegetables and layer the eggplant on top of the rice. Add the meat broth over the rice. You may add additional broth or water, just enough to cover. Cover pot on medium heat and bring to a simmer for 25–30 minutes until rice is tender and the liquid is absorbed. Let rest for 10 minutes. Now for the real "upside down" or "inverting" or flipping the pot over a large enough platter. Remember, with this hot food, lots of care is critical to get all the food out of the serving platter. Upon your success, top the dish with pine nuts and parsley.

Note: Serve with yogurt sauce or cucumber tomato salad or even a refreshing tahini sauce. Enjoy for as long as it lasts.

PASTA

Drunken Pasta ala Romano

Prep time: 15 minutes
Ready in: 20 minutes
Serves: 6

Now, how about pasta in just wine sauce?! Really, no tomato sauce, cream, scampi or even garlic, etc., Yes! This is just wine and cheese, essentially. This is a very easy recipe that can be made in a flash. It is delicious, nutritious and fun.

Nutritional Information

Serving Size: ⅙ recipe • Calories 370, Total Fat 8g, Saturated Fat 2g, Cholesterol 7mg, Sodium 135mg, Total Carbohydrates 57g, Dietary Fiber 6g, Protein 14g

■ INGREDIENTS

1 lb linguini pasta (whole wheat)
1 cup red wine
2 tbsp extra virgin olive oil
½ cup blended Romano and Parmesan cheese
Black pepper to taste
Lemon/orange zest
Chopped parsley (garnish)

■ DIRECTIONS

Cook pasta in lightly salted water with a drop of oil to prevent sticking. Drain pasta. While pasta cooks, heat wine in saucepan. Add drained pasta (while hot) to wine. Stir in olive oil. Add cheese as you toss the pasta. When all liquid is absorbed garnish with black pepper, zest, and parsley. Serve with grilled chicken, sautéed shrimp, pan-seared scallops, or steamed veggies.

Note: I am not advocating "drunken" as much as I am promoting the use of wine flavor into cooking and the absorption method of pasta utilizing wine for great flavor and awesome color other than red sauce. Try this with a variety of wines for an experience. Great freshly ground cheese and black pepper are essential.

GREEK PASTA

Prep time: 20 minutes
Ready in: 30 minutes
Serves: 8

For twenty years, this salad made it to almost every table. Simple, fresh and outstanding.

Nutritional Information

Serving Size: ⅛ recipe • Calories 311, Total Fat 7g, Saturated Fat 3g, Cholesterol 17mg, Sodium 359mg, Total Carbohydrates 50g, Dietary Fiber 5g, Protein 12g

■ INGREDIENTS

1 lb ziti penne
1 cup red pepper chopped
1 cup green pepper chopped
½ cup parsley
½ cup scallions
½ cup of shredded carrots
1 tbsp basil
1 tbsp oregano
½ tsp black pepper
10 oz fresh spinach
½ cup Italian vinaigrette (low fat)
1 cup feta cheese

■ DIRECTIONS

Cook pasta and drain. Mix remaining ingredients in a bowl except spinach, vinaigrette and feta cheese. Add spinach, toss well. Add dressing, toss until well incorporated. Add feta last and gently toss, then serve chilled.

Note: The vibrant colors of this salad can only be achieved by tossing the feta as the last step.

GREEKISH LAMB PASTA

Prep time: 25 minutes
Ready in: 35 minutes
Serves: 8

This flavorful and substantial pasta dish combines the taste of lamb with earthy mushroom, tomato, and feta seasoned with cinnamon and red wine.

Nutritional Information

Serving Size: ⅛ recipe • Calories 559, Total Fat 24g, Saturated Fat 10g, Cholesterol 58mg, Sodium 674mg, Total Carbohydrates 61g, Dietary Fiber 9g, Protein 23g

■ INGREDIENTS

2 tbsp extra virgin olive oil
1 onion chopped
2 tsp garlic chopped
¼ lb sliced mushrooms
1 lb ground lamb
1 quart meatless marinara
¼ cup red wine (dry)
2 tbsp of milk (or milk substitute)
1 tbsp oregano
1 tsp sugar (or sugar substitute)
1 tbsp cinnamon
1 tsp pepper (black or white) to taste
1 lb cooked pasta (whole wheat)
1 cup feta
Parsley for garnish

■ DIRECTIONS

Sauté onions, garlic and mushroom for 4–5 minutes. Sauté lamb separately then drain excess fat. Combine lamb with onion, garlic and mushroom. Add tomato sauce, wine, and milk; mix. Add oregano, cinnamon, sugar and pepper. Mix well and let simmer 10–15 minutes. Serve over cooked pasta. Garnish with feta and parsley. Serve hot.

Note: This lamb sauce is versatile and offers great alternatives such as you can layer it with lasagna sheets or layered squash strips or use as pizza sauce. The sauce will keep for few days, and use for other dishes, and with little adjustments, even soup.

MINTED ORZO PILAF

Prep time: 25 minutes
Ready in: 35 minutes
Serves: 8

Orzo, a seed shaped pasta, has found its way into many dishes around the Mediterranean region. I have used it as a pilaf in soups, salads and stuffing.

Nutritional Information

Serving Size: ⅛ recipe • Calories 177, Total Fat 4g, Saturated Fat 1g, Cholesterol 0mg, Sodium 269mg, Total Carbohydrates 28g, Dietary Fiber 2g, Protein 6g

■ INGREDIENTS

6 cups of chicken broth
2 tbsp extra virgin olive oil
1 large white onion, chopped
2 cups orzo (pasta in the shape of rice)
6 pinches black pepper
⅓ cup chopped fresh mint

■ DIRECTIONS

Bring chicken broth to a boil. Heat oil in saucepan. Add onion until soft. Add orzo and stir 2–3 minutes until well coated. Add broth to orzo 2 cups at a time, cook, stir and repeat until liquid is absorbed. Add pepper. Stir in chopped mint. Serve hot.

Note: You may use vegetable stock in place of chicken broth. I have often added crumbled feta to this dish and even some sliced kalamata olives. The degree of the doneness you cook this pasta to is important for the recipe you are using. For example, this pasta will continue to absorb liquid. As a pilaf, you want to avoid overcooking and ensure no lumping.

Orzo with Feta and Olives

Prep time: 20 minutes
Ready in: 30 minutes
Serves: 8

This is not just any pasta dish. This one is absolutely a way to gain new friends and impress your loved ones.

Nutritional Information

Serving Size: ⅛ recipe • Calories 201, Total Fat 8g, Saturated Fat 2g, Cholesterol 8mg, Sodium 156mg, Total Carbohydrates 27g, Dietary Fiber 2g, Protein 6g

■ INGREDIENTS

2 cups orzo
1–2 tbsp olive oil
1 tsp oregano, crumbled
1 tsp thyme, crumbled
1 tsp basil, crumbled
½ cup crumbled feta
½ cup black olives, pitted and slivered
2–3 scallions chopped finely
Fresh parsley, minced or chopped
Fresh ground black pepper
¼ cup toasted pine nuts for garnish

■ DIRECTIONS

Bring pot of water (with a drop of oil) to a boil. Add orzo and cook 5–7 minutes. Drain well and put in a bowl with olive oil (use enough oil to coat orzo. You can add more later if you desire); toss and let cool. This step prevents the orzo from sticking. Add oregano, thyme, basil, feta, olives, scallions, parsley, and black pepper, and toss well. Add olive oil if needed. Chill thoroughly. Top with toasted pine nuts and enjoy.

Note: For a variation, you can sauté some chopped shallots, chickpeas or white beans and add as a topping. I also like kalamata olives with this dish.

PASTA PRIMAVERA

Prep time: 20 minutes
Ready in: 30 minutes
Serves: 8

This is a seasonal warm pasta and vegetable dish that will satisfy everyone's taste. The one aspect of this dish that offers variation is changing the vegetables.

Nutritional Information

Serving Size: ⅛ recipe • Calories 345, Total Fat 10g, Saturated Fat 4g, Cholesterol 13mg, Sodium 75mg, Total Carbohydrates 55g, Dietary Fiber 8g, Protein 13g

■ INGREDIENTS

1 lb whole wheat pasta
3 oz clipped green beans, cleaned
3 broccoli florets sectioned
½ lb asparagus, trimmed and cut into
    2-inch sections
2–3 tbsp extra virgin olive oil
2 cups red onions chopped
4 cloves chopped garlic
1 cup frozen peas or corn
2 cups halved cherry tomatoes
1 cup half and half
Salt and pepper to taste
4 tbsp basil, chopped
4 tbsp cheese, grated

■ DIRECTIONS

Bring water to a boil in a medium sized pot. Cook cut beans, broccoli and asparagus for 2 minutes, remove and set aside to cool. Return water to a boil. Add pasta; cook and drain.* Heat olive oil in pot. Add onions and garlic, sauté for 3–4 minutes. Return pasta to pot and add peas or corn and cooked vegetables to pasta in pot. Add tomatoes, half and half. Season with salt and pepper and heat for 3–5 minutes. Put in a serving bowl and sprinkle with chopped basil and grated cheese. Drizzle with olive oil and serve.

Note: A change of seasons would be a great reason to vary the vegetables, type of pasta and flavor of this dish.

*If you precook the pasta, put in boiling water to reheat.

Pasta with Mushroom Sauce

Prep time: 20 minutes
Ready in: 30 minutes
Serves: 8

This sauce is very good with different pasta, especially Tagliatelle. Adding a blend of assorted mushrooms, when available, provides an earthy and deeper rich taste (ta3m).

Nutritional Information

Serving Size: ⅛ recipe • Calories 360, Total Fat 10g, Saturated Fat 3g, Cholesterol 8mg, Sodium 454mg, Total Carbohydrates 58g, Dietary Fiber 8g, Protein 15g

■ INGREDIENTS

1 lb pasta (any shape, whole wheat)
3 tbsp oil
1 medium onion diced (shallots also work well)
4 cloves of garlic diced
1 lb sliced mushrooms (shiitake, button, or crimini)
1 16-oz can whole tomatoes, diced
2 cups prepared reduced-sodium marinara sauce
½ cup 2% milk
½ cup grated blend of Romano and Parmesan cheese
Chopped parsley
6 pinches black pepper

■ DIRECTIONS

Cook pasta al dente and drain. Sauté onions and garlic until translucent. Add mushrooms, cook 3–5 minutes until tender. Add tomato and marinara sauce. Bring to a boil, simmer. Add cream or dairy product. Toss in ¼ cup cheese and stir. Toss in chopped parsley at the last minute. Add salt and pepper. Stir well and simmer for 1 minute. Serve on top of pasta. Use remaining cheese for topping.

Note: You may add sundried tomato, olives, pre-cooked chicken, or beef. The beauty of this dish is the simplicity, the robust taste and the richness of the sauce. Sherry or Marsala wine may be added when sautéing the mushrooms for a great depth of flavor.

SALADS

AVOCADO SALAD WITH SESAME VINAIGRETTE

Prep time: 15 minutes
Ready in: 15 minutes
Serves: 8

This is a colorful and zesty variation for a quick and unusual combination of flavors. The toasted sesame oil in this vinaigrette makes this salad very flavorful.

■ INGREDIENTS

Dressing

¼ cup lemon juice
¼ tsp rice vinegar
¼ cup toasted sesame seed oil
⅛ to ¼ cup toasted sesame seeds
A couple drops of hot water

Salad

2 avocados, pitted, peeled, quartered, and thinly sliced
1 cup red cabbage, thinly sliced
1 cup carrots, peeled and julienned
2 cups baby spinach or arugula or broccoli rabe
1 red onion, sliced
1 tbsp toasted sesame seeds

Nutritional Information

Serving Size: ⅛ recipe • Calories 192, Total Fat 17g, Saturated Fat 2g, Cholesterol 0mg, Sodium 28mg, Total Carbohydrates 10g, Dietary Fiber 5g, Protein 3g

■ DIRECTIONS

In a large bowl, whisk together dressing ingredients to blend well. Layer the vegetables into the salad dressing. Mix gently to blend. Garnish with toasted sesame seeds before serving.

Note: If toasted sesame oil is not handy, then you may toast some sesame seeds in canola oil until golden brown to infuse flavor. The vinaigrette can be used as a marinade for chicken breasts; finish in 325° oven. You can serve avocado slices separately. Drizzle with dressing and garnish with toasted sesame seeds before serving.

AVOCADO-ARTICHOKE SALAD

Prep time: 15 minutes
Ready in: 15 minutes
Serves: 8

Colorful, interesting, unique and mmm... good.

Nutritional Information

Serving Size: ⅛ recipe • Calories 179, Total Fat 15g, Saturated Fat 2g, Cholesterol 0mg, Sodium 64mg, Total Carbohydrates 12g, Dietary Fiber 6g, Protein 4g

■ INGREDIENTS

2 tbsp fresh lemon juice, or more to taste
¼ cup extra virgin olive oil
2 pinches of sea salt
2 pinches of black pepper
2 ripe avocados, peeled and quartered,
    sliced and cut in half again
¼ cup red onion, diced
¼ cup cilantro, roughly chopped
2 cups plain artichoke hearts, drained
    and quartered

■ DIRECTIONS

In a bowl, whisk together lemon juice, oil, salt and pepper. Add avocados, onions and cilantro and mix thoroughly. Add artichoke hearts and mix to coat. Allow flavors to meld. Prior to serving, garnish with cilantro, red peppers, and beets.

Note: This salad can also be made by substituting plain cooked beets, sugar snap peas or steamed asparagus for the artichoke hearts. Another option is to add ¼ cup julienned cooked beets or sliced red bell pepper for extra color and taste. Keep avocados, onions, asparagus and peppers cut at the same length for an interesting and appealing salad. Caution, add and toss cooked beets at the end, so the color doesn't bleed into the rest of the salad.

Chickpea Salad

Prep time: 15 minutes
Ready in: 20 minutes
Serves: 10

Simple, delicious and healthy salad made in a minute.

Nutritional Information

Serving Size: 1/10 recipe • Calories 171, Total Fat 6g, Saturated Fat 1g, Cholesterol 0mg, Sodium 424mg, Total Carbohydrates 25g, Dietary Fiber 5g, Protein 5g

■ INGREDIENTS

4 cups cooked, drained and rinsed chickpeas
½ cup diced red pepper
½ cup diced green pepper
½ cup sliced black olives (drained and rinsed)
½ cup diced red onion
¼ cup shredded carrots
¼ cup chopped parsley
3 tbsp each extra virgin olive oil and lemon juice
3 pinches kosher salt
4 pinches pepper
4 pinches of dry mint

■ DIRECTIONS

Combine vegetables and parsley in bowl and toss. Add oil/lemon juice mix. Add salt, pepper, and mint. Toss all ingredients and mix well. Serve as a side dish or first course.

Note: You may add feta cheese or freshly grated cheese for garnish. I have added dried fruit (raisins) to this salad for a wonderful yet new twist on taste.

Eggplant Salad

Prep time: 15 minutes
Ready in: 45 minutes
Serves: 6

This is a Turkish and Eastern Mediterranean style salad that is served with toasted pita bread, hot peppers, and olives.

Nutritional Information

Serving Size: ⅙ recipe • Calories 75, Total Fat 5g, Saturated Fat 1g, Cholesterol 0mg, Sodium 70mg, Total Carbohydrates 8g, Dietary Fiber 4g, Protein 1g

■ INGREDIENTS

1 eggplant
1 small red onion, diced
1 large tomato, wedged thin
2 tbsp chopped parsley
2 cloves garlic, chopped
2 tbsp vinegar
4 pinches each of salt and pepper
2 tbsp extra virgin olive oil

■ DIRECTIONS

Bake eggplant at 350° for 30–40 minutes; peel and dice. Add onion, tomato, parsley, and garlic. Add vinegar, salt and pepper. Toss lightly. Top with extra virgin olive oil and serve. Garnish with parsley.

Note: You may vary the method of cooking the eggplant such as grilling it. Also, using cilantro and lime alters the flavors.

Fruit and Vegetable Salad

Prep time: 20 minutes
Ready in: 25 minutes
Serves: 8

Fresh, sweet, tangy, hot and delicious. That's how it is described by those who've made it or tried it. Thinly sliced fruit and vegetables combined with tomatoes and dried fruit make good partners in this salad.

Nutritional Information

Serving Size: ⅛ recipe • Calories 138, Total Fat 0g, Saturated Fat 0g, Cholesterol 0mg, Sodium 7mg, Total Carbohydrates 35g, Dietary Fiber 5g, Protein 2g

■ INGREDIENTS

¼ cup cider vinegar (rice wine vinegar)
1 tbsp brown sugar
½ cup water
1 cucumber, 2 cups
1 red onion, 1 cup
8 pineapple slices
1 sliced apple
2 cups sliced strawberries
1 each sliced peppers (red and green)
2 cups sliced tomatoes
½ cup dates, pitted and halved

■ DIRECTIONS

Combine the dressing ingredients of vinegar, sugar and water, mix well. Toss all fruit and vegetables in a mixing bowl. Drizzle dressing atop salad mix. Toss again and serve.

Note: Honestly, every time I make this salad, everyone raves about it for its simplicity, offbeat idea, and great taste. You may heat the dressing, let cool then drizzle it on your salad. Greek olives and sliced oranges may add vibrant colors and a great new taste.

Garlic Red Potato Salad

Prep time: 20 minutes
Ready in: 40 minutes
Serves: 10

Like a German potato salad, but with a twist.

Nutritional Information

Serving Size: ⅟₁₀ recipe • Calories 367, Total Fat 20g, Saturated Fat 5g, Cholesterol 30mg, Sodium 504mg, Total Carbohydrates 44g, Dietary Fiber 5g, Protein 6g

■ INGREDIENTS

5 lb small red new potatoes
2 cups light mayonnaise
1½ cups reduced-fat sour cream
6 cloves fresh garlic, cleaned and finely diced
3 tbsp minced parsley
½ cup chopped scallions
1½ cups chopped red bell pepper
½ tsp sea salt
White pepper to taste

■ DIRECTIONS

Wash the red potatoes. Bring to a boil in salted water and cook until tender, about 15 minutes. Cool, then cut into 1-inch chunks. In a bowl, combine mayonnaise, sour cream, garlic, parsley, scallions, red pepper. Mix well. This dressing should be smooth. Gently fold in the potatoes. Season with the salt and pepper to taste. Refrigerate or let sit for 20 minutes before serving. It is best served at room temperature or immediately after making it.

Note: If you are adventurous, add some chopped crisp bacon or even chopped sweet relish or both for a great, new taste.

GREEK SALAD

Prep time: 15 minutes
Ready in: 15 minutes
Serves: 8

The success of this salad is heavily dependent on the use of fresh ingredients and topping it with extra virgin olive oil.

Nutritional Information

Serving Size: ⅛ recipe • Calories 185, Total Fat 17g, Saturated Fat 4g, Cholesterol 8mg, Sodium 183mg, Total Carbohydrates 7g, Dietary Fiber 2g, Protein 3g

■ INGREDIENTS

Dressing

½ cup extra virgin olive oil
Juice of 1 lemon
3 pinches of oregano or thyme
Ground black pepper

Salad

1 head romaine lettuce, cleaned and chopped
4 vine-ripened tomatoes, wedged
1 medium cucumber seeded, partially peeled and sliced
½ cup feta, crumbled
2 spring (green) onions, trimmed and sliced
½ red onion, cleaned and sliced
2 oz (½ cup) black or pitted Kalamata olives

■ DIRECTIONS

Whisk ingredients for dressing in a bowl. Put all ingredients for salad in a large bowl. Toss lightly. Pour dressing over salad mixture. Toss lightly again and serve. May serve with toasted pita or crusty bread.

Note: Ripened grape tomatoes, sliced bell peppers and marinated artichoke hearts add great variation and color to this salad.

Lebanese Fattoush Salad (Mountain Bread Salad)

Prep time: 15 minutes
Ready in: 20 minutes
Serves: 10

Fresh ingredients, a great dressing, fresh herbs and you got it—the perfect balance between toasted pita and greens. Serve this salad as an appetizer or to accompany grilled shrimp, lamb or grilled chicken.

Nutritional Information

Serving Size: 1/10 recipe • Calories 112, Total Fat 6g, Saturated Fat 1g, Cholesterol 0mg, Sodium 108mg, Total Carbohydrates 15g, Dietary Fiber 3g, Protein 3g

■ INGREDIENTS

3–4 loaves whole wheat pita bread cut into small pieces

Salad

½ head romaine lettuce chopped
2 cucumbers, quartered and thinly sliced
1 pint cherry tomatoes, cut in half
½ cup diced red onions
½ cup sliced green onions
½ cup red pepper, diced
½ cup chopped parsley
1 lemon diced with peel
1 tsp dry mint or 1 tbsp fresh mint

Dressing

¼ cup extra virgin olive oil
¼ cup pomegranate or lemon juice
2–4 cloves chopped garlic
4 pinches kosher salt
4–6 pinches black pepper

■ DIRECTIONS

Toast pita bread to make chips and set aside. Add all vegetables to lettuce and toss. In a mixing bowl, add oil, garlic, lemon/pomegranate juice, salt, pepper and whisk well. Combine vegetables and dressing. Add pita chips, toss and serve.

Note: This salad is best when all ingredients are combined together and tossed with dressing at the last minute and almost the time of service. You may choose to also add fennel, sliced radishes, sumac, or pomegranate seeds.

ORANGE AND ASPARAGUS SALAD

Prep time: 15 minutes
Ready in: 20 minutes
Serves: 8

This is uncomplicated, simply elegant and offers a wonderful aroma and flavor of the orange and olive oil.

Nutritional Information

Serving Size: ⅛ recipe • Calories 105, Total Fat 6g, Saturated Fat 1g, Cholesterol 0mg, Sodium 60mg, Total Carbohydrates 13g, Dietary Fiber 5g, Protein 3g

■ INGREDIENTS

Salad

1 lb asparagus cut in 2 inch pieces
2 large oranges (seedless) in wedges
3 ripe tomatoes in wedges
1 head romaine lettuce, cleaned and
    chopped

Dressing

3 tbsp extra virgin olive oil
3 tbsp apple cider vinegar
4 pinches salt
4 pinches pepper
Rind of 1 orange for topping

■ DIRECTIONS

Steam asparagus and let cool. Grate the rind of one orange and set aside. Peel and cut both oranges into wedges or segments. Mix all dressing ingredients (oil, vinegar, salt, pepper). Toss asparagus, oranges and tomatoes with dressing. Place on top of the chopped lettuce and serve. Sprinkle with the rind of one orange.

Note: For more depth in flavor, color and variation on taste, you may add sliced bell pepper, red onions, black olives, nuts or raisins. I have used a combination of white and green asparagus to add vibrant color and appeal.

Orange and Date Salad

Prep time: 10 minutes
Ready in: 15 minutes
Serves: 8

A very flavorful and great color salad combination. This may be served as a side dish.

Nutritional Information

Serving Size: ⅛ recipe • Calories 240, Total Fat 4g, Saturated Fat 0g, Cholesterol 0mg, Sodium 7mg, Total Carbohydrates 53g, Dietary Fiber 9g, Protein 4g

■ INGREDIENTS

1 large head of romaine lettuce, trimmed
    and cleaned
6 oranges, peeled and segmented
2 tbsp orange flower water
1 tsp lemon juice
12–14 dates, pitted and julienned
½ cup pistachio nuts or almonds
Powdered sugar

■ DIRECTIONS

Arrange the romaine on a platter. In a separate bowl, toss oranges, orange flower water, lemon juice, and dates together and lay on top of romaine. Top with pistachio nuts and sprinkle lightly with powdered sugar.

Note: One other way to serve this salad is to pile every ingredient next to one another then sprinkle with dressing, chill and serve. You may toast the almonds prior to sprinkling the salad. Instead of romaine, try using your favorite salad mix.

PEAR AND CRANBERRY SALAD

Prep time: 10 minutes
Ready in: 15 minutes
Serves: 6

The combination of sweet and savory along with the buttery taste of Bibb lettuce is truly a delightful taste for a light meal.

Nutritional Information

Serving Size: ⅙ recipe • Calories 161, Total Fat 6g, Saturated Fat 1g, Cholesterol 5mg, Sodium 32mg, Total Carbohydrates 25g, Dietary Fiber 3g, Protein 3g

■ INGREDIENTS

Salad

2 cups peeled and diced pears
½ cup sliced celery
⅓ cup walnuts
¼ cup Craisins
1–2 heads of chopped leafy lettuce
 (Boston bibb)

Dressing

½ cup cranberry sauce
2 tbsp mayonnaise (light)
4 tbsp reduced fat sour cream
4 tbsp milk (optional)
1 tsp lime juice (lemon juice)

■ DIRECTIONS

Mix salad ingredients, toss. Mix dressing ingredients, add to salad, and toss. Place on top of Boston bibb lettuce (or heads of romaine).

Note: This is an outside-the-box salad. It is a favorite around the holidays. You may substitute cranberry juice for milk. Toasting the walnuts with a little brown sugar and cinnamon will add a great new taste.

TABBOULEH SALAD

Prep time: 20 minutes
Ready in: 25 minutes
Serves: 10

This is the traditional Lebanese parsley and bulgur wheat salad. A wonderful, lemony and refreshing salad that combines the freshness of mint, parsley, scallion and tomato.

Nutritional Information

Serving Size: $\frac{1}{10}$ recipe • Calories 121, Total Fat 6g, Saturated Fat 1g, Cholesterol 0mg, Sodium 88mg, Total Carbohydrates 16g, Dietary Fiber 4g, Protein 3g

■ INGREDIENTS

1 cup bulgur wheat (No. 1 fine bulgur)
1 cup cold water
¼ cup extra virgin olive oil
¼ cup lemon juice (fresh)
2 tsp diced fresh mint
7 pinches black pepper
7 pinches sea salt
4 cups chopped parsley
3 cups tomato diced into ½-inch cubes
1 cup scallions, chopped

■ DIRECTIONS

Place bulgur in a mixing bowl and soak in cold water for ½ hour. The dressing can be made as the bulgur is soaking. Whisk together equal parts olive oil, lemon juice, mint, salt and pepper. Add parsley, tomato and scallions to bulgur by layering them in the order given. Pour the dressing over the salad bowl and toss well until evenly distributed. Serve cold and garnish with mint, lemon wedges and pita bread.

Note: Despite all the different spellings of the words "bulgur," "burghul," and "borghul" all are intended to mean the same. Also, others would add cucumbers or more bulgur wheat compared to parsley. Enjoy this bundle-of-health salad. Delicious with kabobs or any outdoor grilled favorite. You may serve as an appetizer with the hearts of romaine lettuce or as a side dish. There is a debate as to how green or grainy this salad should be. Well, how do you like it?

TOMATO-CUCUMBER SALAD

Prep time: 15 minutes
Ready in: 15 minutes
Serves: 10

This salad can be made with many variations. The basic salad is delicious and refreshing and has few ingredients. It is easily made just in advance of meal time.

Nutritional Information

Serving Size: ¹⁄₁₀ recipe • Calories 78, Total Fat 6g, Saturated Fat 1g, Cholesterol 0mg, Sodium 65mg, Total Carbohydrates 6g, Dietary Fiber 2g, Protein 1g

■ INGREDIENTS

3–4 tomatoes (summer ripened tomatoes are best)
2–3 cucumbers (medium)
¼ cup chopped parsley
¼ cup chopped spring onion (scallions)
1 red onion, chopped (medium)
¼ cup extra virgin olive oil
¼ cup lemon juice
6 pinches sea salt
6 pinches black pepper
6 pinches dry mint

■ DIRECTIONS

Cut tomatoes into bite-sized pieces. Cut cucumbers into bite-sized pieces. Add the parsley, scallions, and red onion. Toss with olive oil and lemon juice, then add salt, pepper, and mint. Toss gently and serve.

Note: May serve with olives, pita bread and hot peppers. You may add crushed garlic to this salad and even crumbled feta for a great new taste. Fresh mint gives even more flavor *ta3m* to this dish.

Sauces and Dressings

Apricot Glaze

Prep time: 10 minutes
Ready in: 15 minutes
Serves: 8

Fresh or dried apricots may be used. The need to adjust the amount of liquid is important to achieve the desired consistency.

Nutritional Information

Serving Size: ⅛ recipe • Calories 55, Total Fat 0g, Saturated Fat 0g, Cholesterol 0mg, Sodium 44mg, Total Carbohydrates 14g, Dietary Fiber 1g, Protein 1g

■ INGREDIENTS

1 cup dried apricots
1 cup hot water
2 tbsp sugar
2 tbsp Dijon mustard
½ cup apple juice
1 tsp lemon juice
1 tsp orange zest

■ DIRECTIONS

Bring apricots, sugar and water to a boil until apricots are soft. Transfer apricots to food processor and puree. Add puree to saucepan with mustard and apple juice and increase heat, stirring well. Add lemon juice. Add orange zest. Bring to simmer and cook until good consistency.

Note: I have used this with roasted pork loin, grilled pork chops, grilled skinless chicken breast or duck.

BÉCHAMEL SAUCE

Prep time: 10 minutes
Ready in: 20 minutes
Serves: 12

A variation on a very versatile and classical sauce.

Nutritional Information

Serving Size: $\frac{1}{12}$ recipe • Calories 124, Total Fat 10g, Saturated Fat 6g, Cholesterol 31mg, Sodium 100mg, Total Carbohydrates 6g, Dietary Fiber 0g, Protein 2g

■ INGREDIENTS

6 tbsp butter
6 tbsp flour
3 cups half and half, and milk
   (equal portions)
4 pinches salt
4 pinches white pepper
If desired may add cheese, nutmeg

■ DIRECTIONS

Melt butter in a medium deep sauce pan. Add flour and stir constantly until well incorporated. Add milk product and whisk thoroughly until mixture forms a smooth, creamy, thick sauce. Add salt and pepper and whisk. Remove from heat. Based on your application or use, you may add grated Parmesan, cheddar or Romano cheese or Gruyere.

Note: The Greeks would use grated Kefalotiri cheese when making this sauce for Moussaka. This classic sauce may be used as a topping for vegetable dishes. You may add sautéed onion and mushrooms for additional flavors. Egg yolks may also be used for thickening and to add flavor. The results are delicious; however use caution because it is higher in fat and cholesterol than recommended. Use sparingly and enjoy periodically!

Chutney

Prep time: 15 minutes
Ready in: 25 minutes
Makes: 3 cups, approximately 20 servings at 2 tbsp per serving

Chutney as a condiment may incorporate a wide variety of ingredients, degree of sweetness and hotness. This recipe is one approach for middle of the road.

Nutritional Information

Serving Size: 1/20 recipe • Calories 29, Total Fat 1g, Saturated Fat 0g, Cholesterol 0mg, Sodium 23mg, Total Carbohydrates 4g, Dietary Fiber 1g, Protein 0g

■ INGREDIENTS

½ cup wine, dry red is preferred
⅓ cup orange juice
2 ½ tsp soy sauce
3 oranges, peeled and chopped
½ cup red pepper, cleaned and chopped
½ cup red onion, diced
3 tsp cilantro, chopped
2 tsp ginger, freshly grated
1 tsp sesame oil (toasted is preferred)
¼ tsp crushed red pepper (or the fresh hot pepper variety)
1 tbsp sesame seeds
Zest of the orange

■ DIRECTIONS

Heat wine, juice, and soy sauce in a medium-deep sauce pan. Add oranges, peppers, onions, cilantro, and ginger. Cook for 10–15 minutes. Reduce heat, add sesame oil, pepper, sesame seeds and orange zest, then simmer for an additional 10 minutes on low heat. Check for consistency. You may add some water to achieve the desired consistency and taste.

Note: I have used this on grilled or roasted lamb, chicken, or pork, as well as roasted, hearty vegetables.

CILANTRO-MINT PESTO

Prep time: 10 minutes
Ready in: 15 minutes
Makes: 2 cups, approximately 10 servings
at 2 tbsp per serving

When all else or basil is gone, go
for this.

Nutritional Information

Serving Size: ⅒ recipe • Calories 171, Total Fat 17g, Saturated Fat 3g, Cholesterol 6mg, Sodium 83mg, Total Carbohydrates 2g, Dietary Fiber 1g, Protein 3g

■ INGREDIENTS

½ cup pine nuts, walnuts or almonds
2 cups cilantro
2 cups mint
¼ cup feta cheese
¼ cup Parmesan cheese
½ cup extra virgin olive oil
4 cloves garlic

■ DIRECTIONS

Put all ingredients in food processor, pulse at first then run until smooth. Serve over: red meat, hearty fish, roasted chicken, grilled vegetables.

Note: You may use all pine nuts, walnuts or almonds. I like to use a combination of two types in equal amounts, which gives it great balance. Top with light olive oil and store. It will keep up to 1–2 weeks.

CUCUMBER YOGURT SAUCE

Prep time: 10 minutes
Ready in: 15 minutes
Serves: 6

Cool as a cucumber! I bet you have heard that before. Add yogurt to cucumber and then you create this refreshing dish served everywhere in the Mediterranean. It is well suited to the hot, summer temperatures.

Nutritional Information

Serving Size: ⅙ recipe • Calories 88, Total Fat 4g, Saturated Fat 1g, Cholesterol 5mg, Sodium 144mg, Total Carbohydrates 9g, Dietary Fiber 1g, Protein 5g

■ INGREDIENTS

2 medium/large cucumbers, peeled, seeded, and chopped (seeding is optional)
2 cups Greek yogurt (goat's milk preferred) or strained yogurt
4 pinches dry mint
4 pinches black pepper
½ cup chopped parsley
½ cup chopped scallion
5 pinches salt
Extra virgin olive oil

■ DIRECTIONS

Combine all ingredients except olive oil in mixing bowl and mix well. Keep a little parsley aside for topping. Serve cold, garnished with a little parsley and extra virgin olive oil.

Note: Serve as a salad dressing, as a condiment for grilled lamb, chicken or even as a dip with fresh pita bread. This is also wonderful with grilled eggplant or squash. This is also known as tzatziki. You may prepare it in advance; however, hold the salt until it is ready to serve. Also, make sure you seed the cucumber if you plan to keep it for a day or two.

EGG AND LEMON SAUCE WITH CREAM

Prep time: 15 minutes
Ready in: 25 minutes
Makes: 2½ cups; 8 servings at ¼ cup
per serving

Greeks have mastered this very popular sauce made for soups. The two main ingredients, eggs and lemon, and their frothiness are key. This is the best use of few ingredients that make a great, versatile sauce.

Nutritional Information

Serving Size: ⅛ recipe • Calories 71, Total Fat 5g, Saturated Fat 2g, Cholesterol 62mg, Sodium 139mg, Total Carbohydrates 4g, Dietary Fiber 0g, Protein 3g

■ INGREDIENTS

2 fresh eggs (separate yolk and whites)
2 pinches of kosher sea salt
Juice of 2 fresh lemons
2 cups of stock (beef, chicken, or
vegetable)
2 tsp cornstarch
½ cup sour cream (Greek yogurt may
be substituted)

■ DIRECTIONS

Beat the egg whites vigorously in a deep mixing bowl with 2 pinches of salt. Beat the egg yolks in a separate bowl until frothy. Combine the egg whites and the egg yolks. Slowly add the lemon juice as you whisk the eggs. Combine the stock and the cornstarch, mix well. Continue to whisk the egg mixture as you add the stock mixture. Add the sour cream until well incorporated. Once the mixture becomes smooth and silky, it is ready. You may reheat the sauce on low heat to avoid separation.

Note: Serve over your favorite dish. You may add to rice, top a fish, chicken, or lamb dish, or it may be used as a soup base or another sauce base. Cooked orzo pasta may be added at time of serving for best results.

Egg and Lemon Sauce (Avgolemono)

Prep time: 20 minutes
Ready in: 25 minutes
Makes: 2 cups; 8 servings at ¼ cup
per serving

This is similar to the sauce on the previous page, but without cream. It is simple but great.

Nutritional Information

Serving Size: ⅛ recipe • Calories 42, Total Fat 2g, Saturated Fat 1g, Cholesterol 55mg, Sodium 128mg, Total Carbohydrates 3g, Dietary Fiber 0g, Protein 3g

■ INGREDIENTS

2 fresh eggs (separate egg yolk and
whites)
2 pinches of kosher sea salt
Juice of 2 fresh lemons
2 cups of stock (beef, chicken, or
vegetable)

■ DIRECTIONS

Beat the egg whites vigorously in a deep mixing bowl with 2 pinches of salt. Beat the egg yolks in a separate bowl until frothy. Combine the egg whites and the egg yolks in a saucepan over low heat. Slowly add the lemon juice as you whisk the eggs. Continue to whisk the egg mixture as you begin to add the stock. Once the mixture becomes smooth and silky, it is ready. You may reheat the sauce on low heat to avoid separation. Serve over your favorite dish.

Note: This recipe is a version of the classical Greek avgolemono base for soup or sauce without the cream or Greek yogurt added. Add rice or smaller type pasta (e.g., orzo) for a great soup.

Fish or Pasta Dish Sauce

Prep time: 10 minutes
Ready in: 15 minutes
Serves: 8

This is such a versatile sauce that I have used it on many main dishes, side dishes, and even on toasted French bread with some melted goat cheese.

Nutritional Information

Serving Size: ⅛ recipe • Calories 109, Total Fat 10g, Saturated Fat 1g, Cholesterol 1mg, Sodium 274mg, Total Carbohydrates 6g, Dietary Fiber 2g, Protein 1g

■ INGREDIENTS

1 medium onion, chopped
4 tbsp extra virgin olive oil
3–4 cloves garlic, chopped
4 cups chopped tomato
4 tsp drained capers
½ cup pitted Kalamata olives
4 pinches black pepper
2 pinches cayenne pepper
4 pinches grated cheese
4 pinches chopped parsley

■ DIRECTIONS

Sauté all ingredients except cheese and parsley. Adjust for taste as you need. Add to fish, pasta, ravioli, etc. Garnish with grated cheese and parsley.

Note: Try adding one cup roasted red pepper or one cup artichoke hearts. Use this sauce as described above, but if you add roasted red peppers or artichokes, not only are you adding volume to your dish, but you are increasing the flavor. Also, if you were to add tomato sauce or juice, you then get a hearty soup. Enjoy!

Fruit Balsamic Glaze

Prep time: 10 minutes
Ready in: 15 minutes
Makes: 1 cup, 4 servings at ¼ cup per serving

If you are looking for a simple and zesty glaze, this recipe combines the sweet, citric and the tangy.

Nutritional Information

Serving Size: ¼ recipe • Calories 77, Total Fat 0g, Saturated Fat 0g, Cholesterol 0mg, Sodium 9mg, Total Carbohydrates 18g, Dietary Fiber 2g, Protein 1g

■ INGREDIENTS

½ cup balsamic vinegar
½ cup orange juice
Juice of 1 fresh lemon
4 tsp brown sugar
1 cup chopped fruit or berries

■ DIRECTIONS

Add all ingredients in a saucepan and bring to boil. Reduce heat and simmer for 4–5 minutes until it thickens. Use to drizzle on pan-seared fish or grilled chicken. May add fresh grated ginger or the zest of an orange.

Note: May be served on poached hearty fish warm or at room temperature. Also, you may add to pork, chicken, or duck.

HONEY GARLIC YOGURT SAUCE

Prep time: 5 minutes
Ready in: 10 minutes
Makes: ½ cup, 4 servings at ⅛ cup per serving

One of the easiest and most special sauces that can be served cold or used as a marinade for grilled chicken or fish.

Nutritional Information

Serving Size: ¼ recipe • Calories 64, Total Fat 2g, Saturated Fat 1g, Cholesterol 5mg, Sodium 27mg, Total Carbohydrates 11g, Dietary Fiber 0g, Protein 2g

■ INGREDIENTS

1 tsp chopped garlic
2 tbsp honey
½ cup yogurt (low fat)
2 tbsp sour cream
1 tsp black pepper

■ DIRECTIONS

Combine garlic, honey, yogurt, sour cream, and pepper, mixing until incorporated. Use mix to marinate chicken or fish, brushing before grilling. Other spices may be added including dill, thyme or rosemary for a more savory taste.

Note: You can thicken the yogurt by putting it in a fine cheesecloth in a colander and letting it drain for a few hours. A drop or two of hot sauce will result in a more robust taste.

ITALIAN DRESSING

Prep time: 5 minutes
Ready in: 10 minutes
Makes: 2 cups, 16 servings at 2 tbsp per serving

Great flavoring for a light everyday salad dressing or a quick marinade for chicken, fish, or shrimp.

Nutritional Information

Serving Size: 1/16 recipe • Calories 133, Total Fat 14g, Saturated Fat 2g, Cholesterol 0mg, Sodium 147mg, Total Carbohydrates 1g, Dietary Fiber 0g, Protein 0g

■ INGREDIENTS

1 cup olive oil
½ cup white wine vinaigrette
¼ cup lemon juice
1 clove garlic, crushed
1 tsp sea salt
¼ tsp pepper
1 tbsp dried oregano
1 tbsp dried basil
1 tsp crushed red pepper flakes
2 tbsp water

■ DIRECTIONS

In a mixing bowl or a blender, combine all ingredients including 2 tbsp water and whisk vigorously.

Note: Enjoy on a wide variety of salads including spinach and arugula. I also have used it as a light marinade on grilled shrimp, chicken, beef, and vegetables.

Mango Glaze

Prep time: 5 minutes
Ready in: 10 minutes
Makes: 4 cups, 31 servings at 2 tbsp per serving

This yummy sauce has a citrusy, golden color and an incredible taste which pairs well with fish, chicken, duck or pork.

Nutritional Information

Serving Size: ⅟₃₁ recipe • Calories 12, Total Fat 0g, Saturated Fat 0g, Cholesterol 0mg, Sodium 4mg, Total Carbohydrates 3g, Dietary Fiber 0g, Protein 0g

■ INGREDIENTS

2 cups mango flesh (without skin or pit)
2 cups water
2 tbsp sugar
2 tsp Dijon mustard
¼ cup apple juice
1 tbsp lemon juice
Zest of ½ orange
Juice of ½ orange

■ DIRECTIONS

Boil mango in a saucepan with water until tender. Remove mango and puree with food processor. Keep remaining water in pan. Stir in sugar and mustard into saucepan. Add mango puree back into sauce. Add apple juice, lemon juice, and zest. Stir to thicken. Add orange juice to adjust thickness, taste, and texture. Serve hot or cold.

Note: I love the fact that you can create this great sauce in four steps. Also, I have used walnuts and pomegranate seeds as garnish to finish the perfect presentation of your favorite dish. The colors are stunning.

Marsala Sauce

Prep time: 10 minutes
Ready in: 15 minutes
Makes: 4 cups, 12 servings at ⅓ cup per serving

This is a classic mushroom and Marsala wine sauce that still has a great place on the table with any light meat or fish dish.

Nutritional Information

Serving Size: ¹⁄₁₂ recipe • Calories 129, Total Fat 9g, Saturated Fat 5g, Cholesterol 23mg, Sodium 405mg, Total Carbohydrates 8g, Dietary Fiber 0g, Protein 3g

■ INGREDIENTS

½ cup butter
2–3 cups mushrooms, sliced
3–4 shallots chopped
2 cups Marsala wine
4 cups demiglace* (chicken or beef)
Salt and pepper to taste

■ DIRECTIONS

In a large skillet, sauté shallots and mushrooms in butter. Add most of the Marsala wine and reduce. Add stock and bring to a boil; reduce by a third. Finish with remaining wine, salt and pepper. Serve over chicken breasts or hearty fish.

Note: You may add a tsp of grated cheese, chopped parsley and freshly sliced lemon to add a depth of flavor to your dish.

*Demiglace is a thickened and flavored stock.

Mornay Sauce

Prep time: 10 minutes
Ready in: 15 minutes
Makes: 5 cups, 15 servings at ⅓ cup per serving

This is a simple sauce used in many dishes that are lightly prepared then baked after topping with sauce.

Nutritional Information

Serving Size: ¹/₁₅ recipe • Calories 124, Total Fat 10g, Saturated Fat 6g, Cholesterol 30mg, Sodium 195mg, Total Carbohydrates 4g, Dietary Fiber 0g, Protein 4g

■ INGREDIENTS

6 tbsp butter
6 tbsp flour
2 cups half and half (may use heavy cream)
2 cups chicken broth
1 cup Parmesan cheese

■ DIRECTIONS

Heat butter in saucepan. Add flour and cook 2 minutes over low heat. Add room temperature half and half and chicken broth. Simmer until thick. Add cheese, stir and serve. Use as a topping for grilled vegetables.

Note: I find that this basic sauce can play a role in plating and saucing main dishes such as fish steaks, chicken, beef, pork and roasted vegetables. This sauce is higher in saturated fats than recommended, so use caution and serve with lean protein.

Olive Oil and Lemon Sauce

Prep time: 10 minutes
Ready in: 15 minutes
Makes: 3 cups, 12 servings at ¼ cup
per serving

This is easy, quick, tangy and provides us with multiple uses.

Nutritional Information

Serving Size: ¹⁄₁₂ recipe • Calories 324, Total Fat 36g, Saturated Fat 5g, Cholesterol 0mg, Sodium 34mg, Total Carbohydrates 2g, Dietary Fiber 0g, Protein 0g

■ INGREDIENTS

2 cups extra virgin olive oil
1 cup fresh lemon juice
¼ cup chopped parsley
6 pinches of fresh ground black pepper
4 pinches of kosher sea salt

■ DIRECTIONS

In a mixing bowl, combine all ingredients and whisk vigorously. Serve chilled or room temperature (best at room temperature). May be served on light dishes like steamed vegetables, or poached fish or chicken. May use a lighter extra virgin olive oil for a lighter taste.

Note: You may use this for a salad dressing or as a marinade for multiple uses.

Pesto (Basil)

Prep time: 10 minutes
Ready in: 15 minutes
Makes: 4 cups, 50 servings at 2 tbsp per serving

Now that your main dish is planned, what about side dishes to go along with it? Whether they are hot or cold side dishes, I tell you there is nothing better than a side salad or pasta dish with PESTO. It's easy to make, it's fresh, earthy, healthy and delicious.

Nutritional Information

Serving Size: 1/50 recipe • Calories 79, Total Fat 8g, Saturated Fat 1g, Cholesterol 3mg, Sodium 42mg, Total Carbohydrates 1g, Dietary Fiber 0g, Protein 2g

■ INGREDIENTS

3 cups fresh basil leaves washed and
    towel dried
6 healthy size garlic cloves, peeled
½ cup of shelled walnuts
1 cup pine nuts
½ cup grated Parmesan cheese
½ cup grated Romano cheese
Sea salt to taste
Fresh ground pepper to taste
1 cup extra virgin olive oil
Fresh parsley for garnish

■ DIRECTIONS

Combine all ingredients except olive oil and parsley and mix in a food processor. As processor is running, pour the olive oil steadily and slowly. Scrape side of processor and process again to combine all ingredients. Now it is ready to use. Garnish with parsley.

Note: This can be used cold or heated, depending on use. It is great over cooked pasta of all types, shapes and sizes. Add to mayonnaise for sandwiches or use as a salad dressing. Use for grilling or broiling on fish or meat by brushing on first. Use for poaching a favorite fish, shrimp or scallops. Substitute fresh mint in place of basil and follow same steps above for a great variation on taste. This is excellent with roasted leg of lamb and swordfish.

PESTO (PARSLEY)

Prep time: 10 minutes
Ready in: 15 minutes
Makes: 2½ cups, 20 servings at 2 tbsp per serving

I love this as an alternative to the basil pesto. It is easy to make, fresh, healthy, and tastes great.

Nutritional Information

Serving Size: ¹⁄₂₀ recipe • Calories 43, Total Fat 4g, Saturated Fat 1g, Cholesterol 1mg, Sodium 19mg, Total Carbohydrates 1g, Dietary Fiber 0g, Protein 1g

■ INGREDIENTS

2 cups of parsley leaves
4 tbsp pine nuts (may use almonds or walnuts)
3–4 garlic cloves
¼ cup extra virgin olive oil
4 tbsp Parmesan cheese

■ DIRECTIONS

Combine all and process in blender until smooth. May cover with extra olive oil for better storage life.

Note: Add to mayonnaise or sour cream and apply as a condiment for sandwiches. It may be used hot or cold depending upon use. Add a little fresh mint to achieve a new taste for grilled meats.

TOASTED PINE NUTS

Prep time: 5 minutes
Ready in: 5 minutes
Serves: 1

Pine nuts are one of the most used seeds in many of the Mediterranean dishes across the whole region. The seed from the cone of a Mediterranean family of pine trees is used exclusively in many of the Middle Eastern lamb, rice, stuffing, and fish dishes as well as garnish for vegetable and hummus dishes. It is also used as the filling for many different types of baklava.

Nutritional Information

Serving Size: 1 recipe • Calories 228, Total Fat 24g, Saturated Fat 2g, Cholesterol 0mg, Sodium 1mg, Total Carbohydrates 4g, Dietary Fiber 1g, Protein 4g

■ INGREDIENTS

1 oz. pine nuts
1 tsp olive oil

■ DIRECTIONS

Toast pine nuts in an oven on high heat or in a saucepan with a few drops of oil or butter (use a good amount of oil, so when heated, the caramelization time is very quick). Stir constantly and carefully toss to avoid burning pine nuts. Burnt pine nuts taste bitter and become brittle. When you reach an even light brown color, the pine nuts are at the perfect taste and appearance. Remove immediately and put on a cold plate.

Note: Use it any way you like it. Wow!

POMODORO SAUCE

Prep time: 20 minutes
Ready in: 10 minutes
Serves: 4

Should you ask what is the most used sauce in Mediterranean cooking, don't be surprised if the answer is this sauce. This is a fresh sauce and many versions exist depending upon what tomatoes and what type of oil you use.

Nutritional Information

Serving Size: ¼ recipe • Calories 103, Total Fat 7g, Saturated Fat 1g, Cholesterol 0mg, Sodium 378mg, Total Carbohydrates 10g, Dietary Fiber 2g, Protein 2g

■ INGREDIENTS

2 tbsp extra virgin olive oil
2–4 cloves garlic diced
1 28-oz can whole, peeled tomato with liquid
4 pinches sea salt
¼ tsp black pepper
½ tsp sugar
6–8 leaves of basil

■ DIRECTIONS

Heat oil. Add half the garlic and let simmer 30 seconds. Add tomato, salt, pepper, and sugar. Bring to a boil, then simmer for 20 minutes. Simmer gently until thick (about ten minutes), stirring occasionally. Stir in basil. Stir in remainder of garlic.

Note: Chopped onions may be sautéed and used with garlic. Other methods would eliminate the onion, put garlic in whole and put all herbs into a bouquet-garni, which can then be removed. A bouquet-garni may include parsley, basil, bay leaves, and thyme.

ROMESCO SAUCE

Prep time: 20 minutes
Ready in: 25 minutes
Serves: 4

This is a simple, traditional sauce that incorporates the sweet and tangy taste of fresh tomato and roasted peppers with the heat of the chili peppers. It is great for seafood dishes.

Nutritional Information

Serving Size: ¼ recipe • Calories 152, Total Fat 13g, Saturated Fat 2g, Cholesterol 0mg, Sodium 50mg, Total Carbohydrates 9g, Dietary Fiber 2g, Protein 2g

■ INGREDIENTS

2 ripe tomatoes
3–4 tbsp olive oil
1 onion chopped
4 garlic cloves chopped
1 roasted red pepper chopped
½ tsp crushed red pepper flakes (chili flakes)
¼ cup stock (fish, chicken)
Splash of white wine
1 tbsp red wine vinegar

■ DIRECTIONS

Cut a small cross in the base of each tomato. Put tomatoes in boiling water for 1 minute, cool slightly. Peel skin then coarsely chop the tomatoes. Heat 2 tbsp olive oil in saucepan. Add onions, chopped garlic; cook until soft. Add roasted pepper, tomatoes, pepper flakes, stock, and wine. Cover and simmer for 15 minutes. Add vinegar.

Note: Add a little herb like thyme or oregano when using this sauce with steamed clams, mussels or sautéed shrimp. Crushed almonds may be added to the sauce for a great, crunchy taste. Roasted chili peppers in place of dry chili flakes will add greater depth of flavor.

Tahini Dressing

Prep time: 5 minutes
Ready in: 10 minutes
Makes: 3 cups, 12 servings at ¼ cup per serving

In the Middle East, sesame paste is probably the equivalent to tomato paste in the Western world in terms of frequency of use. Tahini paste, ground up sesame seed, is very versatile, shelf stable and may be used as a hot or cold sauce. With slight variation of other ingredients or herbs, garlic and lemon juice, the taste and flavor it adds is great. I wanted to explain this ingredient so you can have fun with it and practice using it on eggplant, chickpeas, cauliflower, hearty fish or even meat.

One of the interesting properties of the paste is when adding water, the paste becomes thicker and pastier. On the other hand, when adding lemon juice (citric acid and water), the paste dissolves easier and may be mixed well until smooth. For proper density, use equal parts of water and lemon juice.

Nutritional Information

Serving Size: ¹⁄₁₂ recipe • Calories 117, Total Fat 10g, Saturated Fat 1g, Cholesterol 0mg, Sodium 30mg, Total Carbohydrates 6g, Dietary Fiber 2g, Protein 3g

■ INGREDIENTS

1 cup tahini
1 cup water
1 cup lemon juice
4–5 pinches sea salt
4–5 pinches white pepper
1 tbsp finely chopped garlic

■ DIRECTIONS

Mix all ingredients until smooth and use on top of your favorite food. The sauce may be served cold or hot.

Note: I have also used yogurt and cumin as additional ingredients to enhance the depth of the flavor. In this instance, the dressing may be used as a sauce, which may be added to cooked vegetables like cauliflower, fish like swordfish, or meat like Kefta (lamb burger).

Tarragon Cream Sauce

Prep time: 15 minutes
Ready in: 20 minutes
Makes: 2 cups, 8 servings at ¼ cup
per serving

Tarragon adds great flavor and aroma to this sauce. You'll want to use it sparingly, and it should be added toward the end stages of cooking.

Nutritional Information

Serving Size: ⅛ recipe • Calories 87, Total Fat 6g, Saturated Fat 4g, Cholesterol 21mg, Sodium 20mg, Total Carbohydrates 2g, Dietary Fiber 0g, Protein 1g

■ INGREDIENTS

½ bottle chardonnay
1 small onion thinly sliced
3 pinches of black pepper
1 cup heavy cream
1 tbsp grated Parmesan cheese
2 sprigs tarragon chopped

■ DIRECTIONS

Heat wine in saucepan. Add onions and black pepper. Add cream and let simmer. Add grated cheese. Add chopped tarragon. Reduce over heat for 4–5 minutes. Remove from heat and let stand. Serve hot.

Note: This sauce is used for many egg and chicken dishes. I also have served this on a medley of steamed vegetables, asparagus, sautéed wild mushrooms, and steamed cauliflower.

Tomato Vodka Sauce

Prep time: 5 minutes
Ready in: 10 minutes
Makes: 4 cups, 8 servings at ½ cup per serving

A quick variation on a classic sauce with straightforward ingredients.

Nutritional Information

Serving Size: ⅛ recipe • Calories 74, Total Fat 1g, Saturated Fat 1g, Cholesterol 3mg, Sodium 370mg, Total Carbohydrates 7g, Dietary Fiber 1g, Protein 4g

■ INGREDIENTS

¼ cup vodka
¼ cup Marsala wine
1 cup tomato paste
2 cups chicken broth (reduced sodium)
2 tsp green peppercorns
¼ cup Parmesan cheese

■ DIRECTIONS

Mix all ingredients except cheese in saucepan and reduce to the desired consistency or thickness. Whip in cheese. Adjust for taste. Enjoy by adding to pasta, tortellini, shrimp, etc.

Note: You may substitute heavy crushed tomato puree in place of tomato paste or sundried tomato paste. Now if you have time and some great, ripe tomatoes, then make your own tomato sauce. Other ingredients such as fresh basil or crème fraiche may be used to offer an intense new taste.

TUSCANY TOMATO SAUCE

Prep time: 10 minutes
Ready in: 15 minutes
Makes: 4 cups, 8 servings at ½ cup
per serving

Quick, simple, zesty and versatile. Enjoy it on a cool summer night or fall evening with some delicious pasta, grilled chicken, light fish or anything that delights your palate.

Nutritional Information

Serving Size: ⅛ recipe • Calories 50, Total Fat 4g, Saturated Fat 1g, Cholesterol 0mg, Sodium 29mg, Total Carbohydrates 4g, Dietary Fiber 1g, Protein 1g

■ INGREDIENTS

4 cups whole peeled tomatoes
2 tbsp extra virgin olive oil
2 pinches of sea salt
4 pinches fresh pepper
4 cloves of garlic, chopped
4 pinches crushed red pepper
½ cup chopped fresh basil
4 pinches of fresh parsley, chopped

■ DIRECTIONS

Drain tomato and set liquid aside. In a saucepan (2-quart size), combine tomato with oil, salt, pepper, and garlic. Add crushed red pepper, basil, and parsley, and simmer for 5 minutes. Mix well. Add tomato liquid to achieve the desired consistency.

Note: Using quality tomato products is a must. Fresh herbs and spices will set the taste of this dish apart from any other sauce you have tasted.

YOGURT DRESSING

Prep time: 5 minutes
Ready in: 10 minutes
Serves: 8

This is a light and refreshing salad dressing that is very low in saturated fat and is perfect for vegetable dip or as a topping for raw or grilled vegetables.

Nutritional Information

Serving Size: ⅛ recipe • Calories 59, Total Fat 2g, Saturated Fat 0g, Cholesterol 4mg, Sodium 128mg, Total Carbohydrates 6g, Dietary Fiber 0g, Protein 4g

■ INGREDIENTS

1 pint (2 cups) of fat free yogurt (preferably Greek yogurt)
¼ cup light mayonnaise
2 tbsp of freshly chopped chives
1 tbsp of freshly chopped dill
2 tbsp of lemon juice (½ lemon)
4 pinches of black pepper
2 pinches of kosher sea salt

■ DIRECTIONS

In a large mixing bowl mix all the ingredients together till well incorporated and smooth. Chill, serve and enjoy!

Note: This dressing can be used on your favorite mixed greens, as a condiment for a wrap sandwich, or as a dressing for a grilled vegetable, fish or meat. Mint may be substituted for dill. Top with extra virgin olive oil and use as a dip. Another variation on this dressing is to add drained capers to the mixture and use with seared hearty fish.

Soups

BAKED POTATO SOUP

Prep time: 40 minutes
Ready in: 55 minutes
Serves: 10

Out of ideas for soup? Ok then try this one for a hearty soup in less than 1/2 hour. Enjoy!

Nutritional Information

Serving Size: ⅒ recipe • Calories 612, Total Fat 23g, Saturated Fat 11g, Cholesterol 56mg, Sodium 783mg, Total Carbohydrates 81g, Dietary Fiber 9g, Protein 25g

■ INGREDIENTS

6–8 medium baked russet potatoes
  (peeled and diced)
4 quarts chicken stock (or chicken broth)
4 pinches white pepper
4 pinches black pepper
4 tbsp unsalted butter
2 tbsp of light olive oil
1 cup all purpose flour
2 cups white cheddar cheese
2 cups whole milk or half & half

■ DIRECTIONS

Prebake potatoes until soft and tender to the touch, and let cool. Bring stock to a boil. Add white and black pepper and baked potatoes. Cook until potato mixture comes to a boil (about 15 minutes). In separate pan, melt butter with oil and add flour; stir to make roux. Cook roux about 3 minutes. Add roux to potato mixture; whisk and incorporate well. Add cheese and milk. Turn down heat to simmer for about 15 minutes. Serve hot in an appropriate size vessel. Garnish with a dollop of yogurt, crumbled feta, chopped chives, or grated cheese.

Note: Other good melting cheeses may be used, and bacon may be used as garnish or as the starting fat. Add onions to sauté then follow the same as above.

Barley and Asparagus Soup

Prep time: 20 minutes
Ready in: 35 minutes
Serves: 8

This hearty soup incorporates rich flavors and healthy nutrients in one bowl.

Nutritional Information

Serving Size: ⅛ recipe • Calories 206, Total Fat 7g, Saturated Fat 2g, Cholesterol 6mg, Sodium 184mg, Total Carbohydrates 27g, Dietary Fiber 5g, Protein 11g

■ INGREDIENTS

8 cups chicken stock (low sodium) or vegetable broth
2 tbsp extra virgin olive oil
1 chopped onion
4 cloves garlic chopped
1½ cups barley, pearled
1 lb bundle asparagus cleaned and cut at angle into 1-inch pieces
½ cup Parmesan cheese
1 cup dry white wine
2 pinches salt
2 pinches pepper

■ DIRECTIONS

Heat stock or broth. In separate pan heat oil. Saute onion and garlic in oil until soft. Add barley and stir, cook for 2 minutes. Add broth in 5–6 batches, constantly stirring. Add asparagus and cheese at the last batch. Add wine. Season with salt and pepper. Stir and simmer for 3–5 minutes.

Note: "Hulled" or whole-grain barley is the most nutritious form of the grain. Adding broth in batches and stirring avoids sticking and ensures the consistency of soup as you prefer it. Serve with green salad and crusty, hearty bread for a good meal.

BLACK BEAN SOUP

Prep time: 25 minutes
Ready in: 35 minutes
Serves: 6

A hearty soup with a distinctive color that adds a dramatic touch.

Nutritional Information

Serving Size: ⅙ recipe • Calories 276, Total Fat 6g, Saturated Fat 3g, Cholesterol 13mg, Sodium 352mg, Total Carbohydrates 40g, Dietary Fiber 14g, Protein 18g

■ INGREDIENTS

32 oz black beans (can products should be rinsed)
1 cup salsa (choose based on how hot you like it)
1 tbsp chili powder
4 pinches cumin (optional)
1 cup chicken stock (low sodium preferred)
½ cup shredded cheddar cheese
¼ cup sour cream
2½ tbsp chopped parsley (or cilantro)

■ DIRECTIONS

Heat beans in saucepan with ½ cup water (to avoid sticking) for 5–10 minutes; mash about half of the beans in the pot. Stir in salsa. Add chili powder, cumin (if you are using it), and broth. Bring to a boil, simmer 10 minutes. Serve with cheese, sour cream and parsley on the side.

Note: You may use white/cannellini beans instead. For vegetarian soup, you may substitute pureed tomatoes and roasted red peppers instead of chicken stock. You may crisp up some bacon, drain the fat, then sauté some chopped onions and chopped escarole for a great new variation.

Butternut Bisque

Prep time: 45 minutes
Ready in: 60 minutes
Serves: 14

This is one of our most sought after soups for two decades. For a little hard work, there is a great reward at the end.

Nutritional Information

Serving Size: ¹⁄₁₄ recipe • Calories 301, Total Fat 19g, Saturated Fat 12g, Cholesterol 64mg, Sodium 160mg, Total Carbohydrates 32g, Dietary Fiber 1g, Protein 2g

■ INGREDIENTS

1 gallon water
1 large butternut squash
1 cup maple syrup
3 medium shallots, finely chopped
½ cup brown sugar
6 pinches of salt
1 tsp white pepper
1 tsp nutmeg
½ cup flour
½ cup butter
2 cups heavy cream
½ cup sherry wine
¼ cup finely chopped parsley

■ DIRECTIONS

Peel squash, clean, discard seeds and cut into small pieces. Bring water and squash to boil until tender and soft (½ hour). Do not drain. Smash the soft squash while still in pot. Use a large whisk to further break up large pieces. Add maple syrup, chopped shallots, brown sugar, salt, white pepper and nutmeg. Mix well with squash. Continue to simmer on medium heat for 10 minutes. Melt butter, stir in flour, and cook until thickened to make a roux. Whip roux into soup to thicken soup to desired texture. Mix in heavy cream and whip thoroughly. Add sherry and simmer for 10 minutes. Strain soup into a strainer. Puree large pieces in a food processor. Add back to soup through a strainer. Discard the remaining residue. Serve hot and garnish with parsley.

Note: I have added green apples to enhance the tartness level of the soup. I also used a combination of pumpkin and butternut squash in equal amounts for an entirely different flavor.

CARROT DILL SOUP

Prep time: 30 minutes
Ready in: 45 minutes
Serves: 8

A lovely way to use this root vegetable in such a light yet satisfying soup.

Nutritional Information

Serving Size: ⅛ recipe • Calories 111, Total Fat 5g, Saturated Fat 1g, Cholesterol 4mg, Sodium 254mg, Total Carbohydrates 13g, Dietary Fiber 2g, Protein 4g

■ INGREDIENTS

2 tbsp olive oil
1 diced onion
1½ lb carrots cut, peeled, diced, or grated
4 cups chicken/vegetable stock
1 tbsp grated ginger
2 tbsp fresh dill as desired
4 pinches salt
4 pinches white pepper
1 cup orange juice

■ DIRECTIONS

Heat oil in sauce pan. Sauté onion until soft (4–5 minutes). Add carrots, broth, and ginger. Boil until soft (15–20 minutes) and cool. Use hand held blender to puree until smooth. Add dill, salt and pepper. Add orange juice. Simmer for 5 minutes. Serve hot.

Note: You may serve and garnish with a teaspoon of heavy cream or yogurt. You can also thicken slightly with cornstarch.

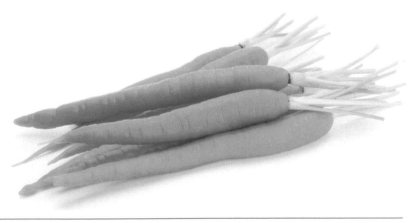

CHILLY CHILI (VEGETARIAN CHILI)

Prep time: 30 minutes
Ready in: 45 minutes
Serves: 20

Sometimes I feel like chili! But have you had a cold chili in the winter? This one is really good. Enjoy it while it lasts.

Nutritional Information

Serving Size: 1/20 recipe • Calories 104, Total Fat 2g, Saturated Fat 0g, Cholesterol 0mg, Sodium 439mg, Total Carbohydrates 19g, Dietary Fiber 6g, Protein 5g

■ INGREDIENTS

16 oz chickpeas (in juice)
16 oz kidney beans (in juice)
16 oz black beans (in juice)
3 oz tortilla chips
2 oz picante sauce
8 oz artichoke hearts (in juice)
4 oz crushed tomatoes
4 oz pureed tomatoes (no salt added)
1 tsp chopped garlic
½ cup finely chopped onions
¼ cup finely chopped red peppers
¼ cup finely chopped green peppers
¼ cup finely chopped scallions
½ tsp coriander
⅓ cup chopped parsley
3 tbsp chili powder
½ tsp white pepper
1 tsp black pepper
½ tsp paprika
½ cup red hot sauce
Tortilla chips, crushed extra fine, for garnish

■ DIRECTIONS

Drain chickpeas, kidney beans and black beans; reserve the liquid and a third of the whole chickpeas and beans. Puree the remaining chickpeas and beans. Mix the remaining ingredients, as well as the reserved whole beans and liquid. Serve chilled with a garnish of kernel corn, crushed tortilla chips and chopped chive, scallion or cilantro. Serve cold or may be served hot.

Note: After a day of enjoying this chili cold, you may put in a pot and cook for 20–25 minutes on a good simmer and serve hot on a chilly night.

CHILLED CUCUMBER SOUP

Prep time: 25 minutes
Ready in: 35 minutes
Serves: 8

As a summer soup, be warned; you will be addicted and love this soup for its ease of preparation and how fresh and clean tasting this soup is.

Nutritional Information

Serving Size: ⅛ recipe • Calories 146, Total Fat 2g, Saturated Fat 1g, Cholesterol 7mg, Sodium 104mg, Total Carbohydrates 26g, Dietary Fiber 2g, Protein 8g

■ INGREDIENTS

1 small honeydew melon, seeded and finely chopped
2 cucumbers, peeled, seeded and finely chopped
1 quart plain, low fat yogurt
1 cup orange juice
1 small red onion, finely chopped
Juice of 1 lime
2–3 jalapeno peppers, chopped
½ tsp mint, fresh is preferred
½ tsp cilantro, fresh is preferred

■ DIRECTIONS

In a food processor, puree half of the amount of honeydew and cucumber. Put in a large mixing bowl. Place the other half of the honeydew and cucumber in the food processor and pulse for a rough chop. Add to the pureed mixture in the mixing bowl. Add yogurt, orange juice, and chopped red onion; mix well. Add lime juice and peppers, and toss again. Taste for sweetness and consistency, Toss in mint and cilantro and mix well. Taste again for flavor, adjust accordingly.

Note: This dish should be fresh, sweet and yet tangy with a little hot aftertaste, so you need to find your preferred taste and adjust accordingly. This soup may be made chunky or smooth.

CHILLED PEPPER SOUP

Prep time: 25 minutes
Ready in: 40 minutes
Serves: 6

This is a light, seasonal soup, great for dunking with freshly made sourdough or wheat croutons.

Nutritional Information

Serving Size: ⅙ recipe • Calories 101, Total Fat 7g, Saturated Fat 1g, Cholesterol 0mg, Sodium 22mg, Total Carbohydrates 9g, Dietary Fiber 1g, Protein 1g

■ INGREDIENTS

1 onion cut into quarters
4 garlic cloves
4 red bell peppers, seeded, cut into
    quarters
2–3 tbsp olive oil
Juice and grated rind of 1 orange
1 chopped ripe tomato (7 oz)
2–3 cups of chilled water
Salt and pepper to taste
2 tbsp fresh chives for garnish
Toasted pita bread for garnish

■ DIRECTIONS

Preheat oven to 375°–395°. Put onions, garlic and peppers in pan and spray with olive oil. Roast 20 minutes until lightly charred and roasted. Add pepper mixture, orange rind, orange juice, tomatoes and water to food processor. Process until smooth, strain if desired. Season lightly with salt and pepper and chill before serving. Serve in bowl, garnished with chives and toasted pita.

Note: The taste of fresh roasted peppers is incomparable. However, if you choose, you can substitute store bought roasted red peppers. I would look for quality labels with less salt.

Fruit Gazpacho

Prep time: 25 minutes
Ready in: 35 minutes
Serves: 8

This is one of my favorites, especially in the summer season. I serve it as an appetizer, soup, or even dessert.

Nutritional Information

Serving Size: ⅛ recipe • Calories 175, Total Fat 1g, Saturated Fat 0g, Cholesterol 0mg, Sodium 272mg, Total Carbohydrates 44g, Dietary Fiber 7g, Protein 3g

■ INGREDIENTS

2 cups tomato puree
3 cup fresh oranges, diced
2 tsp sugar
Zest of 1 orange
Zest of 1 lime
2 cups diced cantaloupe
2 cups diced honeydew
1 mango peeled and diced
1 apple (your favorite kind) diced
1 cup fresh blueberries
1 cup green grapes
½ cup red grapes
½ cup sliced strawberries
2 kiwis peeled and sliced
Fresh mint for garnish

■ DIRECTIONS

In a mixing bowl combine tomatoes, oranges, sugar, orange zest, lime zest, and mix well. Process half of the cantaloupe, honeydew, mango, and apple in a food processor for a rough puree for texture, then add to tomato mixture. Add the remaining diced fruit and the rest of the ingredients to the bowl and toss well. Chill for 2 hours and serve in a bowl, shot glass for sips, or a flute, and garnish with mint.

Note: Enjoy!

GAZPACHO

Prep time: 25 minutes
Ready in: 35 minutes
Serves: 16

This is a bright, fresh and delicious summer vegetable soup. The fresh mint with a little bit of cayenne pepper make this soup a perfect lunch for a hot, summer day.

Nutritional Information

Serving Size: ¹⁄₁₆ recipe • Calories 244, Total Fat 18g, Saturated Fat 3g, Cholesterol 0mg, Sodium 178mg, Total Carbohydrates 18g, Dietary Fiber 5g, Protein 4g

■ INGREDIENTS

8 fresh tomatoes—4 diced, 4 pureed
6 red peppers—3 diced, 3 pureed
8 cucumbers—4 diced, 4 pureed
2 cups roasted red peppers
1 cup artichoke hearts
4 red onions, diced fine
3 scallions diced fine
2 cups red wine vinegar
1 cup olive oil
3 cups Bloody Mary mix
Pinch cayenne pepper
Black pepper to taste
½ cup fresh dill, chopped
½ cup fresh mint, chopped
2 cups parsley, chopped
1 cup crushed tomatoes (canned)
2 cups whole peeled tomatoes (canned)
Sea salt to taste (minimal)

■ DIRECTIONS

Take half of the fresh tomatoes, peppers, cucumber, roasted red pepper and artichoke hearts and puree in food processor. Then dice or rough chop the other half. Combine with remaining ingredients in a large mixing bowl. Mix well. Adjust for taste as you see fit. Chill and serve. Should keep for 2–3 days.

Note: To make bruschetta, take vegetables and add some V-8 juice, just enough so vegetables are still thick, spread on bread, sprinkle with cheese, and toast. Cook your favorite beans and use vegetables as a sauce. Vegetables make a good salsa.

Lentil Soup

Prep time: 25 minutes
Ready in: 35 minutes
Serves: 8

A classical Mid-Eastern favorite soup with many variations on the vegetables used, spiciness or type of lentil used, depending on the region it comes from. You should try to make this soup and its many variations and enjoy.

Nutritional Information

Serving Size: ⅛ recipe • Calories 212, Total Fat 8g, Saturated Fat 1g, Cholesterol 0mg, Sodium 518mg, Total Carbohydrates 28g, Dietary Fiber 9g, Protein 10g

■ INGREDIENTS

4 cups green lentils, cooked (2 cups dry lentils, plus water for cooking)
4 tbsp olive oil
2 onions, 1 chopped and 1 sliced
3–4 cloves garlic, chopped
1 cup each of green and red pepper, diced
2 cups of mushrooms, sliced (optional)
7–8 pinches each cumin, coriander, and pepper
3–4 pinches salt
4 cups water
4 cups reduced sodium vegetable stock
Optional: add 2 pinches of cayenne pepper
Parsley or fresh cilantro for garnish

■ DIRECTIONS

Cook 2 cups of dry lentils in boiling water for 8–10 minutes and then drain. In a stockpot, heat 2 tbsp olive oil and sauté the chopped onion. Add garlic, peppers, mushrooms and spices, stirring for 3–5 minutes. Add lentils and 8 cups of water (or stock). Adjust spices for taste. Cook for 10 minutes or until lentils are soft. In a skillet, sauté sliced onions in 2 tbsp olive oil until golden brown (caramelized). Serve hot with caramelized onion and chopped parsley or cilantro.

Note: Serve with warm pita or bread for dunking or use crispy bread as croutons.

MULLIGATAWNY SOUP

Prep time: 40 minutes
Ready in: 60 minutes
Serves: 10

An incredible fusion of Mideastern, Indian and Moroccan flavors that yield bold flavors—enough to have as a meal on its own.

Nutritional Information

Serving Size: 1/10 recipe • Calories 414, Total Fat 33g, Saturated Fat 16g, Cholesterol 156mg, Sodium 351mg, Total Carbohydrates 7g, Dietary Fiber 2g, Protein 23g

■ INGREDIENTS

2 lb chicken meat (follow procedure
    at right)
2 tbsp butter
3 small onions, chopped
1 large stalk celery, minced
½ red or green bell pepper, chopped
1 tbsp each of curry powder, ground
    coriander and cumin
½ tsp each of ground cardamom, turmeric,
    sea salt, dried thyme
2 quarts chicken broth
1 cup coconut milk, or 3/4 cup milk
    blended with 1/4 cup canned grated
    coconut, or combined with 1 tbsp
    coconut cream
1 large bay leaf
3 tbsp flour
1 cup heavy cream
1 tsp dry mustard
½ tsp granulated garlic
Sea salt and pepper
4 cups hot cooked rice, optional to serve
    on the side with the soup

■ DIRECTIONS

Cut up the chicken to separate breast, thighs, drumsticks and wings. In a large saucepan brown the chicken in olive oil then remove from pot and drain excess fat. Add the butter, onions, celery, pepper and all spices, and sauté 5–10 minutes. Add the chicken broth, coconut milk, bay leaf and deglaze the bottom of saucepan. Put back the chicken. Cover, reduce heat, and simmer for ½ hour. Remove the chicken from the broth and let cool. Remove the bones and skin and strip meat from it. Return meat to the saucepan. Skim 3 tbsp of fat from the surface and put into a small saucepan. Place the saucepan over low heat and stir in the flour to make a roux. Whip the flour mixture into the broth, beating rapidly, and bring to a boil, stirring, another 5 minutes until thickens. Stir in the cream, mustard, and garlic. Bring to a slow simmer. Add salt and pepper to taste. Serve hot and enjoy.

Note: The use of fresh cut up chicken provides the best flavors. You can start with ready chicken meat, but you should compensate for flavor by adding chicken stock or other seasonings.

Potato and Scallion Soup

Prep time: 35 minutes
Ready in: 45 minutes
Serves: 8

Red skin potatoes are tender and full of flavor. The combination of the scallions with cream in a chicken broth yields a delightful flavor to this soup.

Nutritional Information

Serving Size: ⅛ recipe • Calories 158, Total Fat 4g, Saturated Fat 2g, Cholesterol 9mg, Sodium 168mg, Total Carbohydrates 23g, Dietary Fiber 3g, Protein 5g

■ INGREDIENTS

1 tbsp olive oil/butter blend
18 scallions (green onions), sliced
1½ lb red-skinned potatoes (1/2 inch chunks)
½ cup dry white wine
2 cups chicken/vegetable stock (low sodium)
½ cup heavy cream or half and half
½ cup skim, 2% or 1% milk
4 pinches sea salt
4 pinches pepper
Parsley and fresh pepper to garnish

■ DIRECTIONS

Melt oil/butter blend. Sauté onion (scallions). Add potatoes, wine, and broth and boil until tender (15 minutes). Add heavy cream, milk and simmer for 15 minutes. Add the salt and pepper to your taste and stir. Continue to cook until potatoes are tender. Serve hot, sprinkle with parsley.

Note: Leeks may be used in addition to scallions, replacing half the amount of scallions. Shredded Parmesan cheese also may be added to the end of the cooking procedure.

PUMPKIN CURRY SOUP

Prep time: 35 minutes
Ready in: 40 minutes
Serves: 12

Honestly, this beats the carving of a pumpkin any day! This easy-to-make, brightly colored soup is very delicate in flavor, yet very satisfying.

Nutritional Information

Serving Size: 1/12 recipe • Calories 179, Total Fat 9g, Saturated Fat 4g, Cholesterol 19mg, Sodium 275mg, Total Carbohydrates 19g, Dietary Fiber 2g, Protein 7g

■ INGREDIENTS

2 tbsp olive oil (light)
2 tbsp butter
2 cups onion, finely chopped
2 cups celery, finely chopped
4 cloves of garlic, chopped
1 tsp curry powder
1 tsp ground coriander
1 tsp crushed red pepper
8 cups chicken stock or water
64 oz pumpkin puree (or 4 lb pumpkin flesh)
1 cup half and half
1 cup whole milk

■ DIRECTIONS

In a large stockpot, heat oil and butter for 2–3 minutes. Sauté onion, celery, garlic for 3 minutes. Stir curry, coriander and pepper for 2 more minutes. Add stock (or water), bring to a boil. Stir in pumpkin puree and half and half, mix well. Simmer for 5–10 minutes, puree with a handheld machine for the consistency desired. Serve hot.

Note: Another direction for this soup is to use cinnamon, allspice and thyme for a whole different taste. Adding some brown sugar or pureed apples (apple sauce) will certainly surprise you. Adding cooked rice is one more variation.

Red Pepper Soup

Prep time: 20 minutes
Ready in: 30 minutes
Serves: 8

This colorful and vibrant soup is delicately flavored. It makes a great, fresh start to any meal or a great, light lunch with your favorite salad.

Nutritional Information

Serving Size: ⅛ recipe • Calories 393, Total Fat 37g, Saturated Fat 4g, Cholesterol 0mg, Sodium 42mg, Total Carbohydrates 16g, Dietary Fiber 5g, Protein 6g

■ INGREDIENTS

12 roasted red peppers (4 oz per pepper)
5–6 cloves chopped garlic
1 cup almonds
6 pinches cumin
4 tbsp lemon juice
4 tbsp sunflower oil
Salt to taste

■ DIRECTIONS

Clean peppers from charred skin and put in blender; puree until smooth. Add garlic, almonds, cumin, lemon juice, sunflower oil and salt. Blend again. Serve chilled or hot.

Note: Fresh peppers may be used by seeding and cleaning them. Chop peppers fine, then puree in a food processor with the garlic and almonds. Heat in a saucepan with a little oil. Add cumin and lemon juice, and adjust for taste. Simmer for 15 minutes, stir until thickened.

ROASTED VEGETABLE GAZPACHO

Prep time: 40 minutes
Ready in: 50 minutes
Serves: 10

End of the harvest season vegetables, like tomatoes, peppers and zucchini, are great tasting and full of robust flavors, especially in combination. Their flavor is enhanced by roasting them. This is one of my favorite recipes, combining the taste of roasted vegetables in a chilled soup. If you are like me you have a Mediterranean disposition and a great love for this dish!

Nutritional Information

Serving Size: ⅟₁₀ recipe • Calories 114, Total Fat 6g, Saturated Fat 1g, Cholesterol 0mg, Sodium 429mg, Total Carbohydrates 16g, Dietary Fiber 3g, Protein 3g

■ INGREDIENTS

2 lb whole ripe tomatoes
4 red bell peppers
4 yellow peppers
2 large red onions
1/4 cup extra virgin olive oil
1 tsp sea salt
1 tsp cumin
1 tsp ground coriander
¼ to ½ tsp cayenne pepper
1 tsp white pepper
1 tsp black pepper
1 whole bulb of garlic, peeled
4 cups V8 juice or Bloody Mary mix
¼ cup red wine vinegar (or sherry wine vinegar)
Chopped parsley and diced cucumbers for garnish (optional)

■ DIRECTIONS

Cut tomatoes, peppers and onions into small cubes or wedges, toss lightly with extra virgin olive oil, and sprinkle with a little salt and half the spices. Add the peeled garlic and roast in the oven at 350° until caramalization (browning) begins. Let cool once done roasting. Put half the batch into food processor. Process until medium fine texture, and pour into a large bowl. Do the same with the remaining half but process a little coarser. Add V8 Juice or Bloody Mary mix to the mixture of processed vegetables until your desired consistency. Add vinegar and remaining spices. Toss and serve; garnish with parsley and cucumber!

Note: You may serve this hot by cooking in a saucepan and adding some Parmesan cheese and serving with some nice toasted bread!

VEGETABLES

Avocado and Corn Relish

Prep time: 10 minutes
Ready in: 15 minutes
Serves: 8

A great simple summer or fall salad or side dish. Add cilantro for more of a southwestern style salad and taste.

Nutritional Information

Serving Size: ⅛ recipe • Calories 283, Total Fat 22g, Saturated Fat 3g, Cholesterol 0mg, Sodium 345mg, Total Carbohydrates 23g, Dietary Fiber 6g, Protein 4g

■ INGREDIENTS

½ cup extra virgin olive oil
4 cups corn kernels
¼ tsp sea salt
½ tsp pepper
2 ripened avocados, peeled, pitted, ½-inch diced
1 large red bell pepper diced
1 large green pepper diced
Roasted peppers (hot chilies may be substituted)
4 scallions cleaned, trimmed and sliced
¼ cup red wine vinegar

■ DIRECTIONS

Heat oil (¼ cup), sauté corn with salt and pepper. Add avocados, peppers, hot chilies, scallions, vinegar and the rest of the oil. Let cool. Serve with grilled chicken or fish as well as mixed vegetables or greens.

Note: Another variation may be served chopped with sliced tomato, fresh mozzarella, sprinkled with olive oil, lemon juice, and chopped parsley or cilantro.

Basil Tomato Pie

Prep time: 10 minutes
Ready in: 20 minutes
Serves: 8

Simple, very colorful, and delicious. You can use it as a topping for pizza. You can find plain pizza shells that are pan baked.

Nutritional Information

Serving Size: ⅛ recipe • Calories 259, Total Fat 17g, Saturated Fat 6g, Cholesterol 21mg, Sodium 392mg, Total Carbohydrates 18g, Dietary Fiber 1g, Protein 9g

■ INGREDIENTS

15 oz unbaked pie crust (1 crust)
1½ cup shredded mozzarella cheese (6 oz), part skim milk
5 medium Roma tomatoes or 4 medium tomatoes
1 cup loosely packed fresh basil leaves
4 cloves garlic
1 cup low-fat ricotta cheese
½ cup mayonnaise or salad dressing (light)
¼ cup grated Parmesan cheese
⅛ teaspoon ground white pepper
¼ cup fresh basil leaves (optional)

■ DIRECTIONS

Unwrap pie crust according to directions. Place in a 9-inch quiche dish or glass pie plate. Flute edge; press with the tines of a fork, if desired. Line shell with double-thickness of foil. Bake in 400° oven for 4 minutes. Remove foil. Bake 4 to 5 minutes more or until set and dry. Remove from oven. Reduce temperature to 375°. Sprinkle crust with ½ cup of the mozzarella cheese. Cool slightly on a wire rack. Cut tomatoes into wedges; drain on paper towels. Arrange tomato wedges atop cheese in the pie shell. In a food processor bowl combine basil and garlic; cover and process until coarsely chopped. Sprinkle over tomatoes. In a medium mixing bowl combine remaining mozzarella cheese, ricotta, mayonnaise, Parmesan cheese, and pepper. Spoon cheese mixture over basil mixture, spreading to evenly cover the top. Bake in a 375° oven for 12 to 15 minutes or until top is golden and bubbly. Serve warm. If desired, garnish with basil leaves. Makes 8 appetizer servings or 4 main-dish servings.

Note: Be ready. Your friends will request the recipe for this garden-fresh appetizer or entree. Make-ahead tips: Prebake pastry crust; cover and let stand at room temperature for up to 2 hours. Slice and drain tomatoes; let stand at room temperature for up to 2 hours. Prepare cheese-mayonnaise mixture; cover and chill up to 2 hours. You can also use goat cheese instead of mayonnaise and ricotta. You could make your own pie crust, prepared in advance. Also, using prepared pesto would save time and certainly produce a great pie.

BROCCOLI RABE WITH GARLIC AND ANCHOVIES

Prep time: 10 minutes
Ready in: 20 minutes
Serves: 6

Broccoli rabe, also known as rapini, has a slightly bitter taste. Cooking it in boiled water for 2-3 minutes softens its texture and reduces its bitterness.

Nutritional Information

Serving Size: ⅙ recipe • Calories 118, Total Fat 9g, Saturated Fat 1g, Cholesterol 3mg, Sodium 261mg, Total Carbohydrates 5g, Dietary Fiber 4g, Protein 6g

■ INGREDIENTS

2 lb trimmed broccoli rabe
3–4 tbsp extra virgin olive oil
4 tsp chopped garlic (6–8 cloves)
6–8 anchovy filets, chopped
4–5 pinches crushed red pepper (optional)
4 pinches black pepper
4 pinches of salt

■ DIRECTIONS

Boil water, cook broccoli rabe for 2–3 minutes, remove and place in ice water. Rough chop the rabe. Heat sauté pan, add extra virgin olive oil. Add garlic, anchovies, crushed red pepper, black pepper and salt. Stir, cook for 2 minutes. Add broccoli rabe, toss for 2–3 minutes and then serve.

Note: Anchovies are optional. You may add chopped black olives or capers. Use as a side dish, or it is great with pasta, grilled steak or grilled shrimp.

BRUSSELS SPROUTS ALA PROSCIUTTO

Prep time: 15 minutes
Ready in: 20 minutes
Serves: 8

This is a straightforward method of preparing and enjoying Brussels sprouts. You will enjoy the flavor and texture.

Nutritional Information

Serving Size: ⅛ recipe • Calories 109, Total Fat 6g, Saturated Fat 3g, Cholesterol 16mg, Sodium 231mg, Total Carbohydrates 9g, Dietary Fiber 3g, Protein 6g

■ INGREDIENTS

2 lb Brussels sprouts, trimmed, cleaned, halved
½ cup reduced fat sour cream
2 tsp horseradish
½ tsp Dijon mustard
2 pinches salt
4 pinches black pepper
1–2 tbsp Parmesan or cheddar cheese
6 slices Italian ham (prosciutto), crisped, chopped

■ DIRECTIONS

Steam sprouts for 6 minutes (may keep whole). Mix sour cream, horseradish, and mustard in a bowl. Add sprouts, toss well. Add salt and pepper as desired. May add red peppers, diced carrots for color. Sprinkle with Parmesan or cheddar cheese and chopped bacon.

Note: You can also sauté the sprouts with a little olive oil instead of steaming them. You may substitute pancetta or bacon for Italian ham.

CHICKPEA STEW

Prep time: 30 minutes
Ready in: 40 minutes
Serves: 8

Anything with chickpeas is good for you and me. Not only is it healthy, it is a great and easy dish to prepare. This is also a satisfying main dish for vegetarians. If you like cauliflower, this would be a great addition and it complements the entire dish.

Nutritional Information

Serving Size: ⅛ recipe • Calories 371, Total Fat 6g, Saturated Fat 1g, Cholesterol 0mg, Sodium 537mg, Total Carbohydrates 72g, Dietary Fiber 12g, Protein 12g

■ INGREDIENTS

2 tbsp olive oil
2 tsp cumin seed
1 large red onion chopped (2 cups)
6 cloves garlic chopped
1 tsp coriander
4 red potatoes, diced
4–5 cups chickpeas
2 cups hot water
4 tbsp chopped parsley
6 pinches each of salt and pepper
2 tomatoes chopped
Chopped parsley for garnish

■ DIRECTIONS

Heat oil, add cumin seed and cook for 10 seconds. Add onion and garlic and sauté for 4–5 minutes. Add coriander. Add potatoes; cook 2–3 minutes. Add chickpeas and water; cook for 15 minutes. Add parsley and bring to boil. Add 6 pinches of salt and 6 pinches of pepper. Add tomato, let simmer for 3 minutes, let sit for 5 minutes. Serve topped with chopped parsley.

Note: It is important to bring out the intense flavor of the cumin seeds, then follow the directions for cooking the potatoes through the remaining ingredients for great taste. It may be served a day or two later. Caution, the taste will intensify.

CHICKPEAS AND OKRA

Prep time: 20 minutes
Ready in: 25 minutes
Serves: 8

I love okra in season. The canned variety is ok, but frozen is better if fresh is out of season. Meat, like veal, may be roasted and then added to this stew to create a taste sensation.

Nutritional Information

Serving Size: ⅛ recipe • Calories 134, Total Fat 6g, Saturated Fat 2g, Cholesterol 4mg, Sodium 314mg, Total Carbohydrates 18g, Dietary Fiber 4g, Protein 4g

■ INGREDIENTS

1 lb okra
2 tbsp vegetable oil (blended oil)
1 tbsp butter
1 onion chopped
1 tsp garlic chopped
2 slices ginger
1 green chili pepper, chopped
1 tbsp chopped cilantro
1 tsp cumin
1 lb chickpeas, cooked and drained

■ DIRECTIONS

Trim, clean and cut okra. Heat oil and butter. Saute onion and garlic. Add ginger and chili pepper. Add okra and cilantro and cumin. Add chickpeas. Stir and simmer for 3–5 minutes.

Note: Add to rice as a main meal or serve as a side dish for lamb and fish dishes. Chopped, fresh tomato adds a whole other dimension to this dish.

Classic Stuffed Grape Leaves
Vegetarian

Prep time: 35 minutes
Ready in: 55 minutes
Serves: 10

How many can you eat in one sitting!? Sorry, this is one food I can't pass on because I only get to eat it from time to time. You will enjoy this as an appetizer, a side dish or as a meal.

Nutritional Information

Serving Size: ⅒ recipe • Calories 112, Total Fat 6g, Saturated Fat 1g, Cholesterol 0mg, Sodium 647mg, Total Carbohydrates 13g, Dietary Fiber 1g, Protein 2g

■ INGREDIENTS

4 tbsp of olive oil
3 cups diced white onions
1 cup brown rice
½ cup of water
¼ tsp sugar
½ tsp of black pepper
½ tsp cayenne
1 tbsp mint
2 tbsp chopped parsley
½ cup lemon juice
3 tbsp tomato sauce (no salt added)
1 quart of grape leaves in brine, drained

■ DIRECTIONS

Sauté onions in olive oil. Add other ingredients (except lemon juice and tomato sauce) and cook on medium heat 3 minutes (cover half way through). Simmer for 3 minutes on low heat for 3 minutes or until liquid boils away. Remove stuffing and cool down enough to handle. Spoon and roll appropriate amount of rice filling into leaves to form log-like shapes. Place filled leaves on bottom of deep pan and stack; pour in a small amount of water, enough to cover top layer. Mix lemon juice and tomato sauce and pour on top. Place heat-safe heavy dish on top of the grape leaves, so they don't float and come apart during cooking. Simmer for 20–25 minutes on medium to low heat until all liquid is absorbed and rice is cooked through and tender. Let stand before serving. Serve with lemon wedges, yogurt and fresh Greek salad.

Note: This is one of my mom's favorites because it was her way of getting all the kids to enjoy the time making the leaves. We used to hide a piece of the leaf stem inside the stuffing and choose or celebrate the winner who found it in their stuffed leaves. You see, that was a huge and fun-filled meal, and it was healthy for all of us, too!

Eggplant and Chickpea Sauté

Prep time: 20 minutes
Ready in: 35 minutes
Serves: 10

No doubt, this is and always was one of my favorite dishes for our vegetarian clients. Everyone enjoys it. Yes, you need to chop a few things but wait until you see what awaits you at the end. No way will you miss meat. This is perfect for any reason in any season.

Nutritional Information

Serving Size: 1/10 recipe • Calories 280, Total Fat 10g, Saturated Fat 2g, Cholesterol 2mg, Sodium 449mg, Total Carbohydrates 40g, Dietary Fiber 11g, Protein 9g

■ INGREDIENTS

4–5 tbsp of extra virgin olive oil
One large fresh eggplant cut in cubes
4–5 large cloves of garlic chopped
2 cups of chopped white onion (one large onion)
4 cups of ready-made tomato sauce or marinara
4 cups of cooked and drained chickpeas
8 pinches each of cumin, coriander, cinnamon
2 pinches each of kosher sea salt and black pepper

■ DIRECTIONS

Heat extra virgin olive oil in sauté pan. Add eggplant and cook until tender for 5 minutes on high. Add garlic and onion; stir and mix well 3 minutes. Add tomato sauce, reduce temperature to medium. Add chickpeas, stir well. Add spices, salt and pepper, and stir again. Cover and simmer for 10–12 minutes, stirring well every 3–5 minutes.

Note: May serve with couscous, rice pilaf or vegetable orzo pilaf or as a main dish with caramelized onions. Enjoy this heart-healthy dish. To avoid sticking, serve hot.

Eggplant and Tomato Feta

Prep time: 20 minutes
Ready in: 35 minutes
Serves: 8

Amazing—looks good, tastes great and you can bet you will impress your guests.

Nutritional Information

Serving Size: ⅛ recipe • Calories 208, Total Fat 17g, Saturated Fat 4g, Cholesterol 9mg, Sodium 121mg, Total Carbohydrates 12g, Dietary Fiber 4g, Protein 3g

■ INGREDIENTS

½ cup extra virgin olive oil
1 grilled eggplant (sliced into discs)
1 onion, chopped
3–4 cloves garlic, chopped
2 medium ripe tomatoes, chopped
½ tsp oregano (6–8 pinches)
½ tsp thyme (6–8 pinches)
1 cup tomato (marinara) sauce,
     homemade
2 tbsp fresh parsley, chopped
Feta cheese
Salt and pepper to taste

■ DIRECTIONS

Brush eggplant with olive oil and grill on both sides. Remove eggplant and put in roasting pan. In a skillet, add oil and sauté onions, garlic, fresh tomato and marinara. Add seasoning and parsley. Adjust to taste. Preheat oven to 325°–350°. Bake for 5–10 minutes. Remove and top with feta cheese. Pile sauté on top and center of eggplant. Serve hot.

Note: Use and serve as an appetizer or side vegetable dish. You can even use it as a main entrée. Just add some roasted red peppers, artichokes or even Kalamata olives, capers or sautéed onion for a great new taste.

Eggplant Lasagna

Prep time: 15 minutes
Ready in: 45 minutes
Serves: 10

Forget pasta?! Maybe, why not eggplant, squash or zucchini—you know,
those ones that got away and grew
big in your garden! Slicing them
lengthwise makes a whole new
world of lasagna, trust me.

Nutritional Information

Serving Size: 1/10 recipe • Calories 165, Total Fat 8g, Saturated Fat 4g, Cholesterol 24mg, Sodium 224mg, Total Carbohydrates 13g, Dietary Fiber 4g, Protein 11g

■ INGREDIENTS

1 large eggplant sliced the long way
½ cup roasted red peppers, sliced
½ cup artichokes, quartered
1 cup ricotta cheese, part skim
¼ cup Parmesan cheese
3 cups homemade sauce or your favorite
    jarred marinara sauce
½ cup mozzarella cheese, part skim

■ DIRECTIONS

Layer the first 5 ingredients in a large baking dish in an alternating fashion. Try to put the heavier ingredients (eggplant) towards the bottom. Top with sauce and Parmesan cheese. Finish with sauce and mozzarella cheese. Bake at 350° for 25–30 minutes. Let rest for 10–15 minutes and then serve.

Note: You may add the chicken to make it a meat and vegetable dish. Lasagna is traditionally made with pasta. Here you can add chicken and incorporate two favorite ingredients, chicken and eggplant, to satisfy anyone at a dinner party.

Eggplant Roulade

Prep time: 25 minutes
Ready in: 35 minutes
Serves: 10

This variation on eggplant lasagna or pasta filled rolls may be served as an appetizer, side dish or entrée.

Nutritional Information

Serving Size: ¹⁄₁₀ recipe • Calories 412, Total Fat 22g, Saturated Fat 7g, Cholesterol 91mg, Sodium 507mg, Total Carbohydrates 37g, Dietary Fiber 7g, Protein 19g

■ INGREDIENTS

Sliced eggplant (lengthwise)
1 cup all purpose flour (or whole wheat flour)
2 eggs (egg wash—eggs and a little water)
1 cup seasoned bread crumbs (Italian flavors)
½ cup olive oil in a spray bottle
6 cups of marinara sauce (no salt added)
½ cup grated cheese for sprinkling

Filling

2 cups ricotta cheese, part skim
½ cup mozzarella cheese, part skim
½ cup Parmesan cheese
1 tbsp garlic, chopped
¼ cup parsley
1 egg, beaten
4 pinches of pepper
1 tsp oregano
3–4 oz fresh spinach
3–4 roasted red peppers, quartered lengthwise

■ DIRECTIONS

Dredge eggplant slices in flour, then eggs, then press into breadcrumbs. Spray with olive oil and bake in a 350° oven for 8–10 minutes. Remove and cool. For filling, in a mixing bowl add ricotta, mozzarella, Parmesan, garlic, parsley and egg. Season with sea salt, pepper and oregano to taste. Spoon some of the cheese mixture into the middle of each strip on eggplant. Top with spinach and roasted red peppers, and roll up. Place in bottom of a baking pan brushed with olive oil. Top with marinara and sprinkle with grated cheese. Bake in a preheated oven at 325° for 12–15 minutes. Remove and let stand, then serve.

Note: It is a little extra work, yet it is a nice way to offer a different variation on a popular taste. You may add artichokes, roasted onions and even shrimp for a more exotic dish.

FALAFEL– DRIED BEANS CROQUETTE

Prep time: 25 minutes
Ready in: 40 minutes
Serves: 10

These spicy fried "balls" or fritters are typically made from chickpeas, but dried fava beans or a combination of both have been used. It is great as an appetizer, sandwich or even as a stuffing for vegetables.

Nutritional Information

Serving Size: 1/10 recipe • Calories 266, Total Fat 23g, Saturated Fat 2g, Cholesterol 0mg, Sodium 72mg, Total Carbohydrates 12g, Dietary Fiber 3g, Protein 4g

■ INGREDIENTS

2 cups dried chickpeas, washed, cleaned and soaked in lots of water for 10–12 hours
1 medium onion, finely chopped or processed
3–4 garlic cloves, crushed
1 tsp each cumin, coriander
¼ tsp each salt and ground pepper
1 tbsp chopped fresh dill or dry
1 cup chopped fresh parsley or dry
½ tsp cayenne pepper
Vegetable oil for frying (approx. 4 cups)

■ DIRECTIONS

Drain chickpeas and place in food processor until a paste forms. Place in a large mixing bowl and add the onions, garlic, cumin, coriander, salt and pepper, dill, parsley and cayenne pepper. Mix well into a firm paste. Using a small ice cream scooper, form into small balls. In a deep pan, heat vegetable oil. Fry the falafel balls until golden brown. They will float to the top. Remove and drain on a paper towel. Serve in pita bread with salad and tahini sauce.

Note: Serve as a sandwich with pita or a wrap and drizzle with tahini sauce or garlic yogurt dressing. You may also serve falafel over a salad with chickpeas, tomato, and cucumber with a drizzle of tahini.

Garlic Rosemary Roasted "New" Potatoes

Prep time: 5 minutes
Ready in: 45 minutes
Serves: 8

If you like potatoes, this is a great alternative to baked potatoes with butter and sour cream.

■ INGREDIENTS

3 lb small red potatoes, cleaned and trimmed
5 cloves fresh garlic, cleaned and finely diced
1 medium onion, cleaned and sliced
¼ cup olive oil
2 tsp rosemary leaves
¼ tsp black pepper
1 tsp sea salt

Nutritional Information

Serving Size: ⅛ recipe • Calories 221, Total Fat 7g, Saturated Fat 1g, Cholesterol 0mg, Sodium 312mg, Total Carbohydrates 35g, Dietary Fiber 3g, Protein 4g

■ DIRECTIONS

Preheat oven to 375°. Wash the red potatoes and place in baking pan. Rub with diced garlic. Add the sliced onions and olive oil. Sprinkle with rosemary leaves, black pepper, and salt. Place pan in oven and bake 45 minutes until tender. Serve hot.

Note: Should you have access to white and red, or even purple small potatoes, following the same method, you will have a medley of roasted potatoes. Hint: Use the leftovers in soup, frittatas or even salad.

Glazed Orange Carrots

Prep time: 15 minutes
Ready in: 20 minutes
Serves: 8

Inspired by other Moroccan dishes, this simple dish is delicious with many savory couscous and spicy meat dishes.

Nutritional Information

Serving Size: ⅛ recipe • Calories 94, Total Fat 5g, Saturated Fat 2g, Cholesterol 8mg, Sodium 66mg, Total Carbohydrates 13g, Dietary Fiber 3g, Protein 1g

■ INGREDIENTS

1 lb carrots peeled and cut into small
   rounds
1 tbsp olive oil
2 tbsp butter (melted)
1½ cups chopped onions
2 tbsp brown sugar
¼ tsp cinnamon
Juice of 1 orange
Rind of 1 orange

■ DIRECTIONS

Bring carrots to a boil until tender, drain and set aside. In a saucepan heat the oil and butter and sauté the onions. Add the carrots to the onions and toss for 2–3 minutes. Add the brown sugar, cinnamon, orange juice and zest. Reduce heat and sauté for an additional 3–5 minutes.

Note: This could be served as a side dish with fish, chicken, or whatever you please. Any leftover carrots may be used as soup by adding a vegetable or chicken stock. Bring to a boil and puree with a hand-held electric beater or immersion blender until you reach a creamy consistency. Enjoy!

GLAZED ROOTS WITH CINNAMON AND WALNUTS

Prep time: 20 minutes
Ready in: 35 minutes
Serves: 8

Choose your roots! Their great, earthy taste combines well with cinnamon, nuts and dry fruit to make a seasonal fall dish.

Nutritional Information

Serving Size: ⅛ recipe • Calories 322, Total Fat 8g, Saturated Fat 2g, Cholesterol 8mg, Sodium 108mg, Total Carbohydrates 61g, Dietary Fiber 10g, Protein 4g

■ INGREDIENTS

Hot water
3–4 lb assorted cleaned, peeled, chopped
    roots including sweet potatoes,
    turnips, butternut squash and carrots
1 cup apple cider
½ cup brown sugar
2 tbsp butter
½ cup coarsely chopped walnuts
8–10 pinches cinnamon
Handful of dry cranberries, Craisins, or
    raisins

■ DIRECTIONS

Boil roots 6–8 minutes, remove, drain. In saucepan, add roots, apple cider, brown sugar, butter, and walnuts. Cook for 6 minutes, stir until soft (add 6 pinches of salt and pepper if needed). Sprinkle with cinnamon. Sprinkle with Craisins and serve.

Note: All you have to do is be right about your roots and make this dish to impress those Thanksgiving guests or your family any day of the season.

GREEK TIROPITA

Prep time: 25 minutes
Ready in: 45 minutes
Serves: 15

This is a creamy and tangy cheese pie, similar in preparation to the spanokopita dish but it incorporates delicious cheeses that result in a wonderful crispy pie.

Nutritional Information

Serving Size: ⅟₁₅ recipe • Calories 372, Total Fat 30g, Saturated Fat 15g, Cholesterol 125mg, Sodium 671mg, Total Carbohydrates 13g, Dietary Fiber 1g, Protein 13g

■ INGREDIENTS

1 lb feta cheese
1 lb ricotta cheese, part skim
½ lb cream cheese, softened
½ cup grated cheese (Kefalotiri or Parmesan)
4–6 eggs
½ cup parsley
1 tsp dried mint
1 tsp grated nutmeg
8 tbsp each of unsalted butter and olive oil
1 lb filo (12–14 sheets)

■ DIRECTIONS

Combine all cheese and eggs in a mixing bowl to make a paste. Add parsley, mint and nutmeg and mix well. Melt butter and olive oil in a small pan. Cut filo in one-third strips lengthwise. Brush with melted butter. Add one heaping teaspoon of filling close to one end of strip. Fold filo over filling and then fold in sides, fold from edge to edge to make a triangle, tucking end in and placing open end on buttered cookie sheet. Repeat above with each strip. Brush with melted butter. Bake at 350° 20 to 25 minutes until golden brown. Let rest for 5–10 minutes then serve.

Note: If Kefalotiri (Greek cheese) is not available, use a good Romano cheese. Another variation is to use cottage cheese in place of ricotta. To make the pie in a baking pan, follow the same procedures as spanokopita.

GRILLED EGGPLANT WITH TOMATO FETA SAUTÉ

Prep time: 30 minutes
Ready in: 45 minutes
Serves: 8

This tasty variation on a popular Turkish dish offers rich taste and yet may be used as a lighter appetizer or as a topping for a salad. It looks good, tastes great, and you can bet that you will impress your guests.

Nutritional Information

Serving Size: ⅛ recipe • Calories 167, Total Fat 9g, Saturated Fat 3g, Cholesterol 13mg, Sodium 327mg, Total Carbohydrates 20g, Dietary Fiber 9g, Protein 6g

■ INGREDIENTS

2 or 3 fresh eggplant
3 tbsp extra virgin olive oil
1 large onion chopped
3–4 garlic cloves chopped
1 cup chopped roasted or grilled red bell pepper
1 lb fresh chopped ripe tomato
1 cup tomato sauce or marinara
¼ tsp each of dried oregano, thyme and basil
¼ cup fresh chopped parsley
¾ cup crumbled feta cheese
Salt and pepper to taste, optional

■ DIRECTIONS

Preheat oven to 375°. Trim and cut eggplant into round slices, brush lightly with olive oil, and grill for one minute on each side. Arrange in one layer in a roasting pan and set aside. In a sauté pan, heat 3 tbsp olive oil and sauté onions, garlic, the roasted red peppers, fresh tomato, and tomato sauce. Stir in the spices (oregano, thyme and basil). Cook for 5–10 minutes until tender. Add the chopped parsley and stir. Scoop a tbsp on top of each grilled eggplant, then top each with a tsp of feta cheese. Leave in a closed grill for 5–10 minutes or in an oven at 375° for 5–10 minutes. Serve hot or warm as an appetizer or with a sassy salad for lunch or a healthy dinner.

Note: If you use feta cheese or Kalamata olives then skip the salt entirely. You may use this as a warm entrée. Just add artichoke hearts, Kalamata olives and capers. Caramelized onion as a topping will add a whole new dimension and taste.

MOROCCAN STEW

Prep time: 25 minutes
Ready in: 45 minutes
Serves: 12

Couscous is considered the national dish of Morocco. This is another way to stew vegetables and serve with couscous. The use of numerous vegetables in this dish makes it worthwhile for the effort you put into it. It is a one pot meal and easy to make for a crowd.

Nutritional Information

Serving Size: ¹⁄₁₂ recipe • Calories 178, Total Fat 3g, Saturated Fat 0g, Cholesterol 0mg, Sodium 149mg, Total Carbohydrates 36g, Dietary Fiber 6g, Protein 5g

■ INGREDIENTS

2 tbsp olive oil
3 cups chopped onions
3 cloves garlic, minced
1 tsp each cumin, cinnamon, turmeric, cayenne
½ tsp paprika
1 cup sliced carrots
3 cups butternut squash, cooked
1 cup potatoes, cubed
2 cups eggplant, cubed
1 each green and red pepper, sliced
4 cups sliced zucchini and/or yellow squash
2 large tomatoes, chopped
2 cups cooked garbanzo beans, liquid reserved
1 pinch saffron
¾ cup dried currants or raisins
2 cups slivered spinach
¼ cup each of chopped spinach, chopped parsley and scallions

■ DIRECTIONS

Heat olive oil in a heavy-bottomed stew pot with onions and sauté 2–3 minutes. Add garlic and spices, (except saffron) stirring continuously. Add vegetables in order listed, giving each one enough time to cook until color deepens. Stir in the beans, saffron and currants. If stew is dry, add tomato juice or bean liquid. Cover and simmer until vegetables are tender. Add slivered spinach and let simmer for 2–3 minutes. Serve topped with chopped spinach, parsley and scallions.

Note: This dish can also be served with a cucumber yogurt sauce. See recipe.

Okra Tomato Tagine

Prep time: 35 minutes
Ready in: 30 minutes
Serves: 8

Okra is one of the most overlooked vegetables. People don't know a lot about what to do with it. Here is one great way to combine it with tomato, garlic and cilantro.

Nutritional Information

Serving Size: ⅛ recipe • Calories 116, Total Fat 7g, Saturated Fat 1g, Cholesterol 0mg, Sodium 13mg, Total Carbohydrates 12g, Dietary Fiber 4g, Protein 3g

■ INGREDIENTS

1 lb fresh okra
6 large tomatoes
2 medium or 1 large onion
4 tbsp extra virgin olive oil
2 tbsp cilantro, chopped
2 tbsp each chopped garlic, hot peppers
1 tsp hot paprika
Juice of ½ lemon
Marinara sauce (if desired)

■ DIRECTIONS

Clean okra and cut into 1 inch pieces, on the bias. Chop tomatoes into 1 inch pieces. Chop half the onion into ½-inch pieces, slice the remaining onion. Place 2 tbsp oil into skillet, heat medium. Add chopped onion and sauté. Place remaining oil into another skillet, heat to medium and add the sliced onion. Sauté until caramelized (add a little water if necessary); set aside and keep warm. Add cilantro, garlic, hot peppers, and paprika if desired, to the chopped onions. Continue to sauté. Add okra, tomatoes and lemon juice. If you like it saucy, add 1–2 cups marinara sauce. Simmer for 20–30 minutes. Place in a serving bowl, topping with sliced onions. Garnish with toasted slices almonds if desired.

Note: This can also be served on top of rice, as a side dish with a meat, or you can make a soup out of it. You can also cook with veal shanks or lamb chops for additional flavor.

PORTOBELLO MUSHROOM DISH

Prep time: 10 minutes
Ready in: 20 minutes
Serves: 6

One of the favorite appetizers at the restaurant is a baked portobello mushroom with roasted peppers, chopped tomato, and goat cheese. Here it is. Enjoy.

Nutritional Information

Serving Size: ⅙ recipe • Calories 96, Total Fat 7g, Saturated Fat 3g, Cholesterol 8mg, Sodium 90mg, Total Carbohydrates 6g, Dietary Fiber 2g, Protein 4g

■ INGREDIENTS

Olive oil to drizzle
6 portobello mushroom caps
1 cup roasted red peppers, chopped
1 medium ripened tomato, chopped
Goat cheese or feta cheese
3 cloves garlic, chopped
2 tbsp basil pesto

■ DIRECTIONS

Drizzle portobello mushroom caps with oil. Spoon the roasted peppers, tomato, goat cheese, and garlic into the center of the mushroom. Drizzle with pesto. Bake in preheated oven at 300° for 8–10 minutes. Serve hot as an appetizer or on top of mixed greens.

Note: Artichoke hearts may be added for a heartier appetizer or meal. A drizzle of balsamic vinegar adds a tasty and flavorful dimension to the dish. Grill jumbo shrimp and place on top with lemon wedges and serve on the center of the plate.

SPANAKOPITA

Prep time: 25 minutes
Ready in: 50 minutes
Serves: 15

A classic Greek spinach and feta cheese pie—one of the most popular in the restaurant and at catered functions. Always a hit.

Nutritional Information

Serving Size: ¹⁄₁₅ recipe • Calories 295, Total Fat 19g, Saturated Fat 8g, Cholesterol 74mg, Sodium 469mg, Total Carbohydrates 21g, Dietary Fiber 1g, Protein 10g

■ INGREDIENTS

4 tbsp olive oil
½ onion chopped
1 tbsp garlic
2 1-lb bags spinach, chopped
4 scallions chopped
1 tsp mint
4 pinches each of black pepper and
    nutmeg to taste
3 eggs, lightly beaten
1½ cups crumbled feta
2 cups ricotta cheese, part skim milk
Equal amounts of extra virgin olive oil and
    butter (¼ cup of each for brushing)
Filo dough (24 sheets)

■ DIRECTIONS

Heat oil and sauté onions and garlic. Clean and add spinach, cook for 3 minutes. Add scallions, mint and spices to spinach. Add egg and cheeses, then mix well. Cook for 3–5 minutes and then cool to room temperature. Melt butter and oil in saucepan. Brush bottom of baking pan. Line the bottom and sides of the pan with 4 sheets of filo. Spoon spinach mix into pan, cover with 1 sheet of filo. Then brush filo with butter and oil. Continue layering filo, one sheet at a time, using 5–6 filo sheets, brushing each sheet with butter and oil. Continue to brush each sheet. Fold inward any overlapping filo. Brush with butter mix and trim pastry around pan. Cut surface into 3 inch squares, then triangles and bake for 30–35 minutes at 375° or until golden brown. Let rest for 5–10 minutes, then serve.

Note: You also can make individual servings by cutting filo into strips and following the same directions as the tyropita triangles recipe.

SPINACH AND CHICKPEA WITH COUSCOUS

Prep time: 15 minutes
Ready in: 25 minutes
Serves: 8

Makes for a hearty meal or by adding sautéed shrimp or seared scallops. Couscous, fine or thicker Israeli couscous are cooked and prepared differently.

Nutritional Information

Serving Size: ⅛ recipe • Calories 247, Total Fat 11g, Saturated Fat 1g, Cholesterol 0mg, Sodium 285mg, Total Carbohydrates 33g, Dietary Fiber 4g, Protein 8g

■ INGREDIENTS

2 cups low sodium chicken stock
2 cups couscous (fine)
2 tbsp extra virgin olive oil
10 oz chopped spinach (may use Swiss chard)
3 cloves of garlic
1 16-oz can cooked chickpeas
½ cup raisins or currents
½ cup chopped parsley
1 pinch each cumin, black pepper, cayenne pepper
4 pinches of kosher sea salt
½ cup toasted pine nuts

■ DIRECTIONS

Bring stock to boil. Steam couscous by adding stock to couscous and cover 2–3 minutes. Use a fork to fluff couscous. Preheat saucepan, add oil and spinach and wilt down. Add garlic, chickpeas and raisins, parsley when spinach is wilted. Add spices and salt. Cook all until tender and serve alongside steamed couscous, topped with toasted pine nuts.

Note: Frozen spinach or Swiss chard may be used for quick execution. Larger couscous may require additional stock or water to ensure tenderness.

Spinach Korma

Prep time: 15 minutes
Ready in: 25 minutes
Serves: 8

This is one of the most requested dishes during our cooking classes. It is so simple, yet delivers a huge taste. It's just incredible.

Nutritional Information

Serving Size: ⅛ recipe • Calories 145, Total Fat 8g, Saturated Fat 1g, Cholesterol 0mg, Sodium 466mg, Total Carbohydrates 17g, Dietary Fiber 5g, Protein 5g

■ INGREDIENTS

3–4 tbsp canola oil or olive oil
1 cup onion, finely chopped
1 cup red pepper, diced
1 cup green pepper, diced
4–5 cloves garlic, chopped
4 cups frozen spinach, thawed and
　　drained
1 cup tomato sauce (chili sauce or
　　ketchup)
7–8 pinches each of cayenne pepper,
　　cumin, coriander, and pepper to taste
3–4 pinches kosher sea salt

■ DIRECTIONS

In a large skillet, add oil and sauté onion, peppers, and garlic for 3–5 minutes. Add frozen spinach and cook 3–5 minutes. Add tomato sauce and mix well; cook until vegetables are tender. Add spices. Keep an eye on cayenne pepper for degree of hotness. Simmer 5–10 minutes. Serve hot.

Note: You may substitute mushrooms for peppers and can add cooked chickpeas for texture and flavor. Cayenne pepper can make this spicy hot so start with a little and add as you like. Serve with basmati rice.

SPINACH WITH RAISINS AND PINE NUTS

Prep time: 10 minutes
Ready in: 15 minutes
Serves: 8

A great side dish that combines the sweetness of raisins and the nutty flavors of pine nuts.

Nutritional Information

Serving Size: ⅛ recipe • Calories 111, Total Fat 8g, Saturated Fat 1g, Cholesterol 0mg, Sodium 93mg, Total Carbohydrates 9g, Dietary Fiber 2g, Protein 3g

■ INGREDIENTS

⅓ cup raisins
3 tbsp extra virgin olive oil
¼ cup pine nuts
20 oz (2 bags) fresh spinach
2–4 cloves garlic chopped
4 pinches of sea salt
4 pinches of pepper
Homemade croutons or pita chips
   (optional)

■ DIRECTIONS

Soak raisins in warm water for 5 minutes, drain. Heat oil, sauté pine nuts until golden brown, remove and set aside. Add spinach and garlic until wilted in the same saucepan. Toss in raisins and season with salt and pepper. Remove and serve on a platter. Sprinkle with pine nuts and bread croutons or pita chips.

Note: Great as a side dish or even as a snack. For another twist, top with an orange zest. Also, you may use as a filling for pie crust, make empanadillas or in a filo casserole.

VEGETABLE CASSEROLE

Prep time: 20 minutes
Ready in: 35 minutes
Serves: 8

Root vegetables are a must for me, regardless of preparation. They are tasty, earthy and compliment many of the hearty poultry dishes.

Nutritional Information

Serving Size: ⅛ recipe • Calories 153, Total Fat 7g, Saturated Fat 2g, Cholesterol 8mg, Sodium 115mg, Total Carbohydrates 22g, Dietary Fiber 5g, Protein 2g

■ INGREDIENTS

¾ lb carrots
6 small white turnips
2 tbsp butter
2 tbsp olive oil
¼ cup low sodium chicken stock
1 tbsp light brown sugar
Sea salt and pepper to taste
¾ cup frozen peas (see note)
4 tsp chopped fresh dill (see note)

■ DIRECTIONS

Clean and peel carrots, cut approximately 2 inches long. Cook in boiling water until tender. Quarter and peel turnips, trim in oval shapes and cook in boiling water until tender. Heat butter and oil in large skillet and toss carrots and turnips until well coated. Add stock, sugar, salt and pepper, cook over moderate heat until liquid evaporates and vegetables are glazed. Add peas and dill and heat for another 2–3 minutes. Serve hot as a side dish.

Note: This could be done a day ahead. Just reheat and add peas and dill the day you're serving the dish. As a variation, include sweet potatoes, butternut squash or any other favorite root vegetable.

VEGETABLE KORMA

Prep time: 30 minutes
Ready in: 35 minutes
Serves: 10

This is inspired by North African and Eastern Mediterranean infusion of flavors. The larger the amounts you make, the more leftover stew to have with other meal options. Try couscous.

Nutritional Information

Serving Size: ¹/₁₀ recipe • Calories 178, Total Fat 6g, Saturated Fat 1g, Cholesterol 0mg, Sodium 192mg, Total Carbohydrates 29g, Dietary Fiber 4g, Protein 4g

■ INGREDIENTS

¼ cup corn oil, or vegetable oil, or canola oil
1 white onion, chopped
2 carrots, peeled and cut into wheels
3 cloves of chopped garlic
2 sweet potatoes, diced in 1-inch cubes
2 potatoes, peeled and diced
1 red pepper, cleaned and cut into medium size pieces
1 green pepper, cleaned and cut into medium size pieces
2 tomatoes, cored and cut
1 red onion, chopped
1 head of broccoli, cleaned, using crowns and stems
4 oz prepared ketchup or chili sauce
4 pinches kosher sea salt
4 pinches white pepper
4 pinches cumin
4 pinches coriander

■ DIRECTIONS

In a large pot, sauté onions, carrots and garlic in oil. Add remaining vegetables, stir for 3–5 minutes. Add just enough water to cover. Bring pot to a boil. Add ketchup and mix well. Add salt, pepper, and spices. Stir well, let simmer over medium heat 25–30 minutes. Serve with rice pilaf or your favorite chicken or lamb dish.

Note: You should start with those vegetables that are of root origin since it takes longer for them to cook, followed by the remaining ingredients, spices and liquids. The infusion of taste is awesome. Take it all in.

Vegetarian Baked Kibbee BiSanieh

Prep time: 20 minutes
Ready in: 35 minutes
Serves: 8

The bride and groom are vegetarian, so we came up with this variation on the traditional kibbee dish with no animal ingredients whatsoever. It made the local paper.

Nutritional Information

Serving Size: ⅛ recipe • Calories 153, Total Fat 7g, Saturated Fat 2g, Cholesterol 8mg, Sodium 115mg, Total Carbohydrates 22g, Dietary Fiber 5g, Protein 2g

■ INGREDIENTS

1 medium eggplant
3 lbs. potatoes
3 tbsp olive oil
1½ cups chopped onions
½ cup pine nuts
1 tsp allspice
¼ tsp ground cinnamon
1 tsp sea salt or to taste
1 tsp freshly ground black pepper
¼ cup cooked chickpeas
2 tbsp chopped parsley
1 tsp olive oil
1½ cups fine bulgur wheat
½ cup cold water
2 cups finely minced onion
½ tsp sumac
Additional pine nuts for topping

Note: A great variation of the original classic kibbee dish. This was very successful and when we make it at the restaurant, our customers appreciate the great combination of herbs, spices and the vegetables, which all come together.

■ DIRECTIONS

Stuffing

Peel eggplant and cut into long slices (¼ inch thick). Oil the base of a baking sheet and add a layer of eggplant brushed with olive oil and bake until soft and tender (8-10 minutes in 350° oven). Repeat this step to bake all of the eggplant. Set aside. Boil potatoes until firm yet tender. Peel and cut ½ the amount in to very small pieces; set remaining half aside for kibbee. Sauté 1½ cups chopped onions in 3 tbsp olive oil until tender. Add pine nuts until they turn light golden color (you may do this separately). Add allspice, cinnamon, ½ tsp each salt and pepper and set aside. Add chickpeas, potato pieces and parsley to the sautéed onions and spices mixture, stirring well; set aside to cool.

Kibbee

Peel remaining potatoes and mash in food processor. Add 1 tsp of oil and some water to moisten. In a mixing bowl, soak bulgur with ½ cup cold water and set aside for 15 minutes. Mix mashed potatoes with minced onions, then combine with the softened bulghur wheat and mix thoroughly. Working the mixture with hands, add ½ tsp salt and ½ tsp pepper and knead into a soft doughy mixture. Divide the dough in half. Oil the bottom and sides of a 9 by 12 inch baking pan. Evenly spread half the potato and bulgur mixture on the bottom; smooth by hand. Place one or two layers of baked eggplant on top and sprinkle with sumac. Add the stuffing mixture, spreading evenly. Add the rest of the potato bulgur mixture, smoothing the top using a few drops of chilled water. Score the top by cutting the layers into square or diamond shapes. Sprinkle with pine nuts. Bake in a preheated oven at 350° for 25 minutes.

Practical Tips and Strategies for Heart Healthy Eating

Get to know you

- Find out what works for you and find the healthy way to cook and eat. Then commit and stay there.
- What are your daily eating habits? Question the routine and identify then reduce your personal pitfalls.
- Small changes are key, but don't make huge sacrifices. Remember the 80/20 rule, perhaps it's the 20% of the food you eat that you need to worry about, because the other 80% may be just fine.
- Adopt what I call the 10:1 ratio—for every 10% reduction in bad calories you should be able to permanently reduce 1 lb of body fat (weight) over a short period of time, e.g., 30 days.
- Apply consistently and in consultations with your dietician or physician. You should be able to reduce 200 calories a day and lose 20 pounds in a short order and permanently.

Think green, and give red, orange, and other colors a chance

- Don't only focus on the center of the plate, e.g., the main protein on your menu, but also focus on the side dishes you are serving with it.
- Boost your meal with varying color vegetables. Dare to think outside the "crate" and add spinach, collards, garlic, broccoli, fennel, beets, and yellow squash.
- Put your greens in soups, add to rice, bake in casseroles and simmer in stews.
- Boost a meal with healthful servings of vegetables to reduce calories from fat and feel better.
- Frozen vegetables (preferably unprepared) might do the trick when short on time, and they are hassle free for a quick meal.

Think lean and bean then mean it!

- When I think lean I tend to add more grains, nuts, seeds, green leafy vegetables (less starchy vegetables), and fruits, rather than lean steak, hamburger, pork roast or fatty steak.
- Lean means to get down with beans (whole grain, oatmeal, brown rice and whole wheat which are high in fiber and vitamins, especially vitamins B and E).

- Beans are full of fiber, protein, iron, folic acid and are a good source of omega-3 fatty acids.
- Grains and legumes are easy to prepare, fun to have and produces a big bang for the buck both health wise and pocketbook wise.
- Use fortified cereals, a variety of beans, grains and add your favorite nuts like almonds, walnuts and pine nuts.

Get the facts on fats

- The wording and terminology of what the fats are is very confusing to all of us.
- All fats (saturated) have more calories per gram than carbohydrates or protein, almost a 2:1 ratio.
- The golden rule, decrease fat to maintain or lose weight.
- Polyunsaturated and monosaturated are considered good fats with lots of health benefits (e.g., olive oil, nuts, vegetable oil, oily fish).
- Omega-3 reduces the risk of heart disease and is associated with numerous health gains.
- Saturated or trans fats are bad fats (e.g., dairy, beef, pork, palm and coconut oil, French fries, and baked products).
- The U.S. Food and Drug Administration mandates that everything should have clear labels including the reduction of the amount of trans fats. Products that contain .5 grams or less trans fats per serving are allowed to be labeled as 0 trans fats. Read the label: hydrogenated or partially hydrogenated vegetable oil is a trans fat.

What's in a portion?

- A portion is the amount of food you consume at a meal time. That is not the serving size. If you're starving, you could eat more than a serving size until you are full. Serving size is a unit of measure to calculate nutritional facts.
- Reduce the portion size each time you eat. Be inspired to eat less because you know you can eat again for sure.
- When eating out, avoid large portions or supersizing. The larger the portion, the more likely they include more fat, sodium and sugar than you need.
- Be inquisitive and be aware of how your food is prepared. Ask questions of your server.
- Take half of your meal home or share it with others.

Don't fill up on beverages

- Eat your calories, don't drink them. You eat the same amount of food even when you drink a 150-calorie drink. Growing up, we drank only water before, during and after a meal.

He who has health has hope, and he who has hope has everything.

Be a savvy shopper

- The core of the store is a bore. It is typically filled with canned and boxed products.
- Know your grocery store layout and bypass those sections with food products to avoid.
- Resist temptations and avoid middle isles, processed foods, trans fats, sugar, and sodium.
- Read the label, both the front and back, of each product and compare the nutritional facts, not just the dollar value of the item.
- Know the meaning of "reduced" or "less" on the labels of products you purchase. Sodium or other flavoring agents are added to compensate for taste.
  1000mg calcium—bone health
  25g fiber—heart/diabetes
  210mg magnesium—muscles/nerves (nuts, bran, fish)
  4700mg potassium—blood pressure (yogurt, bananas, tomatoes)
  2310mg vitamin A—vision (leafy vegetables, greens)
  25mg vitamin C—immune system (fruit, vegetables)
  15mg vitamin E—(fortified cereal, peanut butter)

What to do to avoid overeating

- Eat slowly and enjoy your food more. It takes 20 minutes for your stomach to tell the brain that you are full.
- Eat a salad or soup or drink water before and during your main meal.
- Add vegetables to snack on during dinner. Dip in oil and balsamic vinegar. Don't just have bread and butter.
- Share large "portions" at a restaurant with a buddy or take some home.
- Avoid all you can eat places, "supersizing" and "oversizing."
- Don't drink (guzzle) your calories (e.g., beer). Sip with a straw, drink hot tea (green), coffee or water.

Easy Salt Reduction Tips

- Buy fresh vegetables or frozen with no salt (sodium) added.
- Use fresh chicken, fish or lean meat, not canned or processed.
- Use herbs and spices, not salt, for seasoning.
- Cook pasta and rice without adding salt. Use drops of oil instead.
- Eliminate frozen/microwavable dinners, canned sauces, canned vegetables, canned soups and dressings as much and as often as possible.
- Rinse all canned vegetables.
- Check all packaged foods for low or reduced sodium or no salt added.
- Check for breakfast cereals low in sodium.
- Cut out desserts high in sodium like cereals and premixes.
- Cut out drinks high in sodium.

Time Saving Tips

- Begin with boiling water before starting. It cuts down cooking time as you plan the meal.
- Keep mixed greens and vegetables on hand.
- Cook bigger meals, save the leftovers and alter them later for varied taste.
- Buy food that lasts longer in storage but that is healthy and is not compromised.
- Buy whole fruit or vegetables easily prepared or eaten.
- Go nuts—walnuts, pistachios, almonds and pine nuts—always have them available to add to salads, rice and cereals.
- Eat half of your healthy take-out and save the rest for later and eat in place of bad snacks.
- Eat with a buddy who believes in the same approach and has the same goals as you do.
- Exercise or walk with a buddy frequently and commit to it.

How and What to Eat Better

- Use olive oil as the main source of fat for cooking, dressings, snacking and for all meals.
- Choose a variety of foods and sources of nutrients.
- Eat sensible portions at each meal and eat smaller, healthy snacks throughout the day.
- Consume a plant food diet and emphasize fruits and vegetables.
- Buy whole foods rather than processed foods.
- Eat low fat dairy in proper proportion to the other food source.
- Eat fish, lean meats and poultry.
- Use herbs and spices.
- Stop at your local farmer's market more often.
- Grow a garden. It's not only an activity, it's a source of lots of nutritional and medicinal benefits.

Eat less, sleep better.

Heart Healthy and Eating Facts

The facts

- More than 60% of Americans are overweight
  More than 1/3 of Americans are obese
  More than 20% of preschool children are overweight
  One third of our teens are overweight
- 40%–70% of children and teens live with obese parents
- Obese adults develop high risk factors for high blood pressure, high cholesterol and diabetes; there is an alarming increase in diabetes due to the obesity epidemic
- About 80% of diabetics will develop and die from cardiovascular disease. 75% of cardiovascular disease patients will die of coronary heart disease. Coronary disease, in this country, begins at the ages of 5 and 6. One out of six high school grads gets a diploma and atheroma (high cholesterol).

Now for other facts

- Fast food, fatty foods, super-sizing, calorie loaded foods, highly saturated fats, and trans fats are all great at clogging up our kids' arteries
- We consume lots of food, more of it, more often and without good balance
- We try quick fixes with diets, but we don't change our habits or lifestyles
- We take more drugs thinking it will fix things, and they don't, most of the time
- We take a pill for everything and more is on the way
- We eat because it's there and think it will make us happy
- We eat to take the stress away

And more

- We eat badly at school as kids
- We eat badly at home because of lack of time
- We eat badly and frequently while at work
- We go out and eat where the kids want to go, not where we should go
- We eat out not knowing what we are eating, let alone how it was prepared

So what, or then what?

- We need to learn about what's right and wrong and what is good and bad for us
- When it comes to food, it's not only at home, school, work or at your in-laws, it's necessary to implement a significant change
- It's a change in will and ways

It's time to adopt the Mediterranean way of life and style of food and habit of cooking. This is the way to a healthy society, a happy family, and fit individuals.

I would love to have the opportunity to discuss this further. As a business, we are committed to the heart healthy alternative. We specialize in the Mediterranean cuisine and diet or lifestyle. Numerous studies support and validate the idea that this diet helps reduce the risk factors associated with heart disease, cardiac death, diabetes and cancer.

So the next time you're out shopping or eating out, ask what is in the food and how it was prepared. Don't be shy, ask! It's your health.

The archer hittith the mark partly by pulling and partly by letting go.

Conversions

Length

1 inch = 2.5 centimeters

1 foot = 30 centimeters

1 yard = 0.9 meter

1 mile = 1.6 kilometers

1 inch = 25 millimeters

Volume

1 teaspoon = 4.9 milliliters

1 tablespoon = 14.8 milliliters

1 cup = 0.24 liter

1 pint = 0.47 liter

1 quart = 0.95 liter

1 gallon = 3.79 liters

Weight

1 ounce = 28.4 grams

1 pound = 0.45 kilogram

2.2 pounds = 1 kilogram

10 pounds = 4.5 kilograms

Temperature

0°F = −18°C

32°F (water freezes) = 0°C

98.6°F (body temperature) = 37°C

212°F (boiling point) = 100°C

Excellent Sources of Calcium

Food Type	mg-Calcium	Amount
Yogurt-plain	452 mg	8 ounces
Parmesan cheese	390 mg	1 ounce
Ricotta cheese	337 mg	½ cup
Skim milk	302 mg	1 cup
Buttermilk (low fat)	285 mg	1 cup
Swiss cheese	272 mg	1 ounce
Collard greens (cooked)	226 mg	1 cup
Sesame seeds (unhulled)	175 mg	2 tablespoons

Excellent Sources of Dietary Fiber

Food Type	g of Fiber	Amount
Lentils (cooked)	16 g	1 cup
Figs (dried)	12 g	½ cup
Kidney Beans	11 g	1 cup
Artichokes	7 g	1 medium
Potato (baked)	7 g	1 medium
Blackberries (fresh)	7 g	1 cup
Barley	6 g	1 cup
Split Pea	6 g	½ cup
Wheat Bran	6 g	¼ cup
Apple	6 g	1 large
Oatmeal	4 g	1 cup

Key Minerals

Mineral	Benefits	Sources
Calcium	• Bone and teeth health • Regulates heartbeat • Muscle contraction	Dairy products, fatty fish (salmon), dark, leafy greens, yogurt, cheese
Iron	• Formation of hemoglobin in red blood cells, certain components of enzymes and proteins	Lean meat, legumes, nuts, tuna, spinach, whole grains
Magnesium	• Helps bone growth • Helps in nerve and muscle function • Helps us use insulin	Whole grains, leafy greens, avocados, bananas, spices
Potassium	• Helps blood clotting • Regulates fluid balance • Maintain blood pressure and heart function	Green vegetables, bananas, potatoes, yogurt, orange juice
Zinc	• Boosts immune system • Reduce inflammation • Cell growth and repair	Oysters, crab meat, eggs, milk, lean protein

Key Vitamins

Vitamin	Benefits	Sources
Vitamin A	• Eyes and night vision • Healthy skin, bones • Keeps tissue healthy	Yellow, orange, and dark green vegetables, beta carotene, eggs, cheese
Vitamin B_6	• Produces red blood cells • Aids in the protein and amino acid chemistry	Beef, poultry, fish, fortified cereals
Vitamin B_{12}	• Formation of red blood cells, • Nervous system function	Seafood, meat, poultry, dairy, eggs, soy milk
Vitamin C	• Antioxidant • Reduces the risk of cancer • Helps in making connective tissue • Enhances iron absorption	Citrus fruit, berries, red and green peppers, broccoli, spinach
Vitamin D	• Maintains strong bones and teeth • Reduces risk of colon cancer	Dairy products, fatty fish, exposure to sun
Vitamin E	• Antioxidant • Reduces risk of heart disease • Protects muscle and red blood cells	Nuts, seeds, whole grains, vegetable oil, leafy greens, avocados
Vitamin K	• Normal blood clotting • Calcium absorption	Broccoli, leafy greens, milk, eggs, cabbage

What Does that Food Label Really Mean?

Accompanying each recipe in this book, you will find that you have also been provided with the nutrient content of each recipe. This nutritional information was determined using www.nutritiondata.com, and has been provided as an additional information source as well as an educational tool. The Nutrition Facts Label is included on food packages to assist you in making healthier food selections. Unfortunately, this little box is often too confusing for many of us to interpret, so it is often ignored. By understanding how to read a these labels, making healthier food selections will become as easy as 1, 2, 3 . . . 4, 5. With these five simple steps, you will be able to understand what these labels mean for you as a both a consumer and now, as a cook, as you begin cooking your way through this book of delicious recipes. Now, let's get started using the sample Nutrition Facts Label displayed here.*

Step 1

Begin at the top left of the label by finding the serving size.

Step 2

Now look just below this number, to find the total number of servings in the container. By doing this, you can often better determine how much of the recipe or product you will actually eat. Using the box of macaroni and cheese example provided, will you eat only half of the box, one serving, or the entire box, which would be a total of two servings?

Step 3

Look at the number of calories in one serving. How many servings did you say you will have?

Sample Label for Macaroni and Cheese

Start Here

Nutrition Facts
Serving Size 1 cup (228g)
Servings Per Container 2

Amount Per Serving	
Calories 250	Calories from Fat 110

	% Daily Value*
Total Fat 12g	18%
Saturated Fat 3g	15%
Trans Fat 1.5g	
Cholesterol 30mg	10%
Sodium 470mg	20%
Total Carbohydrate 31g	10%
Dietary Fiber 0g	0%
Sugars 5g	
Protein 5g	

Vitamin A	4%
Vitamin C	2%
Calcium	20%
Iron	4%

*Percent Daily Values are based on a 2,000 calorie diet. Your Daily Values may be higher or lower depending on your calorie needs:

	Calories:	2,000	2,500
Total Fat	Less than	65g	80g
Sat Fat	Less than	20g	25g
Cholesterol	Less than	300mg	300mg
Sodium	Less than	2,400mg	2,400mg
Total Carbohydrate		300g	375g
Dietary Fiber		25g	30g

Limit these nutrients

Get enough of these nutrients

Footnote

Quick guide to %DV

5% or less is low

20% or more is high

Now, multiply the number of calories in one serving by the number of servings you will be eating in order to determine the number of calories you will be eating.

calories per serving x number of servings you will eat = total number of calories

Step 4

Look at and choose items *low* in fat, saturated fat, trans fat, cholesterol, and sodium.

- Time Out: You are probably thinking, "What in the world does 'low' mean?" An item is considered *low* in a nutrient if the number in the right column, the % Daily Value (%DV), is 5% or less. A nutrient is *high* if the number in the right column is 20% or more. The % DV is a recommendation based on the needs of someone consuming a 2,000 calorie diet, and allows you to interpret the nutritional facts without needing to know the recommendations for each individual nutrient in terms of milligrams, grams, calories, etc.

- Unfortunately, no %DV is provided for trans fat as no specific recommendation has been established at this time. However, due to the association between trans fats and increased LDL cholesterol, limiting trans fats as much as possible is suggested until further recommendations are made available.

- Now remember, if you decided you will eat 2 "servings," this means you will not only be eating twice the amount of calories listed, but also twice the amount of fat, saturated fat, trans fat, cholesterol, and sodium!

Step 5

Lastly, look at and choose items *high* in fiber, vitamin A, vitamin C, calcium, and iron.

- Most of us don't get enough of these nutrients, so for these items, the higher the better! And the same rules apply from Step 4. An item is high in these specific nutrients if an item has 20% or more of the DV. And remember, just like in Step 4, if you eat greater than 1 serving, you also multiply the %DV of these specific nutrients by the number of servings you eat! Nutritious and delicious! Your ultimate goal is to reach 100% of these nutrients by the end of the day.

Now you understand what exactly those nutrition labels have been trying to explain to you all these years! Practice these five steps as you cook your way through this book, and before you know it, you will be a Nutrition Facts Label pro!

*Sample label retrieved from U.S. Food & Drug Administration. For further information on the Nutrition Facts Label, please visit www.fda.gov.

Epilogue

OK! Somehow it feels like I am at, what you may call, the end of this book. But, you may also know this could mark the beginning of a new journey, or charting a new course or chapter of some sort, that only you or I could chart. As for my part, this is a different ending or maybe a "beginning." As you can see from this book, it's a mosaic or a quilt of life lessons that are yet to be experienced, enjoyed, or completed. One thing you have asked me is to continue to chart the next course, or to complete the story which is this journey. This story is simply my interpretation of the path on which this life journey has taken me— where it began and where it has taken me over four decades. The exploration of food, culture, family, the fun of cooking, and tying it all together are a real joy and a great part of my life.

So, as I continue to explore and invent delicious food to share with you, I would like very much for you to do the same. But please remember and employ all those ideas, tips, and suggestions I've offered in this book to eating better, fresher, and smarter. After all, it is about you, your health, and the health of those you love, especially our kids, from now till the rest of our lives.

So now, it is your turn! I would like for you to chart your own way to loving food, cooking healthy, and sharing with others, for the next meal or the next extravaganza. Explore a new recipe, a good cookbook, or a blog about your newfound love of wholesome and healthy food. Just remember this: I salute you with a great glass of wine and say "cheers and here's to your health!" So gather your friends, talk much, stay long, and eat well!

Please take a moment, send me your creation, and share with us your love of food and your cooking stories. This cookbook's community is waiting to hear from you and for you to share with all of us your healthy cooking adventures.

Be sure to visit www.TheMediterraneanDigest.com to learn more. Enjoy all the *ta3m* you create! Thank you. Till next time.

My best regards,
Shaw

References and Bibliography

Adamson, Eve and Cloutier, Marissa, MS, RD. *The Mediterranean Diet*. New York: HarperCollins.

Amendola, J. & Rees, N. *Understanding Baking: The Art and Science of Baking* (3rd ed.). New York: John Wiley & Sons, 2003.

Anthony, Dawn, Elaine, and Selwa. *The Lebanese Cookbook*. Brooklyn: SFF, 2002.

Aronne, Lou, M.D. *Weigh Less, Live Longer: Dr. Lou Aronne's "Getting Healthy" Plan for Permanent Weight Control*. New York: John Wiley & Sons, 1997.

Ask Dr. Weil. http://www.drweil.com.

Attenborough, David. *The First Eden: The Mediterranean World and Man*. Boston: Little, Brown, 1987.

Bourdain, Anthony. *Kitchen Confidential: Adventures in the Culinary Underbelly*. New York: HarperCollins, 2000.

Bowden, Jonny, Ph.D., C.N.S. *The 150 Healthiest Foods on Earth*. Beverly, MA: Fair Winds Press, 2007.

Cadwell, Karin, Ph.D., R.N. and Tibbetts, Edith. *Healthy Heart Cookbook*. New York: Barnes and Noble Books.

http://www.caff.org. Promotes community agriculture and publishes the *National Organic Directory*.

Casas, Penelope. *Tapas: The Little Dishes of Spain*. New York: Alfred A. Knopf, Inc., 1985.

Castelvetro, Giacomo. *The Fruit, Herbs & Vegetables of Italy*. Gillian Riley, Trans. New York: Viking, 1989.

Center for Science in the Public Interest. 1875 Connecticut Avenue NW—Washington, D.C. 20009. (202) 332-9110. www.cspinet.org/home.html. Publishes *Nutrition and Action Newsletter*.

Child, J. *The Way to Cook*. New York: Alfred A. Knopf, 1989.

Community Alliance with Family Farmers. P.O. Box 363 Davis, California 95617. (916) 756-8518.

The Complete Step-by-Step Cooking Class Cookbook. Lincolnwood, IL: Publications International Ltd., 1994.

Cook, Gay. *Mrs. Cook's Kitchen*. Vancouver: Whitecap Books, 2000.

Cooking Light Magazine.

Corriher, Shirley O. *CookWise: The Hows & Whys of Successful Cooking with over 230 Great-Tasting Recipes*. New York: HarperCollins, 1997.

Corti Brothers. P.O. Box 191358 Sacramento, California 95819. (916) 736-3800. Organic olive oils.

Crazy for Chocolate. Australia: Bay Books, 2008.

Doncaster, Lucy, ed. *Best-Ever 400 Budget Recipes*. London: Hermes House, 2008.

Dr. Andrew Weil's Self-Healing: (800) 523-3296

Easy Healthy: Easy Recipes, Easy Cooking, Great Food. UK: Parragon Books LTD., 2007.

Eating Well Magazine.

Environmental Nutrition: (800) 829-5384

Environmental Working Group. 1718 Connecticut Avenue NW—Suite 600 Washington, D.C. 20009. (202) 667-6982. Provides information about dangers of agrichemicals.

Fair, Chris. *Cuisines of the Axis of Evil and Other Irritating States: A Dinner Party Approach to International Relations*. Gilford, Ct: Globe Pequot, 2008.

Ferro-Luzzi, A., and S. Sette. "The Mediterranean Diet: An Attempt to Define its Present and Past Composition." *European Journal of Clinical Nutrition* (Suppl. 2) (1989).

Fidanza, Flaminio. "The Mediterranean Italian Diet: Keys to Contemporary Thinking." *Proceedings of the Nutrition Society,* 50 (1991).

Food Network: http://www.foodnetwork.com

Fox, Robert. *The Inner Sea: The Mediterranean and Its People*. New York: Knopf, 1993.

Frieda's. 4465 Corporate Center Drive Los Alamitos, California 90720. (800) 241-1771. http://www.friedas.com. Specialty fruits and vegetables.

Fungi Perfecti. P.O. Box 7634 Olympia, Washington 98507. (800) 780-9126. http://www.fungi.com. Gourmet and medicinal mushrooms.

Gold Mine Natural Food Company. 7805 Arjons Drive San Diego, California 92126-4368. (800) 475-3663. http://www.goldminesnatural.com. Organic grains, nuts, beans, sea vegetables.

Goldbeck, Nikki, and David Goldbeck. *The Healthiest Diet in the World: A Cookbook and Mentor*. New York: Dutton, 1998.

Great Tastes: Comfort Food: More than 120 Easy Recipes for Every Day. Australia: Bay Books, 2010.

Hazan, Marcella. *The Classic Italian Cook Book*. New York: Knopf, 1976; revised and reprinted in *Essentials of Classic Italian Cooking*. New York: Knopf, 1992.

Herbst, Sharon Tyler. *The New Food Lover's Companion: Comprehensive Definitions of Nearly 6000 Food, Drink, and Culinary Terms*. Hauppauge, NY: Barron's Cooking Guide, 2001.

Hoffman, Susanna and Wise, Victoria. *Adventures in Greek Cooking: The Olive and the Caper*. New York: Workman Publishing.

Hurst, Jacqui and Lyn Rutherford. *A Gourmet's Guide to Mushrooms and Truffles*. Los Angeles: HP Books, 1991.

Jacobs, Susie. *Recipes from a Greek Island*. New York: Simon & Schuster, 1991.

Jenkins, Nancy Harmon, and Antonia Trichopdou. *The Mediterranean Diet Cookbook: A Delicious Alternative for Lifelong Health*. New York: Bantam Doubleday Dell, 1994.

Kremezi, Aglaia. *The Foods of Greece*. New York: Stewart, Tabori & Chang, 1993.

Kochilas, Diane. *The Food and Wine of Greece*. New York: St. Martin's Press, 1990.

The Mail Order Catalog for Healthy Eating. P.O. Box 180 Summertown, Tennessee 38483 (800) 835-2867. http://www.healthy-eating.com. Vegetarian cookbooks and products.

Mallos, Tess. *The Tess Mallos Fillo Pastry Cookbook: And Introducing Kataifi Pastry*. London: Merehurst Press, 1983.

Man, Rosamond. *The Complete Meze Table*. London: Ebury Press, 1986.

McConnell, Carol and Malcolm. *The Mediterranean Diet: Wine, Pasta, Olive Oil, and a Long Healthy Life*. New York: Norton, 1987.

McGee, Harold. *On Food and Cooking: The Science and Lore of the Kitchen*. New York: Scribner, 1984.

Mothers and Others for a Livable Planet. 40 West 20th Street New York, New York 10011-4211 (888) 326-4636. http://www.mothers.org/mothers. Promotes sustainable and organic agriculture.

National Restaurant Association Educational Foundation. *ServSafe Course book*. Hoboken, NJ: John Wiley & Sons, 2008.

Natural Health Magazine.

Nutrition Action Health letter: (202) 332-9110

Ortiz, Elisabeth Lambert. *The Encyclopedia of Herbs Spices & Flavorings*. London: Darling Kindersley, Inc., 1992.

Price, Jessie et al. *Eating Well in Season: The Farmer's Market Cookbook*. Woodstock, VT: The Countryman Press, 2009.

Ratner, Shauna and Frances Johnson. *Eating Light Eating Right: Simple Recipes for a Healthy Life*. Vancouver: Whitecap, 2001.

Reader's Digest. *Eat Well Stay Well: 500 Delicious Recipes Made With Healing Foods*. Pleasantville, NY: Reader's Digest Association, Inc., 1998.

Rigante, Elodia. *Italian Immigrant Cooking*. Cobb, CA: First View Books, 1995.

Roden, Claudia. *A Book of Middle Eastern Food*. New York: Vintage, 1974.

Roizen, Michael F., M.D. and Mehmet C. Ox, M.D. *You Staying Young: the Owner's Manual for Extending Your Warranty*. New York: Simon & Schuster, Inc., 2007.

Russo, Julie and Sheila Lukins. *The New Basic Cookbook*. New York: Workman Publishing, 2009.

Roth, June. *How to Cook Like a Jewish Mother*. Secaucus, NJ: Castle Books, 1993.

Rua, Jim. *Café Capriccio: A Culinary Memoir*. Albany, NY: Capriccio Press, 1992.

Sauces, Dips and Salsas. Australia: Bay Books, 2008.

Schulman, Martha Rose. *Mediterranean Light: Delicious Recipes from the World's Healthiest Cuisine.* New York: Bantam, 1989.

Simopoulos, Artemis P., M.D., and Jo Robinson. *The Omega Diet: The Lifelong Nutritional Program Based on the Diet of the Island of Crete.* New York: HarperCollins, 1999.

Techamaunvivit, Pim. *The Foodie Handbook: The (Almost) Definitive Guide to Gastronomy.* San Francisco: Chronicle Books, 2009.

Tufts University Health & Nutrition Letter: (800) 274-7581

U.S.D.A. Food and Nutrition Information Center: http://www.nal.usda.gov/fnic

Vegetarian Cooking: A Common Sense Guide. Australia: Bay Books, 2010.

The Vegetarian Resource Group: http://www.vrg.org.

Vegetarian Times Magazine.

Weil, Andrew, M.D. *Eating Well for Optimum Health: The Essential Guide to Food, Diet, and Nutrition.* New York: Knopf, 2000.

Weir, Joanne. *From Tapas to Meze: First Courses from the Mediterranean Shores of Spain, France, Italy, Greece, Turkey, the Middle East, and North Africa.* New York: Crown Publishers, Inc., 1994.

Willett, Walter C., M.D., and Frank M. Sacks, M.D., "More on Chewing the Fat: The Good Fat and the Good Cholesterol." Editorial, New England Journal of Medicine (Dec. 12, 1991).

Wolfert, Paula. *Couscous and Other Good Food from Morocco.* New York: Harper & Row, 1974.

Wood, Rebecca, et al. *The New Whole Foods Encyclopedia: A Comprehensive Resource for Healthy Living.* New York: Penguin, USA, 1999.

World Health Statistics Annual/Annuaire de statistiques sanitaires mondiales, 1991. Geneva: World Health Organization, 1992.

Note: Websites may change over time.

A sponge wipes away the past, a rose sweetens the present,
a kiss greets the future.

A

B

cucumber
    in gazpacho, 247
    in salad, fattoush, 205
    in salad, fruit and vegetable, 202
    in salad, Greek, 204
    salad, tomato-cucumber, 210
    in salmon with scallions and yogurt, 154
    sauce, cucumber-yogurt, 216
    soup, chilled, 244

D
dairy. *See* cheese; milk; yogurt
date(s)
    in cake, chocolate spice, 120
    cookies, mamool, 122
    in couscous, Moroccan, 175
    in salad, fruit and vegetable, 202
    salad, orange and date, 207
    tart, date and nut, 121
desserts, 111–134
    about, 50
    baklava, 115
    bread pudding, 116
    Brie en croute, baked, 114
    cake, chocolate lava, 119
    cake, chocolate spice, 121
    cake, saffron, 124
    cake, semolina, 128
    cake, sour cream vanilla, 129
    chocolate ganache, 118
    cookies, date mamool, 122
    crepes, almond peach, 112
    crepes, chocolate, 117
    date and nut tart, 121
    fruit gazpacho, 246
    ganache, white vanilla, 134
    kataifi, 126
    pie, apple, 125
    pie, pumpkin, 133
    pudding, rice, 127
    smoothie, avocado, 113
    streusel topping, 131

tiramisu, 132
    yogurt cream, 139
dill
    about, 60
    in asparagus salmon scramble, 150
    in casserole, vegetable, 280
    in dressing, yogurt, 236
    in gazpacho, 247
    in salmon, herb roasted, 160
    in salmon with scallions and yogurt, 154
    salmon with yogurt-dill sauce, 163
    soup, carrot dill, 236
    in swordfish with puttanesca sauce, 158
dips and spreads
    babaghanooj. *see* chickpeas
    cucumber-yogurt sauce, 216
    hummus, bi-tahini, 138
    hummus, hot pepper, 137
    yogurt cream, 139
dolma, 262
dressings
    about, 51–52
    cucumber-yogurt sauce, 216
    Greek, 204
    Italian, 222
    tahini, 232
    vinaigrette, 206
    vinaigrette, sesame, 198
    yogurt, 236
    See also sauces
drinks. *See* beverages

E
eggplant
    in babaghanooj, 136
    in casserole, meat and rice (magloobah), 187
    grilled, with tomato feta sauté, 272
    kibbee bisanieh (vegetarian), 282
    lasagna, 265
    in moussaka, 185
    roulade, 266

parsley
about, 62
in chicken, pomegranate, 103
in falafel, 267
in gazpacho, 247
pesto, 228
in pesto, garlic, 104
in salad, Greek pasta, 191
in salad, Lebanese fattoush, 205
in sauce, cucumber-yogurt, 216
in spinach and chickpeas with couscous, 277
in tabbouleh, 209
in tiropita, 271
pasta, 189–196
ala Romano, drunken, 190
with lamb, Greekish, 192
with mushroom sauce, 196
orzo with feta and olives, 194
pilaf, minted orzo, 193
primavera, 195
salad, Greek, 191
shrimp scampi, 166
tomato-olive sauce for, 219
See also sauces
pastries. *See* desserts
pastry. *See* filo pastry; puff pastry
peach and almond crepes, 112
pear and cranberry salad, 208
peas
in pilaf, bulgur pomegranate, 172
snap, in avocado-artichoke salad, 199
in vegetable casserole, 280
peppers, hot
in chicken kabobs, 99
in chicken with yogurt, 105
in cucumber soup, chilled, 244
in hummus, hot pepper, 137
in tangine, okra tomato, 274
peppers, sweet
in brown rice and sautéed vegetables, 171
in chicken cacciatore, 93
in eggplant lasagna, 265

in eggplant roulade, 266
in gazpacho, 247
in gazpacho, roasted vegetable, 253
in jambalaya, 97
in korma, spinach, 278
in korma, vegetable, 281
in lamb kabobs, 183
in lentil sauté, 174
in mushrooms, stuffed, 275
in relish, avocado and corn, 256
in salad, chickpea, 200
in salad, fajita, 98
in salad, fruit and vegetable, 202
in salad, Greek pasta, 191
in sauce, for fish or pasta, 219
in shrimp Creole, 165
soup, chilled, 245
in soup, lentil, 248
soup, roasted red pepper, 252
in stew, Moroccan, 273
pesto
basil, 227
in basil tomato pie, 257
cilantro-mint, 215
garlic, 104
parsley, 228
in quiche, cheese and tomato, 144
phyllo pastry. *See* filo pastry
pies
apple, 125
basil tomato, 257
pumpkin, 133
tiropita, 271
pilaf
basmati rice, 170
minted orzo, 193
pine nuts
in cake, semolina, 128
in kibbee bisanieh (vegetarian), 282
in meat and rice casserole (magloobah), 187
in pesto, cilantro-mint, 215
in pesto, parsley, 228

All things are difficult before they are easy.